Sports Turf & Amenity Grassland Management

Endorsed by The Institute of Groundsmanship

Stewart Brown

The Crowood Press

First published in 2005 by
The Crowood Press Ltd
Ramsbury, Marlborough
Wiltshire SN8 2HR

www.crowood.com

British Library Cataloguing-in-Publication Data
A catalogue record for this book is available from the British Library.

ISBN 1 86126 790 8

Dedication
To my wife, Dawn, our children Harry, Hannah and Hayley, for their
unfaltering support, belief and patience.

Acknowledgements
The author is grateful to the following companies for their support and the
pictures they provided for the book: Agria Outdoor Power Equipment Ltd;
Allen Power Equipment Ltd; Barenbrug UK Ltd; Bayer Environmental
Science; BLEC Landscaping Equipment Co. Ltd; Bomford-Turner Ltd;
Campey Turfcare Systems; Connectomatic Ltd; Earthquake Turfcare Ltd;
Ecosolve Ltd; GreenTek; Hardi Ltd; Hayter; John Deere; Rainbird;
Ransomes Jacobsen; Scotts Company (UK) Ltd; Simon Tullet Machinery
Company Ltd; SISIS Equipment (Macclesfield) Ltd; Sovereign Turf Ltd.

Disclaimer
All tools and equipment used in turf management should be used in strict
accordance with both the current health and safety regulations and the
manufacturer's instructions. The author and the publisher do not accept any
responsibility or liability of any kind in any manner whatsoever for any error
or omission, or any loss, damage, injury or adverse outcome incurred as a
result of the use of any of the information contained in this book, or reliance
upon it. If in doubt about any area of turf management readers are advised to
seek professional advice.

Line-drawings by Annette Findlay

Edited and designed by OutHouse!
Shalbourne, Marlborough, Wiltshire SN8 3QJ

Printed and bound in Great Britain by Biddles Ltd, King's Lynn, Norfolk

Contents

Foreword

Turf management is regarded by most people unconnected with the industry as a rather odd and specialized occupation of limited appeal. But it is amongst turf professionals that I have encountered the most fanatical enthusiasts, and I guess I would have to count myself as one of them.

There are reasons for this. To grow a golf green from seed and see the trueness and pace of the putts played upon it when it is finally being mown every day at just 4mm gives a very real sense of satisfaction. Maintain a lawn composed of a pure stand of one of the better cultivars of Smooth-stalked Meadow Grass and you will be the envy of your neighbourhood. Or look at the diversity of plant and insect life that can exist and enjoy the sight of the beautiful fine seed-heads in a low-maintenance area of red fescue – delightful.

The turfgrass industry is large and varied, involving many of our most popular sports, a crucial part of our urban landscape and, of course, our national obsession – gardening in all its forms. There are many ways in which turf practitioners can utilize their imagination and creativity. I remember the parks manager who mowed out of longer grass a labyrinth, a sort of maze but one that allowed you to see where to walk. He produced a beautiful feature that was both visually pleasing and fun. To some, walking the labyrinth in that town park became an almost spiritual experience.

Turf managers often pay tremendous attention to detail. There are products you can buy that coat the grass leaves in silica, like hairspray, so that they stay stiff and are cut more cleanly to produce a better finish. I know a First Division soccer ground manager who mows his pitch with one of the larger pedestrian mowers and turns the machine on a board at the end of each pass so as not to wear out the turf on the sidelines. There are many people that take turf very seriously indeed.

So one can get passionate about turf, and I would argue that showing people the best examples of what can be achieved can extend that enjoyment to others. Certainly, to maintain the ultra-smooth surfaces of, for example, a golf green takes a lot of work. But with an understanding of the grasses and how turf of different forms can be created and maintained, the turf practitioner is able to choose from a palette of options and offer the best surface within whatever resource limitations might be imposed.

I hope that readers of this book will be inspired to enhance the turf they look after (and most of us have some), both for their own pleasure and for that of others.

Dr Tim Lodge was formerly Southern Area Manager for the Sports Turf Research Institute (STRI) and is now Principal Consultant of Agrostis Turf Consultancy (www.agrostis.co.uk)

Introduction

Grasslands are an enormously important vegetation type throughout the world. Amenity grassland has been defined as grass that has a recreational, functional or aesthetic value, and for which agricultural productivity is not the primary aim. They vary enormously in terms of composition, use and cost of management, and they make up a large part of the responsibility of any organization that is involved in urban landscape management. In the United Kingdom, local authorities, private and commercial sports clubs and other organizations annually spend significant amounts of money on turf and grassland maintenance – it is often the largest component of total landscape expenditure.

An initial classification of amenity grasslands might place them into functional, ornamental or sports turf types. While there are overlaps between these three categories, there are certain generalizations that might be drawn about each category in order to

---

Table 1: A classification of amenity grasslands (from Shildrick, 1990*)

Use	Intensity and cost of maintenance:		
	High	*Medium*	*Low*
Sports facilities	Golf (putting) greens and tees; tennis courts; bowling greens; cricket squares	Grass pitches and playing fields for games such as football, hockey, rugby, polo; golf fairways; horse-racing tracks	
Other trampled areas		Urban parks and open spaces; urban and suburban road verges; domestic lawns; other lawn areas (institutional, industrial, cemeteries)	Rural road verges; country parks; golf roughs
Untrampled areas			Motorway and railway embankments; canal banks and riverbanks; airfields

* Shildrick, J., 'The use of turf grasses in temperate humid climates', in: Breymeyer, A (Ed), *Managed Grasslands: Regional Studies, Ecosystems of the World*, Vol. 17A, pp 255–99, Elsevier, (Amsterdam), 1990.

separate them. Functional turf, for example, has the lowest intensity of management and some types of sports turf the highest. Table 1 gives a classification of grasslands showing how the levels of intensity of management of different grass types are related.

Functional grasslands are used for purposes such as erosion control, slope stabilization and other similar applications where function is likely to be more important than appearance. Locations for functional grasslands include road reserves, airports, some categories of park, and golf-course roughs. Typically, these grasslands are composed of both grass and non-grass species. They will be cut infrequently and long, and they will be relatively open, that is, there will be relatively few shoots or stems per unit area.

Ornamental grass and lawn areas are found in a range of circumstances. They include domestic lawns, parkland, surrounds for buildings and public areas, and road verges in built-up areas. An important feature of these grass surfaces is their visual appeal, which, in the conventional view, requires a uniform, green, dense, relatively short sward. The turf acts as a decorative or passive recreation surface in its own right, or as a foil for other plantings or for the buildings around which the turf is planted. In contrast with functional grasslands, these surfaces will be mown shorter and more frequently and will be of less varied composition: often the preference is for grasses only.

As the public changes its views of the costs of government and of the environmental impacts of some horticultural activities, the inputs required to maintain ornamental turf will come under increasing scrutiny. As a consequence, the traditional views of what makes good turf and what is acceptable quality may change and a broader experience of turf may be permitted.

The last category of managed grasslands is that of sports turf. Sports played on these surfaces include golf, bowls, football, rugby, cricket, hockey, tennis and horse racing. These turfs will share the characteristics of ornamental turf, and often involve very short, frequent mowing, particularly for golf and bowling greens. In addition to meeting the requirements of the game and maintaining the appropriate appearance, ideally the vigour of the surface allows it to recuperate from the damage caused by use. The reality is often far removed from the ideal, particularly with turf used for contact sports such as football over the wetter periods of the year. The inability of sports turf to stand up to some sorts of wear has led to increased use of artificial surfaces. Tennis and hockey are examples where artificial surfaces are now more common than turf in first-class games.

The management of this range of turf surfaces involves the use of maintenance inputs at various levels. At the minimum, this may be infrequent mowing, perhaps only once a year, as in the case of some road verges. As the expectation of the user and the level of use increase, however, the management inputs must increase. The increase of mowing frequency, irrigation, fertilizer application, weed control, aeration, topdressing and renovation are all associated with turf maintenance where higher quality outcomes are expected, such as golf greens. It is important that turf managers make appropriate resource allocations to grasslands in their control. It is possible to waste resources on facilities that do not require them. Similarly, it is important to recognize that some quality outcomes are possible only with appropriate levels of expenditure and, if this is not done, the turf surface will not provide the experience expected of it.

The input levels required by a particular grassland can be described as the intensity of management or culture. Intensity of culture is determined by user expectation and intensity of use. The lowest intensity of culture will be found where both these factors are low, for example on roadsides. The highest levels will be found where either user expectation and/or intensity of use are high. Examples include golf greens and sports fields, but could also include prestige ornamental lawns. Intensity of culture will obviously determine the cost of turf maintenance.

CHAPTER 1

Grasses and Their Uses

Grasses occur naturally in most parts of the world. Perennial pasture grasses, together with annual species that have been developed as cereals, are the most important agricultural plants on earth. In nature, grasses are most successful when in competition with other species in continental regions that have rather low and seasonal rainfall. These climatic areas are now the main cereal-growing regions of the world, typified by the prairies of North America and parts of Continental Europe and Asia.

The reason that grasses in grazed or clipped conditions are successful and persistent is that during vegetative growth their regenerative meristematic zones are close to the soil surface; they therefore remain undamaged by grazing animals and mowing machines. Annual grasses are of little use in turf because they have evolved to survive situations of stress by producing seed. This survival characteristic, involving death of the vegetative plant, is of no value in turf where increasingly there is a demand for year-round use. Annual Meadow Grass (*Poa annua*), which dominates many turf areas, behaves as a vegetative perennial in moist temperate climates, but retains the advantage of profuse seed setting even at close mowing heights.

The Grass Family

Grasses belong to a family of plants known as Poaceae (formerly recognized as Gramineae). This is one of the largest flowering plant families on earth, comprising 635 genera and 9,000 species of annual, perennial and rhizomatous herbs, and even woody and tree-like plants such as the bamboos. The family is economically the most important as it includes the cereals (barley, wheat, maize, millet, rice, oats, rye), sugarcane, pasture and fodder crops. Many species are sources of alcohol, aromatic and edible oils, waxes, fibres and paper pulp.

The root system of grass plants is usually fibrous, often augmented by adventitious roots, which branch or tiller from the base to form a rosette or tussock. Endo-mycorrhizae are often associated with roots; and plants often spread laterally by stolons or rhizomes. Vegetative propagation is very important in many species. The grass stem (or culm) is jointed, with hollow internodes. Leaves are borne alternately in two rows on opposite sides of the stem, with open sheath and an elongated blade. Auricles and ligules are often present at the junction of the leaf blade (lamina) and sheath. Ligules are usually membranous, or reduced to a hairy fringe, but are rarely absent. Flowers are usually wind-pollinated, bisexual (less often unisexual), and produced in one- to many-flowered spikelets. The seed is actually a fruit and is called a caryopsis.

Cool and Warm-Season Grasses

Turfgrasses are commonly divided into two main groups according to their temperature tolerance. Those that grow predominantly in a temperate climate (UK, northern Europe,

---

SOME COOL- AND WARM-SEASON TURFGRASSES

Cool-season grasses

Browntop Bent

Creeping Bent

Red fescues

Perennial Ryegrass

Smooth-stalked Meadow Grass

Hard Fescue

Annual Meadow Grass

Warm-season grasses

Bermuda Grass

Zoysia

Buffalo Grass

Seashore Paspalum

St Augustine Grass

Kikuyu Grass

Crabgrass

North America and other regions of the northern hemisphere), and have a temperature optimum of 15–24°C, are known as cool-season grasses; those that grow best in subtropical or tropical climates (including Asia, South America, Africa and southern China), and have a higher optimum temperature requirement of 26.5–35°C, are known as warm-season grasses.

The distinction between the two groups shown in the box above may seem obvious: warm-season grasses live in warm places while cool-season grasses are happy enough in cooler environments such as those in the UK. There are, however, more fundamental differences between the two groups. One difference is in the way the plants fix carbon from the carbon dioxide (CO_2) in the atmosphere in order to grow. (This is part of the complicated process we know as photosynthesis.) They also differ anatomically as well as in their temperature and sunshine requirements, and in their rates of water consumption.

Photosynthesis
Cool-season grasses fix one carbon atom into a compound with five carbon atoms. The compound splits into two molecules containing three carbon atoms each. Cool-season grasses are therefore known as C-3 plants. In warm-season grasses, the carbon from atmospheric CO_2 joins straight onto a three-carbon molecule to form a four-carbon molecule. So these are called C-4 plants.

Types of Grass Leaf
Under the microscope, anatomical differences between the cool- and warm-season grasses are apparent. It will be seen that the leaves of warm-season grasses have a ring of thick-walled cells around the vascular cells (veins). This ring is known as the bundle sheath. Such distinct cells (Kranz cells) are absent from cool-season grasses. Kranz cells are packed with chloroplasts, mitochondria and other organelles to ensure that their overall rate of photosynthesis is rapid.

In warm-season grasses, C-4 compounds are passed quickly into the Kranz cells, where they release the CO_2. This CO_2 is then utilized just as it is in the cool-season grasses, and the products can be shunted directly into the veins for transport to those parts of the grass where they are needed for the promotion of growth.

Temperature and Sunshine
The energy for driving both C-3 and C-4 photosynthesis comes from the sun. Warm-season grasses need more sunshine than do cool-season grasses to complete this process. Provided they can get this, however, the whole C-4 process is very fast and efficient. At high light intensities, and at high temperatures, warm-season grasses are at least twice as efficient at making dry matter as cool-season grasses. Although such efficiency is a huge advantage, warm-season grasses need high temperatures to survive and so they cannot be supported by the temperate UK climate.

Water Consumption

Stomata (the little holes in the surfaces of the leaves) vary in diameter to control the in-flow and outflow of gases and water. The efficiency of the C-4 process is such that very little CO_2 is wasted. Even with the stomata nearly closed, the C-4 process can continue and comparatively little water is lost, which makes warm-season grasses very efficient users of water. Under equivalent conditions of temperature and sunshine, they will use much less water than will a cool-season grass. In places where fresh water for irrigation is a rare and expensive commodity, this is a major advantage of the warm-season grasses.

The Turfgrass Plant

The term turfgrass is used loosely to describe species that when mown (or grazed) are capable of forming a more or less tightly knit and uniform vegetated surface. Some grasses are intolerant of regular mowing or grazing. Typically, these are found on wasteland or as weeds of arable land where cir-cumstances do not expose them to regular defoliation. Couch Grass (*Agropyron repens*) is an example of a species of this type that cannot be considered a turfgrass.

Once established, unmown grasses grow vegetatively until flowering is initiated. After this, a high proportion of the carbohydrate fixed by the leaves is diverted to flowering and seed production. This results in a marked decrease in the growth rate of leaves and roots of perennial grasses in mid-season. If grasses are mown regularly, thus preventing flowering, the pattern of growth throughout the summer will be more even that it would be if left unmown. Although there is always a surge of growth in late spring, variations in leaf-growth rate throughout the summer are influenced mainly by nutrient and water supply.

Grasses grow by cell division and elongation at their base. Thus, the oldest part of a leaf is its tip and the youngest its base. Mowing removes the mature parts of leaves, which, through photosynthesis, make the main contribution to the energy balance of the plant. Severe mowing may not damage

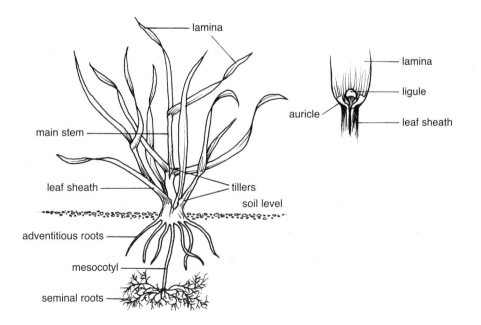

Table 2: Common UK turfgrasses and their uses

Species	Area of usage
Agrostis canina	Fine turf; amenity areas; ornamental lawns
Agrostis capillaries/castellana	Fine turf; amenity areas; ornamental lawns
Agrostis stolonifera	Fine turf; amenity areas; ornamental lawns
Festuca arundinacea	Amenity areas; sports fields; race tracks
Festuca longifolia	Fine turf; amenity areas; ornamental lawns
Festuca rubra ssp. *commutata*	Fine turf; ornamental lawns
Festuca rubra ssp. *rubra*	Fine turf; amenity areas; ornamental lawns
Lolium perenne	Amenity areas; sports fields; race tracks
Poa annua	Fine turf; sports fields
Phleum bertolonii	Amenity areas; sports fields; race tracks
Poa pratensis	Amenity areas; sports fields; race tracks

---

meristematic tissues, but it does remove much of the active photosynthetic tissues, leaving stem bases and immature leaves that may not be energy self-sufficient.

Since grasses are found in a wide diversity of habitats, they show a considerable measure of ecological adaptation. Even so, the grass plant is something of an all-purpose structure, and the descriptive morphology of growth habit and the progress of the life cycle conforms to a widely recognizable pattern.

Stems

The shoot is the main functional part of the turfgrass plant. It consists of a short central stem, with levels or branches borne alternately at successive nodes. The stem is the main stalk or body of a plant, which may take one of the following forms: a crown (unelongated internodes with closely stacked nodes); a stolon or rhizome (laterally elongated internodes with interspersed nodes); or a culm (upright elongated internodes terminating in an inflorescence, or 'grass flower'). The crown is that part of the turfgrass plant that includes the stem apex, the unelongated internodes, and the lower nodes from which roots are initiated.

The node is a jointed or enlarged area of a stem containing meristematic tissue from which leaves, roots or branches of stems arise. Usually visible as a slight swelling of the stem, it is a key structure in the plant's potential to recuperate from wear, stress and disease or pest injury, as well as in its ability to survive drought, heat and low temperature dormancy. Internodes are the regions of stem between two successive nodes. Severing an internode, such as by mowing, stimulates the adjacent node on each side to form new shoots and roots.

Successive leaves are initiated by the stem apex, which in most species remains short during vegetative development so that leaves arise close together. The majority of species delay stem development until shortly before flowering. When stem development does occur, the structure is fairly uniform: long and narrow, with either solid or hollow internodes separated by solid nodes.

The anatomy of the mature grass stem is superficially simple, with longitudinal vascular bundles embedded in parenchymatous ground tissue. In species with solid stems, such as those of *Zea* and *Saccharum*, the central parenchyma provides a large store for carbohydrates, which may later be used during seed development. In species with hollow stems, the vascular bundles are arranged in one or two concentric rings. Where stems are solid, however, the bundles can be more widely distributed, although they are usually more concentrated towards the outside. Columns of strengthening sclerenchyma develop in close proximity to the vascular bundles.

Leaves

A leaf is a lateral outgrowth of a stem, borne alternately; it consists of a flattened upper blade and a lower basal sheath that encircles the stem. The main structure contains chlorophyll, the green pigment involved in light-energy capture for photosynthesis. The leaf sheath, the basal tubular portion of a leaf surrounding the stem, also contains some chlorophyll.

As the plant develops, the shoot (or culm) becomes conspicuous. At this stage it consists solely of a series of concentric leaves, with the oldest on the outside and the youngest ones forming in the centre and pushing upwards until they finally emerge. As the seedling develops, the emerging leaves show variations in structure, which are most important for species identification. The mature leaf blade is sometimes very narrow – little wider than its thickness – resulting in a hair-like or setaceous appearance. In most species, however, the blade is flat or capable of being flattened (laminate). The many species with folded or rolled leaf blades fall into this latter group. Some (mainly tropical) grasses have very stiff setaceous leaves, referred to as needle-like or acicular. In species with laminate leaves, the arrangement of the young leaf – whether it is rolled or merely folded at its midrib – before it emerges through the surrounding leaf sheath is important. The most important variation in leaf sheaths is in whether they possess free margins that overlap or margins that are fused to form a complete tube.

The ligule is one of the most important diagnostic features of grass leaves. It is always present, although its texture, size and shape vary widely. Most commonly it is a membranous structure, but this can become stiffened to a scale, or reduced to a fringe of hairs.

Separate from the ligule, the leaves of some species have auricles, ear-like projections that also form at the junction of leaf sheath and lamina, as in many turfgrasses.

Branching and Vegetative Reproduction

Buds in the axils of leaves on the initial grass shoot develop into new shoots. These are called tillers, and the number and vigour of tillers controls the density of leaves in the sward. Tillering is affected by several environmental factors, including temperature, light intensity and mineral nutrition. The optimum temperature for tillering in temperate grasses is around 18–24°C, and tillering is favoured by high light intensities. These conditions favour net photosynthate accumulation by the plant.

Tillers, or lateral shoots, arise in the axils of the first-formed leaves on a shoot. Where these are retained within the surrounding leaf sheath, tillering is referred to as intravaginal, and produces the familiar tufted or caespitose growth habit. An alternative form of tillering is termed extravaginal, and occurs where the lateral stem does elongate, and bursts through the side of the surrounding leaf sheath to produce a spreading growth habit. Extravaginal tillers form either rhizomes (horizontally spreading stems that bear scale leaves only) or stolons (the aboveground equivalent, which possesses fully

---

STOLONIFEROUS OR RHIZOMATOUS?

Stoloniferous turfgrasses include:

• *Poa annua* ssp, *reptans* (Annual Meadow Grass).

• *Agrostis stolonifera* (Creeping Bent).

Rhizomatous turfgrasses include:

• *Poa pratensis* (Smooth-stalked Meadow Grass).

• *Festuca rubra* ssp. *rubra* (Strong Creeping Red Fescue).

developed leaves). Both forms then root and produce new shoots at the nodes, permitting a single plant to spread over a wide area.

In stoloniferous species, the distinction between a horizontally spreading stem and a vertically growing shoot is often rather vague, so that a fallen upright stem might root at the nodes and permit vegetative spreading, whilst a horizontal stem may (particularly if it becomes reproductive) turns upwards.

Rhizomatous species are similarly distinguished by their type of branching. In monopodial growth, the apical meristem of the rhizome continues horizontal development, and lateral buds give rise to aerial shoots. In sympodial growth, the apical meristem turns upwards, and an axillary bud continues rhizome growth.

In some weedy grasses, the underground development of a complex mass of monopodial or sympodial rhizomes can make eradication very difficult: Couch Grass (*Agropyron repens*) is a notorious example. On the other hand, situations where soil stabilization is necessary can utilize this growth habit. In habitats of shifting soils, where the grass may become buried, genera such as *Vetiveria* can be used to create contoured terraces, and *Ammophila*, found on coastal sand dunes, can progressively substitute higher nodes as the effective stem base as the soil or sand accumulates. Tiller, rhizome and stolon growth can all lead to vegetative reproduction.

Roots

The seminal root system consists of a primary root and a few (between two and seven) first-order branches. This root system is progressively replaced by adventitious roots, which arise at stem nodes and push out through the subtending leaf sheath. Adventitious roots develop from the leaf bases, and eventually replace the seminal roots that grew from the initial seedling. The anatomy of grass roots is very similar to that of other monocotyledons.

Much of the root system of perennial grasses is annual or shorter in persistence. There is a turnover of roots during the growing season depending upon mainte-

nance regime and mowing in particular. However, there is a major loss of roots over winter, the degree of which varies between species. Active root growth occurs at lower temperatures than does leaf growth, and substantial growth of new roots occurs in early spring before significant leaf growth is apparent. As the season progresses, changes in light input and temperature, plus maintenance regime, influence the amount of live root material.

Root development requires an input of energy. This is provided in spring through the mobilization of energy stored over winter in stem bases and through the translocation of sugars fixed by leaves. In the growing season, roots obtain all their energy from sugars produced in the leaves. Thus, while stems and leaves depend on roots for their supply of essential mineral nutrients, roots require energy derived from photosynthesis for maintenance and growth.

Although internal control is affected by plant-growth regulators, the interdependence of tops and roots affects their relative performance. One predictable consequence is that severe mowing, which decreases photosynthesis, reduces the energy available for root growth. Following on from this, it can be seen that severe defoliation will be followed by a rapid loss of roots. Regular close mowing causes a less extreme decrease in photosynthesis, but in general closer mowing brings about a decrease in living root mass. The level of plant-nutrient supply affects root development and the relative growth of roots and shoots.

Factors affecting root growth
Environmental factors that affect root growth include:

- Temperature. Cool-season turfgrass requirements are 10–18°C.
- Soil reaction. Acidic soils with a pH below 5.5 limit root growth.
- Soil texture. Loamy sands and sandy loams allow for easier root growth.
- Soil aeration. Oxygen movement through soil air spaces to roots is required for their

growth, plus the outward movement of potentially toxic gases.

- Soil compaction. This limits root growth. It is prevented by the use of root–zone mixes or corrected by turf cultivation practices such as spiking or coring.
- Soil waterlogging. This limits root growth. Suitable drainage should be provided and excessive irrigation avoided.
- Toxic chemicals. Certain pesticides and heavy metals, including copper and zinc, limit root growth.
- Salinity. High salt levels limit root growth. Excess salts can be flushed through the soil profile via deep irrigation at rates higher than the evapotranspiration.

Cultural practices that affect root growth include:

- Mowing. The higher the cutting height, the deeper the root system.
- Nitrogen nutrition. Moderate, judicious levels of nitrogen aid root growth.
- Potassium nutrition. High levels aid root growth.
- Irrigation. Moderate, judicious amounts of water applied at depth aid growth.
- Thatch. To encourage root growth, thatch accumulation should be minimized by scarification.

The Maturing Plant

Throughout vegetative growth, the apical meristem of the grass plant remains close to ground level and initiates new leaves. Eventually, however, reproductive development begins. The apex increases its growth rate and initiates the inflorescence, while the condensed internodes underneath the meristematic region begin to elongate. As this happens, the inflorescence is pushed upwards and eventually emerges from within the enclosing leaves, carried on the main stem, or rachis. The switch to flowering is usually permanent, so far as any single stem is concerned.

Many grasses flower and seed during their first year of growth, but reproductive growth may be long delayed. Even where flower formation occurs, it is not always particularly effective. Not surprisingly, at the climatic extremes for any species, a seedling may develop and persist, but only in the vegetative state, being unable to reproduce sexually. Failure to produce seed can delay or postpone indefinitely the senescence of the vegetative parts of the plant.

The Grass Inflorescence

In most grasses vegetative growth is followed by reproductive development. In ephemeral grasses the life cycle might be completed in as little as three months, while in some species flowering may be long delayed. The switch to reproductive development in annual or monocarpic species is followed by the death of the parent plant. Even in true perennials, however, the individual reproductive shoot is monocarpic, and the continued survival of the plant depends on the further creation of vegetative tillers. Generally, seed fertility is higher in annuals than in perennials, a situation readily explained since the latter need not depend entirely on the seed for propagation and spread.

The grass inflorescence is a complex structure involving panicles, spikelets and florets.

The Panicle

The typical grass inflorescence is the panicle, a branching system of varying complexity that supports the spikelets. In some grasses the branching is so reduced that spikelets (in groups of one to three) are directly attached to the main stem (or rachis). Such inflorescences are conventionally referred to as spikes. In some grasses, such as *Alopecurus* and *Phleum*, the inflorescence is a tight spike in which branching is not apparent on first inspection. Closer examination shows that these inflorescences can be understood as tightly condensed branching panicles. This is an important point, since these inflorescences are defined as panicles in floras, and must be correctly identified when using keys.

The Spikelet

One or more florets are grouped together into a spikelet in a way broadly consistent throughout the *Poaceae*, but with variation in detail. The spikelet is subtended by (usually) two glumes. Within a floret, male and female organs may mature at different times and there may be individual flowers that are hermaphrodite, male or female only, or one or more of each.

The Floret

In most species, the grass floret (or flower) consists of a pistil with two stigmas. Around this are either one or two whorls of three anthers; beyond these are usually two lodicules. Each floret is enveloped by a pair of structures, the palea (the inner) and the lemma. An awn may be present as a projection from the lemma. Awns can be terminal (attached to the end of the lemma as a projection of the midrib), or dorsal (arising from some way down the back of the midrib). Sometimes, the awn is hygroscopic and twists on being hydrated. This acts, after shedding, to move the dehisced grain away from the mother plant or assist in its insertion into the soil.

Pollination and Fertilization

Windborne pollen is deposited on the stigma, which produces a sticky secretion that allows the pollen grains to adhere to it and stimulates them to germinate. Thereafter, germination and entry of the pollen tube and its passage to the egg cells is completed. Grasses are self-incompatible.

The turfgrass seed is actually a fruit. It is a one-seeded, non-dehiscent fruit termed a caryopsis. The caryopsis contains the true seed, which in a typical grass has a relatively elaborate embryo situated at one end of the fruit next to a generous supply of endosperm. The relative proportions of embryo and endosperm vary among the grass subfamilies. The grass fruit can vary enormously in size. The embryo contains the single cotyledon or scutellum, a large elliptical structure appressed to the endosperm. The embryonic shoot and root axes are found at the centre of the scutellum. Depending on species, a small scale of tissue, the epiblast, may also be present on the outside of the embryo. When germination begins, the developing shoot expands within a protective modifed leaf, the coleoptile, which splits through the caryopsis. Similarly, the primary root pushes through its protective organ, the coleorhiza.

Desirable Characteristics of Turfgrasses

Spreading Ability

In general, grasses that are able to spread vegetatively by stolons (creeping above-ground stems) or rhizomes (underground stems) produce the most tightly knit turf. Examples include bents (*Agrostis* species), Smooth-stalked Meadow Grass (*Poa pratensis*) and Strong Creeping Red Fescue (*Festuca rubra* ssp. *rubra*).

In regularly mown turf this creeping behaviour is also shown by other species not normally recognized as having this ability. The process is called aerial tillering and involves the production of new tillers away from the parent plant on shoots extending above ground within or slightly above the turf. These tillers form roots in the protected moist environment. Annual Meadow Grass has this ability, as do some cultivars of Perennial Ryegrass (*Lolium perenne*). The tightly knit and even turf produced by species that spread by stolons or rhizomes is normally advantageous but can also be difficult to manage.

Verdure

Verdure is a qualitative assessment of the fresh green colour of turf, and good verdure throughout the year is deemed desirable for many turf uses. The shade of green may vary, but in essence greenness reflects active growth. A rare exception to this rule is a cultivar of Meadow Fescue (*Festuca pratensis*) whose senescent leaves remain green. Many naturally selected strains of turfgrass species in the UK (especially those in the uplands) have a short growing season and are visually unattractive or at least non-green for around half of the year. It must be remembered, though, that lush green grass created with plentiful supplies of fertilizer or irrigation will not necessarily provide the best surfaces for play.

Wear Tolerance

Tolerance of wear and regular mowing are requirements of most turf, but especially of sports turf. The games of golf and bowls demand a closeness of mowing that can be tolerated by very few species. Only species of bent, fine-leaved fescues and Annual Meadow Grass of the temperate species can produce a tightly knit and reasonably vigorous turf when mown at heights of 3–8mm. Other sport and amenity uses of turf do not demand such close mowing, and turfgrass cultivars of broadleaved species, including Perennial Ryegrass, Timothy and Smooth-stalked Meadow Grass, grow well provided the cutting height is not much below 20mm.

There are two components of wear. One is compression, through treading, to which all used turf is subjected to a greater or lesser extent. The other is tearing-type wear, which is especially important in the winter games of soccer and rugby. Wear tolerance also has two components. One is durability, the inherent resistance of grass to compression, scrubbing or tearing, which is especially important when weather conditions result in slow growth. The second component, which is a major asset when growing conditions are good, is the ability to recover rapidly from damage inflicted.

All turfgrasses have a high tolerance of compression, and the key differences in wear tolerance arise from the relative sensitivity to scrubbing or tearing and the ability to recover from damage. The tight mat-forming grasses typified by the bents and Smooth-stalked Meadow Grass are very tolerant of scrubbing wear, but the tightly knit nature of the turf means that studded boots tend to tear out sections of it (divots). In contrast, studded boots tend to slide through Perennial Ryegrass turf, without tearing out rooted tillers, because of its open growth habit. Despite the poor ability of Perennial Ryegrass to spread vegetatively, its vigour and its low susceptibility

to tearing-type wear means that in long-term practical situations it is more successful in winter games turf than any other sown species.

Important Grasses for Sports and Amenity Turf

A checklist of the most important grasses are shown in the box below. The particular grass chosen will depend on its intended use and, more importantly, on how it withstands that use – in other words, its resistance to wear and tear. It will need to have distinct characteristics suitable for the intended purpose, and these in the main are those already described in the last section.

The number of species used in amenity situations is actually quite limited, although for each species there are often hundreds of cultivars. The list of grasses overleaf are the most important and frequently used in both sports turf and amenity situations.

Identification of Grass Seeds and Turfgrasses

The seeds of turfgrasses vary with the species. It is usually possible to identify the seeds of an individual species on its morphological appearance alone, but sometimes it is possible only to identify seeds as belonging to a group of species (such as the fine-leaved fescues). Nevertheless, the ability to recognize species seeds is useful because it enables unwanted species to be recognized in seed mixtures (such as Perennial Ryegrass in a ryegrass-free mix).

The identification of grasses is much simpler when seed-heads are present, but in turf that is mown frequently and closely, the only species able to produce seed is Annual Meadow Grass. Seed-heads are produced in some amenity grassland situations, such as roadside verges, when mowing is carried out only once or twice per year. Not only are seed-heads absent from most turf, but the amount of vegetative growth may be very short. The number of grass species likely to be present is quite small, and it is usually possible to make an accurate identification from vegetative characteristics.

CHECKLIST OF IMPORTANT GRASSES

Agrostis capillaris (Browntop Bent)

This is the main bent grass used in the UK. It is a tufted perennial plant, some 10–70cm in height, which spreads by means of short rhizomes and sometimes by stolons, forming a loose or dense turf. Browntop Bent is well adapted to the maritime climate of the UK and is predominantly used for fine sports turf and other areas that are close mown.

Agrostis stolonifera (Creeping Bent)

Creeping Bent has been used extensively in the USA and Mediterranean countries and is becoming more frequent in its use in the UK. The plant, a tufted perennial 8–40cm high, spreads by leafy stolons and forms a close turf. Creeping Bent is also used for fine turf situations, although it requires a higher soil pH than does Browntop Bent. The vigorous stolons need to be controlled by verti-cutting to restrict the 'nap' or 'grain' formation that would otherwise occur.

Agrostis castellana (Highland Bent)

Originally thought to be a cultivar of Browntop Bent but now considered a separate species, Highland Bent has been used extensively in sports and amenity turfs. The plant is a densely to loosely tufted perennial, vigorously spreading from stout, short rhizomes. Highland Bent is often used in conditions that receive heavy wear as its new growth from rhizomes aid recovery.

Agrostis canina ssp. *canina* (Velvet Bent)

Velvet Bent is finer leaved than Browntop Bent and produces a dense sward with good drought resistance. A tufted perennial 15–75cm high, it spreads by slender creeping stolons that root at the nodes. It is, however, seldom used because its density may cause fibre accumulation and possible disease occurrence. The stolons may also form a 'nap' within the turf.

Lolium perenne (Perennial Ryegrass)

This is the main turfgrass in the UK for both heavy-duty sports turf and comparable turf for general landscape purposes. The plant is a loosely to densely tufted perennial some 10–90cm high. It has a fast establishment rate, vigorous growth and persists well under traffic and heavy wear. It is best if cut at not less than 20mm, although the finer-leaved cultivars will withstand closer cutting.

Festuca rubra ssp. *commutata* (Chewing's Fescue)

A major grass used in fine sports turf and high-quality ornamental lawns. It is a densely tufted perennial, 20–90cm high, but it is without rhizomes. It adapts well to dry and infertile conditions but is unable to fill bare patches owing to its lack of rhizomes. It is fast to germinate, tolerant of heavy wear, and shows some resistance to *Fusarium* and take-all patch diseases.

Festuca rubra ssp. *litoralis* (Slender Creeping Red Fescue)

A densely tufted or mat-forming perennial, with numerous closely packed tillers that spread by short, very slender rhizomes. Slender Creeping Red Fescue is fine-leaved and low-growing, and it survives close mowing well. It will withstand abrasive wear when established and recovers from such wear moderately well. It is very tolerant of salt and persists well in coastal areas.

Festuca rubra ssp. *rubra* (Strong Creeping Red Fescue)

Strong Creeping Red Fescue is unsuitable for fine turf, as it does not persist under close mowing. The perennial plant grows to approximately 22–100cm high and spreads by means of very long, slender, scaly creeping rhizomes. It is most often used in mixtures for heavy wear such as winter sports and for soils of high fertility and pH (alkaline). In summer, relatively few shoots are produced from rhizomes, although growth is vigorous.

Phleum pratense bertolonii (Small-leaved Timothy)

Used to some extent for medium-fine sports turf and comparable areas that receive heavy wear, this loosely to compactly tufted perennial, 10–50cm high, sometimes produces leafy stolons, it is tolerant of wet, heavy soils and blends well with fescues and bents in colour and texture.

Phleum pratense (Large-leaved Timothy)

Large-leaved Timothy is used in the main where maximum wear tolerance is required and mowing is not less than 15–20mm. It is a loose to densely tufted perennial, some 40–150cm in height. This hard-wearing grass establishes easily and is tolerant of wet, heavy soils.

Poa pratensis (Smooth-stalked Meadow Grass)

This grass is slow to establish, but once it has it can be tough, hard-wearing and persistent, particularly if mown no closer than 10–15mm. The plant itself is very variable and forms a loose to compact tuft, 10–90cm high, and spreads by means of slender creeping rhizomes, which give good recovery from wear and some drought resistance; indeed, in dry conditions it may dominate Perennial Ryegrass. It performs best on well-drained soils of high fertility that are somewhat neutral to alkaline in soil reaction (pH).

Poa trivialis (Rough-stalked Meadow Grass)

This can be a substitute for Smooth-stalked Meadow Grass in wetter situations, in which it is more tolerant. It is a loosely tufted perennial, 20–100cm high, with creeping leafy stolons. It is faster in establishment than Smooth-stalked but generally less wear-tolerant. In some non-intense cases it may be used instead of Perennial Ryegrass to provide rapid ground cover; it is slightly less rigorous initially than that species, but lower growing in the long term.

Cynosurus cristatus (Crested Dog's-tail)

Crested Dog's-tail is of limited use for ornamental lawns and perhaps some sports turf situations. It produces a tufted plant that attains 5–75cm in height. It is still used for some fine turf mixtures with fescue and bent, but it does not blend well with these grasses. It is not too tolerant of close mowing, and under such conditions only scattered plants will persist.

Deschampsia caespitosa (Tufted Hair Grass)

A densely tufted perennial originating from wet and badly drained soils, marshy fields, rough grassland and moorland. It forms large tussocks 20–200cm high. It was considered a coarse, worthless grass unsuitable for turf and amenity grassland, but a new cultivar of the species is claimed to have good shade and wear tolerance when maintained at 10–15mm height. It is reported to form a dense sward, comparable to Smooth-stalked Meadow Grass, and to be well suited to winter games use and shaded landscape situations.

Deschampsia flexuosa (Wavy Hair Grass)

A 'natural' shade species of which seed is usually available in the UK, Wavy Hair Grass can be used in lawn mixtures but is not tolerant of regular mowing. The plant is a densely tufted perennial 20–100cm high, sometimes with slender rhizomes. It may be used as a lawn grass on very acid soils and in open woodlands on similar soils.

Festuca tenufolia (Fine-leaved Sheep's Fescue)

This grass persists quite well and is tolerant of wear and close mowing, but it is limited in its use because of its growth habit: it grows in unattractive whorls that generally make it unsuitable for fine sports turf (Chewing's Fescue performs better in this situation). It is a densely tufted fine-leaved perennial, some 10–45cm in height, but without rhizomes. It may be of use in acid, dry and infertile soils and semi-natural grassland situations.

Festuca longifolia (Hard Fescue)

Good cultivars of this species are comparable in their tolerance of close mowing and wear to good cultivars of red fescue. They may be of use in situations with dry infertile soils when mixed with red fescue. The grass is a densely tufted perennial and grows to 15–70cm high, but it lacks rhizomes. Hard Fescue is only fair in its tolerance of heavy wear and is not worth considering for winter sport or similar areas of intense wear.

Festuca arundinacea (Tall Fescue)

In recent trials, newer turf-type cultivars of this tufted perennial have proved comparable to Perennial Ryegrass. It will grow to 200cm high, lacks rhizomes and forms large, dense tussocks. The leaves, even of turf-type cultivars, are considerably larger and coarser than those of Perennial Ryegrass and form a more robust, broadleaved sward than UK users are accustomed to.

Poa annua (Annual Meadow Grass)

Annual Meadow Grass is not sown deliberately as a turfgrass but predominates in many established grass areas of all types. It has a unique status in UK turf! Depending upon the actual area in which it occurs, it is regarded either as a useful turfgrass or as an extremely successful and indestructible weed. It is more often regarded as a weed in fine turf situations than in those areas that receive heavy wear (for example, winter sports), where it will provide 'cover', and in other general amenity situations with less intensive maintenance requirements.

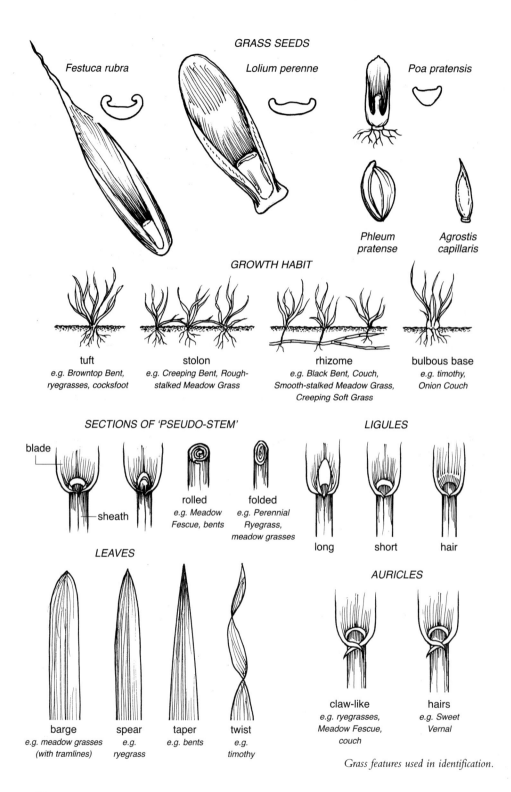

GRASS SEEDS

Festuca rubra *Lolium perenne* *Poa pratensis*

Phleum pratense *Agrostis capillaris*

GROWTH HABIT

tuft
e.g. Browntop Bent, ryegrasses, cocksfoot

stolon
e.g. Creeping Bent, Rough-stalked Meadow Grass

rhizome
e.g. Black Bent, Couch, Smooth-stalked Meadow Grass, Creeping Soft Grass

bulbous base
e.g. timothy, Onion Couch

SECTIONS OF 'PSEUDO-STEM'

blade

sheath

rolled
e.g. Meadow Fescue, bents

folded
e.g. Perennial Ryegrass, meadow grasses

LIGULES

long short hair

LEAVES

barge
e.g. meadow grasses (with tramlines)

spear
e.g. ryegrass

taper
e.g. bents

twist
e.g. timothy

AURICLES

claw-like
e.g. ryegrasses, Meadow Fescue, couch

hairs
e.g. Sweet Vernal

Grass features used in identification.

18

Two basic keys for identification of the most common turfgrass species are provided below and overleaf. There are, however, many more detailed keys and texts available that should be consulted for more precise identification.

The morphological features used to identify grasses are often physically small and a magnifying lens is essential. The ability to identify the common turfgrasses is important, for without this it is not possible to appreciate the effectiveness of over-seeding, the relative persistence of particular species and their susceptibility to disease, or indeed to monitor changes in turfgrass composition in response to wear or maintenance.

QUICK KEY TO TURFGRASS GENUS LEVEL

The main difficulties most people seem to find in identifying grasses lie in distinguishing *Lolium perenne* and *Poa trivialis*, *Agrostis* and *Phleum*, and *Phleum* and *Dactylis*. To avoid confusion, work your way methodically down the following key:

Festuca

Mature leaves are rolled, needle-like. Fescues of turf are small, fine, low-growing grasses. Pinky rhizomes near the surface indicate *F. rubra rubra* species; no rhizomes indicate *F. rubra commutata*.

Holcus

Hold leaves up to the light. If leaves are covered with hairs on both surfaces it is *Holcus*. The leaves are usually paler in colour than in most other grasses, and are coarse and tufted in appearance.

Poa

Unfold a leaf, hold it up to the light. If two pale, thin, parallel lines (tramlines) are visible either side of a darker midrib, the grass is a *Poa*. If the expanded leaves are dull and keel-shaped, this confirms *Poa*. If the grass is red at the base it is probably *P. trivialis*. This is easily confused with *Lolium* (*see* below). Some keys say that *Poa* are not ribbed, but this all depends on what you mean by ribbing – to the layperson, many do appear distinctly ribbed.

Lolium

Hold the leaf up to the light; if it is deeply ribbed over the upper surface only, with a midrib but no tramlines, it is probably a *Lolium*. To check, look at the lower surface: if it is shiny and waxy, with visible auricles clasping the stem, it is *Lolium*; if the shoot bases are pink, it is *Lolium perenne*.

Phleum

Grub about at the base of the plant. If there are no stolons or rhizomes, and the bases of the shoots are markedly swollen – onion- or leek-shaped (but not nodular) – then it is probably a *Phleum*. If the leaves are twisted, this confirms *Phleum*.

Dactylis

Grub about at the base of the plant. If the stems look flattened and form a sort of fan-shape, this is probably *Dactylis glomerata*.

Agrostis

Grub about at the base of the plant. If there are stolons or rhizomes, and it is not a fescue, it is probably *Agrostis*. Narrow, fine stems and blades confirm this. Some *Agrostis* have little bead-like lumps at the stem bases – nodules.

SIMPLE GRASS KEY

1. Older, expanded leaves are rolled, and not easily flattened out.

   Deschampsia: leaves dark green and waxy to touch.
   Festuca rubra rubra: pinkish rhizomes just under the surface; leaf sheath densely hairy.
   Festuca rubra commutata: no rhizomes; sheath hairless.

2. Young leaves rolled, round in section.

   Holcus lanatus: sheaths and leaves very hairy; no rhizomes.
   Lolium multiflorum: shoots often pink at bases.
   Phleum: shoot bases thickened to the point of being bulbous; leaves have characteristic twist; sheath bases white.
   Agrostis: shoots not thickened at base; rhizomes or stolons present.

3. Young leaves folded, flat in section.

   Go to 4 or 5.

4. Leaf blade ribbed above, smooth and glossy below.

   Lolium perenne: base of sheaths red/pink when young.
   Cynosurus cristatus: leaf sheath hairless; leaf blade trough-shaped at junction with sheath.

5. Leaf blade not ribbed above or below.

   Dactylis glomerata: sheaths compressed, fan-shaped; no tramlines present either side of midrib.
   Poa annua: tramlines; seed-heads present; pale green.
   Poa pratensis: tramlines; rhizomes; leaves blue-greyish.
   Poa trivialis: tramlines; leaf glossy underneath; some red at base.

CHAPTER 2

Mowing

Mowing is the most significant practice in the management of turf and amenity grassland areas. It has profound effects not only upon the sward but on most other maintenance operations. In the maintenance of any natural grass surface or area, the highest management costs will be those of labour and machinery. Mowing can account for more than 75 per cent of labour costs in the cutting season, and the machinery involved is often expensive to purchase and to maintain. Thus the importance of mowing cannot be underestimated for its effects upon the grass sward, other maintenance requirements and the management costs.

Mowing is an operation familiar to many people and the one that is most readily associated with lawn and turf maintenance. This familiarity is not always a good thing, as mowing is also one of the maintenance practices most misunderstood and most abused by both amateur lawn carers and, too frequently, 'professional' turf maintenance personnel. Fundamental errors in mowing practice cause significant damage to the grass and to the integrity and appearance of the sward. For example, mowing too closely and mowing too infrequently often lead to bare patches and the ingress of diseases or weed species, which results in loss of surface uniformity. Follow a few basic principles and you will be rewarded with better quality surfaces and a more efficient mowing operation.

Many turf surfaces used for sport are the subject of media interest, so it is imperative that the surface not only fulfils the needs of a particular sport but also looks its best. Grass growth, surface performance and aesthetic quality will all be significantly better if the basic principles of mowing are understood and effectively implemented.

Reasons for Mowing

It was not until the invention of the lawn-mower in 1830 by Edwin Budding that mowing became possible on the scale we know today. Prior to this date, so-called lawns were maintained by men using scythes or they were grazed by livestock, most frequently sheep. The quality of these surfaces, although acceptable, cannot have been anywhere near the manicured surfaces attainable today with modern technology. There have been many advances in mowing-machine technology since 1830, as a result of which lower cutting heights and more frequent mowing give much better surface uniformity and appearance. What has not changed to any real extent is the underlying reasons for mowing any area of grass.

These are:
- To maintain the grass at a specific desired height.
- To promote turfgrass density and ground coverage.
- To maintain the turf's aesthetic quality (i.e., visual appearance).
- To develop and sustain a surface for sport, play or other recreational activity.

- To inhibit (or eliminate) any undesired plant species (i.e., weeds).

The Effects of Mowing

The most important point to remember about mowing is that from a plant's viewpoint it is detrimental, often causing significant stress. The mowing operation has a direct impact on the grass in a number of ways and can adversely affect its physical health, even if only temporarily. This is often exacerbated by incorrect or poor mowing practice.

Mowing removes grass leaves, shoots and stems, and this has immediate repercussions. These tissues, especially the leaves, are the sites of plant photosynthesis, whereby the plant is able to synthesize its own sugars and carbohydrates utilizing natural resources. Immediately following mowing there is a decrease in sugar production, and the plant must utilize what remaining carbohydrates it has stored to facilitate new vegetative growth. There will also be a temporary cessation to root growth. The plant seeks to maintain a balance between leaves, shoot and root mass, so the plant's natural reaction is to shed some roots (as the root mass cannot now be sustained by the reduced leaf area with its lessened photosynthetic capacit). As a result, water uptake is reduced, and water loss through the severed plant tissues increases. These sites also offer themselves as entrance points for any prevailing plant pathogens that can then more readily enter the plant and cause disease. This problem is made worse when the leaves are not cut cleanly: torn tissues have a greater surface area, which calluses slowly.

Grasses tolerate such defoliation because of their ability to grow from the base of the plant. Meristematic tissues, from where new buds grow into new shoots, are located at the interface of the soil and aerial environment. In some grasses this is quite prominent (often being referred to as the crown). This area of plant tissue, as well as the lower parts or the stems, are passed over by the mower and so are able to generate new growth. This ability to re-grow from the base is an adaptation that has evolved as a result of grazing by herbivores for millennia.

Mowing directly affects sward density because it encourages new shoots to grow, thus forming a denser carpet of leaves. Root growth is directly related to top growth, so new roots as well as the extension of existing root will arise in order to support such shoot growth. New shoots and leaves require more nutrients and water from the roots to sustain their development and plant physiological processes.

The growth habit of grasses is in part a property of its genotype but this also is affected by mowing. In particular, mowing height is often a significant determinant of whether the plant grows in an upright, or vertical, orientation or has a procumbent, trailing habit. The botanical composition of the sward (that is, which grasses actually survive or persist) is directly affected by mowing. Mowing height and frequency are both important here as grass species vary in their tolerance to these two factors. Very few grasses will persist satisfactorily if continually mown at heights of cut below 5mm. As well as grasses, other plants found in grassland communities are also significantly affected by the mowing operation. Mowing is often the key to the successful management of longer grass swards such as wildflower meadows. In close-mown turf, relatively few broadleaved species can survive. Those that do often exhibit plant modifications or adaptations that allow them to do so.

Mowing Factors

Several variables are important in determining the mowing regime to be implemented on any given area of turf or amenity grassland. These are:

- Height of cut.
- Frequency of cut.
- Clipping return or removal.
- Direction of cut.

Height of Cut

This is the height at which, ideally, the grass is to be left after mowing. It is essentially the distance between the base of the mower roller, wheel or skid and the plane of cut. There are two components to mowing height:

1. Bench setting: this is the height of cut at which the mower is mechanically set in the workshop or maintenance facility by the mower operator.
2. Effective cutting height: the grass is actually cut in the field at this height.

It is important to recognize that these two components are rarely, if ever, the same and that the height setting on the machine will not be that at which the grass is actually cut. The mowing machine rides atop compressed grass shoots, leaves, and thatch layers within the soil or root zone, and this means in practice that effective cutting height is often higher than the bench setting. Surface condition, topography and ground water status will also have an influence here.

Grass species vary in their tolerance to mowing, but it is actually mowing height that is most influential in determining which species survive. Most species have a range of cutting levels at which they will persist within the sward. It should not be forgotten, however, that there is a great difference between mere survival and healthy, strong vigorous grass growth, which is usually what is desired. It is as mowing height decreases that the most

dramatic effects occur to the plant and resulting sward. Lower cutting heights will encourage tillering, the production of side shoots, and new growth from the base of the plant. This increases density of coverage and creates the carpet effect of a continual green sward. Since root depth and mass is related to shoot growth and height, they will decrease with lower cutting heights.

The closer grass shoots and leaves are mown, the smaller they will be. To a degree, closer mowing can produce a more aesthetically and visually appealing turf and is often the requirement in some cases, but it is achieved at the expense of the grass's tolerance to environmental stresses and plant pathogens. Closely mown turf is more prone to stress from heat, cold, drought and traffic. This is why fine-turf surfaces require intensive management systems and higher levels of resource input to sustain them. There is a greater level of technical expertise required to manage such fine-turf surfaces as golf and bowling greens. The resulting shorter root systems mean that more frequent irrigation and fertilizer application is needed to compensate for the plant's reduced ability to extract water and nutrients form the soil. The manager of such surfaces must also be ever vigilant for plant pathogens and other harmful organisms or phenomena.

Another consideration with close mowing is that if you mow at low cutting heights you will also need to mow more frequently to maintain such surfaces. There is an eco-

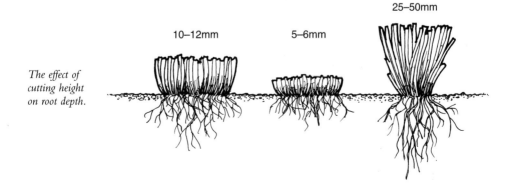

The effect of cutting height on root depth.

25–50mm

10–12mm   5–6mm

Table 3: Minimum height of cut (mm) to ensure persistence and relative speed of growth			
Species	**Persistence at (mm)**	**Temporary minimum (mm)**	**Speed of growth**
Browntop Bent	5	3	Slow
Creeping Bent	5	3	Slow
Chewing's Fescue	7	5	Slow
Slender Creeping Red Fescue	7	5	Slow
Strong Creeping Red Fescue	8–12	12	Medium
Hard Fescue	7	6	Slow/medium
Sheep's Fescue	12	12	Slow
Smooth-stalked Meadow Grass	10	8	Medium
Annual Meadow Grass	5	3	Medium
Timothy (Small-leaved)	15	15	Medium
Perennial Ryegrass	12	8	Fast

nomic factor here. At the extreme, close mowing will result in a thin sward, with often-significant bare patches and weed or moss invasions. Mowing too closely often leads to scalping, with the inevitable exposure of bare ground and stubble.

Generally there are more positive aspects in increasing mowing heights than in reducing them. For example, with increases in mowing height there will be greater root penetration into the soil, allowing for enhanced drought resistance as the grass plant can then source moisture from a deeper reservoir of water. A disadvantage is that water use can increase by up to 25 per cent (although there are gains in overall plant vigour and greater resistance to environmental stresses and pathogens). Grass that is very tall will place the lower parts of the plant in shade, which will inhibit the growth of new side shoots, or tillers, which are essential if you want to create a dense ground cover. Long grass, as well as failing to achieve a high shoot density, may often be limp and procumbent, making mowing more difficult or less effective. Grass growing in areas of reduced natural light will also be further stressed by close mowing as there

is less sunlight for photosynthesis and the leaf area is being reduced. This often leads to moss growth, especially in the autumn. Stress from mowing will also be greater in hot conditions. At times like this, raise the height of cut to compensate for the stress caused to the plant by lack of moisture.

Bear in mind when determining cutting height that it is generally advisable to remove no more than 50 per cent of the standing height of the grass at any one mowing. Indeed, it is preferable, especially on intensively managed surfaces, to remove no more than 30 per cent. Thus if the grass is 30mm tall, mowing should not remove more than 10mm. When changing the mowing height, do so gradually over a period of time. Smaller, incremental changes to cutting height will allow the grass plants to adapt more readily, helping to negate any harmful effects to the plant or sward. It is also important when selecting a particular mowing height to consider the particular grass or other plant species present and the intended use of the surface or grass area. For turf surfaces used for sport it is the nature and requirements of the particular game that will largely determine the height of cut.

To summarize, the key determinants in selecting an appropriate height of cut will be:

- The physiological and growth effects on the turf, especially root growth.
- The purpose for which the turf is to be used.
- The specific grass species involved.
- Ground and environmental conditions.

Frequency of Cut

This is simply the number of cuts per unit of time. It is often expressed as the number of mowing occasions per week, month or even year. As we have already seen, it is necessary to mow fine-turf areas most frequently to maintain the low grass heights required. Golf greens are often mown daily at the height of the growing season and even twice a day during golf competitions or tournaments. At the other extreme, areas of rough grassland or scrub may be cut only once a year or even less frequently. Thus, for most turf or grassland areas, mowing frequency is inextricably linked with mowing height and especially so where a dense grass coverage is required for a uniform lawn or sports surface. Infrequently mown turf is coarser and more open than turf under a more intense mowing regime. Long grass areas will be reduced to stubble after mowing closely. This is not necessarily a problem for areas such as wildflower swards, where maintaining the actual individual species is more important than having a dense ground cover containing a limited number of turfgrasses.

The most notable effects of very frequent mowing include less rooting, reduced rhizome growth, increased shoot density, decreased shoot growth, decreased carbohydrate reserves, and increased plant succulence. Mowing should be sufficiently frequent to minimize stress, which is primarily determined by the proportion of leaf tissue removed rather than the actual height of cut. Remember the one-third or 30 per cent rule that constitutes a sound basis for mowing.

Do not neglect mowing in autumn or winter if grass growth is taking place. The main period of grass growth in the UK occurs during late spring to early summer, when there is vigorous top growth naturally culminating in flower production around late June and early July. Flowering and seed production restrict vegetative growth, so mowing is usually required less frequently. At the height of the summer period, in late July and August, normally hot, dry weather also limits grass growth. During the autumn, there is often a second flush of growth, triggered by rain and warm conditions, and mowing will necessarily be more frequent again. It will then tail off again for the winter, when shorter days and lower temperatures restrict grass growth. To maintain surface uniformity and density, it is necessary to adapt mowing frequency (and cutting heights) in accordance with prevailing environmental conditions. A reduction in mowing frequency is justified when growth is slow during periods of dry weather or throughout the winter, but must never be neglected totally. If grass growth is taking place and other environmental factors allow it, then mow! 'Topping' the grass during such slow growth periods will help to maintain a dense, uniform carpet of grass that will fulfill its intended function and be more visually attractive.

Many lawn owners, amateur gardeners and even professional turf operatives ignore these fundamental principles, resulting in poor turfgrass swards that are sparse, weed infested, and stubble-like with poor visual or functional characteristics. To maintain the best possible surface, mow frequently at a suitable height of cut.

Set the cutting height at the maximum that can be tolerated for that surface and mow it regularly – at least weekly for most surfaces – during the cutting season. Specialist sports turf surfaces have very specific requirements for mowing height and frequency that must be adhered to.

Mowing frequency is therefore determined by:

- Shoot-growth rate.
- Ground and environmental conditions (affecting grass-growth rates).

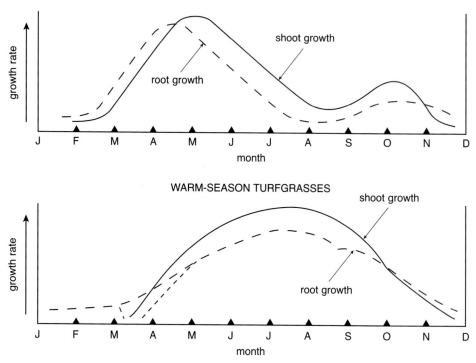

Typical seasonal growth patterns for warm- and cool-season grasses.

- Cutting height – a lower cutting height means more frequent mowing.
- The use of the turf or grass area.

Clipping Return or Removal

The key question is whether grass clippings should be collected and removed from the surface or left in situ where they fall.

There are many obvious benefits from the removal of grass clippings from the mown surface. Often it is important to remove the clippings for presentation reasons, to leave the surface 'tidy' and free from clumps of grass. Sometimes the clippings spill on to paths or planted borders, which is also often undesirable. As well as being unsightly, large clumps of grass clippings can have adverse effects on the lawn or turf.

They can smother underlying grass plants, inhibiting their development and often leading to yellowy brown patches in the turf. They may also create the warm, moist conditions that often foster disease development. In most surfaces used for sport, grass clippings would have an influence upon the game and would affect such performance factors as ball roll. Those who maintain fine-turf surfaces, especially those used for sport, also use the removal of grass clippings as a cultural technique to control Annual Meadow Grass (*Poa annua*). This grass occurs frequently in many turf surfaces and has the capacity to flower and set seed at very low cutting heights. Removal of the flower heads helps to limit the plant's spread throughout the turf surface.

Table 4: Recommended mowing heights and frequencies

Use	Mid-spring to late summer: maximum growth period		Autumn to early spring: growth slowed or stopped	
	Height (mm)	Cuts per week	Height (mm)	Cuts per week
Fine ornamental lawns	12	1–2	20	CWG
Utility lawns	25	1	25	–
Parks / landscape areas	25	1	25	–
Flat bowling greens	3	3–4	8	CWG
Crown bowling greens	5	3–4	8	CWG
Cricket outfields	12–20	1	25	–
Cricket tables (maintenance)	6–8	1–2	12	CWG
Cricket tables (for play)	3	–	–	–
Tennis courts	6	2	12	–
Hockey pitches	20	1	20	CWG
Football pitches	25	1	25	–
Rugby pitches	25–50	1	50	–
Horse-racing tracks	100	1	100	CWG
Golf greens	5	5–6	8	CWG
Golf tees	8	2	12	CWG
Golf fairways	15	1	20	CWG
Golf semi-rough	50	(fortnightly)	50	–

CWG = cut when there is growth in order to maintain the required height.

For most lawns, park and amenity grass areas, clippings will not be of any detriment to the surface if they are dispersed over it. Indeed, they can be positively beneficial as they do in fact return nutrients to the soil. Grass clippings contain plant nutrients, especially nitrogen (N) at around 3–5 per cent concentration by weight. Phosphorus (P) and potassium (K) are also present. On many lawns and amenity grass areas, this may be the only input of these essential plant nutrients. Thus it follows that the removal of grass clippings necessitates the application of additional fertilizer to compensate for the nutrients that are lost as a result. Nutrient application is essential in intensively managed turf where the grass is cut frequently at low cutting heights.

Grass clippings returned to the soil can also be beneficial in sustaining soil organic matter. Such plant residues returned to the soil break down rapidly at first and then progressively more slowly in well-aerated soils, helping to maintain soil moisture, microbial activity and earthworm populations. For most turf and amenity grassland situations, this is highly desirable. For intensively managed surfaces used for sport, there are a number of issues with this approach to grassland management, but in such instances clippings are in any case almost always removed. In intensive systems we have often to resort to other supplementary management practices to assist turfgrass growth and surface development where the soil is devoid of natural aerators and nutrient providers. The argument relating to thatch development resulting from grass clippings is now considered dated. The contribution that clippings make to thatch development is believed to be minimal, since leaf-blade tissues contain little lignin and are readily decomposed.

If clippings are to be returned to the grass surface, do not mow in wet conditions as clumps are easily formed. In dry conditions, clippings are readily dispersed during mowing. Mow frequently to limit the volume of clippings and consider using rotary-type, 'mulching' mowers where appropriate. The design of these machines means that clippings are finely cut, so that they integrate more easily into the turf sward instead of sitting on the surface.

Clipping removal can also be an expensive option. It is time-consuming and you have to dispose of the collected clippings. You can perhaps disperse them over rough ground, or you can compost them. Grass clippings, however, do not compost well on their own and are best mixed with other vegetative material. This can provide a useful source of compost or mulch for landscape areas but often means investing in handling equipment and machinery if you are working on a commercial scale. For large sports grounds, golf courses and parks departments, it is the environmentally friendly way of disposing of large quantities of grass clippings. It has been estimated that in swards dominated by ryegrass, clippings can amount to over 8,000kg/ha per year, and even in fine-turfgrass swards dominated by fescues and bents half of this amount is often encoutered – which is still a significant volume of plant material.

In wildflower meadows, or other semi-natural grassland areas, clippings will be removed as an important management practice. For these areas, it is important to maintain a low soil-nutrient status for the desired species to thrive. The return of grass clippings would increase soil fertility and be detrimental to the biodiversity of the grassland plant species. In such areas, mowing often involves cutting long vegetation infrequently, raking clippings off and removing them from site. Large mechanical rakes and collectors are often used for this purpose.

To summarize, remove grass clippings if:

- They would interfere with the purpose for which the turf is maintained.
- They would adversely affect visual appearance or desired effect.
- If clippings will be excessively thick and therefore damaging to the sward.
- If disease development would be enhanced by their presence.

Always remember, however, that – with the exception of wildflower areas or lower quality landscape areas – if clippings are removed, more nutrient input will be necessary in many instances; for most sports surfaces it will be essential.

Direction of Cut

Varying the direction of cut each time you mow has several key advantages. Mowing in alternate directions produces a striping effect often sought by both amateur gardeners and professional turf managers. This striping effect is caused by the reflection of light from the grass leaves. Differences in reflectivity between the upper and lower leaf surfaces of many species (but especially ryegrass) result in light and dark stripes after mowing as they lie in opposite directions.

This allows intricate patterns to be created by professional turf managers with dramatic effect, as often seen on golf courses or football grounds hosting major sporting competitions or tournaments. Presentation of turf and lawn areas is important both for ornamental areas and for surfaces used for sport. Striping patterns on sports turf surfaces can assist the player when judging distance in play or shot control.

Notwithstanding the significance of aesthetics, there are also sound agronomic reasons for varying cutting direction. In fine turf especially, grass leaves and shoots will develop horizontal orientation in a particular direction if mown consistently in that direction. This is often termed 'grain' or 'nap' and, on fine-turf surfaces such as golf and bowling greens, can be detrimental to play. A ball rolling against the grain will be slowed, while a ball rolling with the grain will gain speed. Grain or nap may also cause the ball to be deflected off course. Mowing in a different direction each time you mow will help to alleviate such conditions and allow truer playing surfaces to be maintained.

Another problem encountered from failing to change cutting direction is that areas where the machine is turned or manoeuvred will be more prone to surface damage, scarring and compaction. Mowing in one direction continually will also increase the likelihood of wheel or roller markings occurring on the turf surface. This is again particularly significant on fine-turf areas where sport is to be played and true surfaces are required for optimum ball roll and speed.

Verti-cutting (Vertical Mowing)

Verti-cutting, or vertical mowing, has developed in recent years with some simple advances in mower technology and is now common practice on most fine-turf surfaces, especially those used for sport.

Mowing grass, especially fine-turf areas, at an appropriate height and frequency of cut does not guarantee that an even, uniform sward will be maintained. This is because grasses grow both vertically and horizontally. Several species produce significant lateral growth from stolons, rhizomes, trailing stems or aerial tillers. These are desirable attributes in many grasses used in turf culture as they help to ensure the grass covers the soil and produces a dense carpet.

However, to keep these grasses in check and to stimulate further lateral growth for enhanced density of coverage, this growth needs to be controlled. If not controlled, fine-turf surfaces can become soft and 'puffy', with increased grain formation. This affects surface playability and, ultimately, appearance. Excessive lateral growth also shades developing basal growth and seedlings to give a false picture of complete turf cover. It is necessary to lift this growth so that it can be mown at the general height for the sward. Various implements can be used with mowing machines to provide 'lift' for cutting such lateral growth. Combs and brushes are often fitted to fine-turf cylinder mowers for this purpose. When fitted behind the front roller, they lift procumbent growth so that it can be severed with the vertical grass shoots and leaves.

All well as promoting density and sward coverage, these tools help to alleviate grain or nap and significantly enhance playability in sports such as golf and bowls that depend upon fast, true rolling surfaces. Specialist units with vertically rotating blades can often replace the conventional cutting cylinder for vertical mowing. These units are set to sever lateral growths at or just below the soil surface. There is a fine line here between vertical mowing and scarification, but these are different operations and seek to achieve different objectives. Vertical mowing units are intended to sever only lateral growths such as trailing stems and stolons and not to penetrate deep into the soil or turf root zone. Scarification is an extreme operation where revolving vertical blades are used to remove thatch and other material from the turf grass surface. This is often a renovation practice where more robust blades or tines must be used than those used for vertical mowing. Light verti-cutting practised regularly causes negligible damage to the sward or surface especially if conducted when conditions, favour rapid grass growth and recovery.

Growth Retardants

Plant growth retardants are used for some areas of amenity grassland to limit mowing and reduce maintenance costs. They are not suitable for fine turf, where rapid recovery from wear and visual appearance is important. In the UK products currently available are Maleic hydrazide, Mefluidide and Trinexapac-ethyl. These products have different modes of action and different effects upon the sward. Maleic hydrazide and

Mefluidide are primarily absorbed through the foliage and inhibit cell division and differentiation in meristematic regions. They are inhibitors of vegetative growth and interfere with seed-head development. Their growth inhibition is rapid, occurring within four to ten days, and lasts for six to eight weeks. Trinexapac-ethyl is also absorbed through the foliage but suppresses growth through interference of gibberellic acid biosynthesis, a hormone responsible for cell elongation. It is slower in growth suppression than Maleic hydrazide or Mefluidide, and its effects last for four to seven weeks.

The timing of application is important, and swards should have been mown two to three days prior to treatment. Application is best carried out when the grass is actively growing in April or May. Uniform coverage and a period of eight to twelve hours of dry weather post spraying are essential for full effectiveness. Only mature swards that have been established for one season or more should be treated with these chemicals. Where floral diversity is not important, herbicides can be mixed with growth retardants to control dicotyledonous species. A product that contains Maleic hydrazide, Dicamba and MCPA is currently available for this purpose.

These products are most useful for the maintenance of untrampled grassland where other forms of management are impractical. Such areas include roadside verges, road and rail embankments, cemeteries and churchyards. With all these products, the number of treatments per year is restricted and some form of mowing is still required at least once during the year to prevent invasion of woody plant species.

Mowing Machines

There are four different cutting mechanisms found on machines for cutting grass:

- Cylinder or reel.
- Rotary.
- Flail.
- Reciprocating knife.

Cylinder or Reel Mowers

The highest possible mowing quality and close, even cutting is obtainable with properly maintained and operated cylinder mowers, which makes them the perfect choice for sports surfaces and for high-quality lawns and recreational areas.

This type of machine has a number of helically mounted blades on a rotating cylinder that cuts the grass against a fixed bottom blade or bed knife. This gives a very effective shearing or scissor-like cutting action. This is the most advanced cutting technology and provides the highest quality of cut available in mowing machinery. The basic design has not changed since Edwin Budding developed the first machine in 1830. The point of cutting between the bottom blade and the blades mounted on the cylinder is termed the shear point.

There are some important concepts to understand about the way in which cylinder mowers work. One of these factors is known as the 'clip'. This is the forward distance travelled between cutting contacts taken from the shear point. The clip is affected by:

- The number of blades on the cylinder.
- Ground speed of the mower.
- Rotational speed of the blades.

If the set height of cut and the clip measurement are not approximately equal, the cylinder blades will not provide sufficient cuts per metre, and this will result in ribbing or a wavy appearance in the cut sward (this effect is also known as marcelling). This problem most frequently arises when the forward speed of the mower is too great and the grass is too long for that particular cylinder-type machine.

The bottom blade gathers grass to the cylinder where it is cut by one of the helically mounted blades passing against it. As the height of cut is reduced, so the thickness of the bottom blade must be reduced, in order that it does not touch the ground. Fine-turf machines have very thin bottom blades. Mowing quality is directly affected by the sharpness of the blades and the adjustment

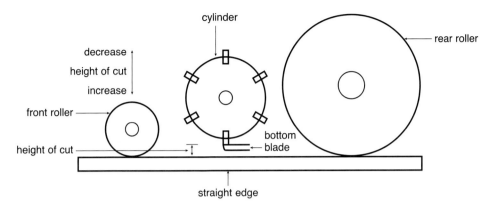

Cylinder mower layout (height of cut adjustment).

between the bottom blade and the cylinder blades. Blunt or dull blades and/or poor adjustment of the cutting action results in torn or bruised grass leaves, which will die back and turn brown. As well as looking unsightly and adversely affecting the visual quality of the turf, these damaged grass tissues are easy sites for disease entry. This condition is often more pronounced with grass species such as Perennial Ryegrass (the most popular turfgrass in the UK), which has tough vascular tissues that resist cutting.

When adjusting the cylinder to bottom blade or cutting action there are two commonly encountered mechanisms: a fixed bottom blade with a moving cylinder or a fixed cylinder with a moving bottom blade. In either case, it is most important that this adjustment is checked and adjusted both frequently and correctly. When set properly, the cylinder must be able to rotate freely when turned by hand and, in the case of fine-turf machines especially, cut a single thickness of paper. In theory it is the 'juices' from the cut-grass tissues that provide the lubrication and prevent metal-to-metal contact. Many professionals now advocate that the cutting action is set with no contact between the blades and that if sharpness is maintained there will be a far more effective scythe cut, which is less likely to tear grass leaves.

Checking the blade sharpness and integrity is imperative for efficient cutting action especially for fine turf that is cut both low and frequently and where a very high standard of surface uniformity is expected. There are a number of manual grinders and centrifugal spin grinders available for sharpening blades on cylinder mowing machines. Blade sharpness can also be maintained on many modern machines by a process known as 'back lapping': the cylinder can be driven in a reverse direction, which helps to remove any burred edges from the cutting blades. This procedure is usually augmented with the use of a lapping compound applied to the blades beforehand. An emery-based slurry in oil or detergent applied to the blades when back lapping helps to maintain a sharp cut between grindings. Apply sufficient compound to the blades and adjust the gap between cylinder and bottom blade to maintain minimal contact when back lapping. Remove any excess compound when the process is complete. and reset the cutting action (and height of cut if necessary). Remember to treat and adjust all cylinders the same on machines with multiple units.

Both the diameter of the cylinder and the number of blades will affect desired cutting height and quality of cut, and will therefore determine the machine's suitability for different surfaces. Fine-turf machines have smaller diameter cylinders with many blades, usually ten to twelve, while cylinder mowers for longer grass areas have fewer blades, four to five, on a cylinder with a larger diameter cylinder. The longer the grass, the larger the diameter of the cylinder needs to be, so that the grass can be physically gathered within the cylinder and cut by the rotating blades.

Pedestrian cylinder mower designed for fine turf surfaces. (Photo: John Deere)

The maximum cutting height of a cylinder mower is the distance from the cutting edge of the bottom blade to the horizontal centre shaft of the cylinder. Grass extending above this will be pushed away, rather than pulled in, by the cylinder.

The cylinder width typically varies from 500–760mm, with some specialized machines for larger areas being 910mm. If a wider cut is required, you will need a number of cutting units – three, five, seven, nine or more. These wider machines will be the ride-on or tractor-operated type. If you wish to cut fine turf you will need a narrow-width machine, because you will be cutting very low. A wide machine will either scalp or miss cutting grass. The typical arrangement for pedestrian machines is one where the cutting cylinder is placed between a smaller front roller and a larger rear roller. The rear roller is often powered (especially on professional machines) to provide forward drive for the machine. This rear roller pushes the grass forward in the direction of travel, creating a striping effect on the finished surface. Depending upon machine width, the roller will be split into two or three sections, which allows for easier turning and greater manoeuvrability. For fine-turf surfaces, the roller should be smooth so as not to leave any markings on the turf surface. On larger machines, especially those with trailed seats, the roller may be ribbed to aid traction. Some machines have rubber-coated rear rollers, which, being much quieter, are useful where the machine has to

Table 5: Number of blades mounted on the cylinder		
No. of blades	**Cuts per metre (approx.)**	**Type of area**
10 or 12	150	Fine-turf surfaces, greens, and so on
7 or 8	90	Good ornamental lawns
5 or 6	65	General lawns with grass collection
5 or 6	36	Sports fields and large park areas without grass collection
3 or 4	28	Longer grass areas that are cut less frequently/road side verges, and so on

be transported over hard surfaces to the mowing site.

The front roller supports the front of the machine, carries the grass-collection box and, most significantly, is used to adjust the cutting height of the machine. Height of cut is set by placing a straight-edge so that it rests upon the front and rear rollers, measuring the distance between the straight-edge and the top of the bottom blade and then moving the front roller up or down until the desired height is reached when the front roller is tightened into position. The front roller does limit the length of grass that can be cut because longer grass and seed-heads will be pushed over and missed by the cutting blades. For fine-turf machines, a comb or brush attachment fitted behind the front roller, to lift the grass, will help overcome this problem.

On cylinder machines designed for longer grass the front roller is situated behind the cutting cylinder, and the larger-diameter rear roller is moved further backwards or, as often as not, replaced by wheels either side of the cutting unit (as, for instance, with gang mowers). Some machines have skids instead of rollers or wheels.

Although there are some specialist cylinder mowers for longer grass areas, most cylinder machines do not work well in long grass and do not cut flowerheads or seed stalks effectively. They are not reliable when cutting grass higher than 40mm, and other mower types should be considered for such areas. Also, unless fitted with comb or brush attachments, they will not reliably lift prostrate growth for cutting.

Cylinder mowers are the most expensive to buy and to maintain. They can be easily damaged – especially their blades, when stones or other objects become trapped. They are best used, therefore, in relatively short grass where such debris can easily be seen and removed prior to mowing. Another feature of cylinder mowers is that the cutting action tends to pull and uproot the grass as the revolving blades cut the grass against the bottom blade. This should not occur with properly adjusted machines but may occur, and be a problem, when mowing young seedling turf where the plants are not yet sufficiently rooted. For this reason a rotary mower is often recommended for the first few cuts on young turf.

In their favour, cylinder mowers have a higher speed of operation than other mowers and can cut large areas quickly. Multiple units (gangs) have a high work capacity and can cover larger areas more quickly than other mower types. The design of cylinder mowers is also the most efficient in collecting grass clippings. The revolving cylinder throws the grass forward and it can easily be collected in a grass box in front of the cutting cylinder. Moreover, in recent years developments in machine technology have

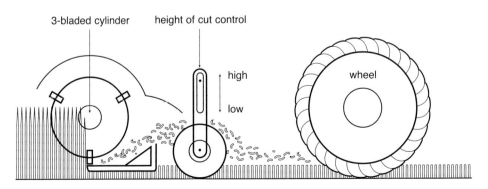

Cylinder mower layout for long grass areas.

significantly improved evenness of cut, closeness of cut and width of cut. There are a wide variety of pedestrian, ride-on and tractor-operated cylinder mowing machines available today for a range of different situations and particular surfaces. For regularly mown grass below 35mm, there is no better mower option.

Gang Mowers

A gang mower consists of a number of cylinder cutting units that are held together on a frame or chassis. It is used for mowing large areas. The cutting unit often has a larger-diameter cylinder and a thicker bottom blade than pedestrian or smaller machines, and is generally more robust in construction. Gang

ABOVE: *Ride-on cylinder mower designed for longer grass areas. Roadside verges in urban areas are often mown with such machines. (Photo: RansomesJacobsen)*

LEFT: *Pedestrian cylinder mower designed for longer grass areas. (Photo: Hayter)*

mowers are either towed behind or mounted on to the rear of a tractor (or other comparable power unit) and can have three, five, ,seven or nine cutting units. There are machines available with more units but these are not common and are used only where there are very large areas to cut, for example on turf farms.

Trailed gang mowers have cutting units driven by land wheels on the sides of each unit, belt drives via the tractor's power-take-off (PTO) or, in some cases, by hydraulic motors supplied by a pump powered by the tractor's PTO. Wheel-driven units are simple in design and relatively cheap and reliable but still very efficient for mowing in all but the most adverse of conditions. Units powered by either belt or hydraulic motor have the advantage of positive cutting in wet conditions, where wheel-driven units would often slip. Wheel-driven units have a clutch mechanism to disengage the cutting cylinders for transport. Land wheels can be of either the pneumatic tyre type or steel. Steel wheels are normally used only on machines where they remain on one site, such as on large sports grounds where no

moving between different sites is needed. Tractor-mounted gang mowers typically have five or seven cutting units on a frame attached to the tractor's three-point linkage system. The tractor PTO shaft provides the power source for a hydraulic pump that then supplies the individual motors on each cutting unit. Variable cutting speed is possible as is back-lapping for blade sharpening or for clearing blockages when mowing. Individual units can be isolated from use and lifted to manoeuvre around obstacles as required. Varying cylinder speeds and tractor forward speed provides a near infinite combination of operating options.

Ride-on gang mowers Most machines consist of a four-wheel-drive power unit with five mounted cutting units, usually three up front and one on each side of the chassis, where the operator sits. These have become increasingly popular, especially for mowing large amenity areas and other specialist areas such as golf-course fairways. They offer some advantages over conventional tractor gang units including their shorter length and greater manoeuvrability, which

This trailed gang mower, with seven cutting units powered by hydraulic motors and the tractor PTO, is suitable for large amenity grass areas. (Photo: Hayter)

is a significant attribute when mowing in confined areas or those containing frequent obstacles. Grass collection is often possible, and many machines can be fitted with different units such as thatch control, rollers or verti-cutting units instead of the grass-cutting cylinders themselves. Their versatility and manoeuvrability provides greater opportunities for varying the direction of cut, controlling grain formation and creating mowing patterns, generally increasing the standards of presentation. They have become very popular in the golf-course sector and other professional sports surfaces.

Triplex or Triple Mowers
These have three cutting cylinders mounted on a power unit. The type includes the specialist machines used for mowing fine-turf surfaces such as golf greens. They usually have hydraulic drive to the cutting units and hydrostatic drive to all three wheels, making them very manoeuvrable and fast mowers, capable of mowing closely, following ground contours and collecting grass clippings. The usual layout is two cutting units out front and one centrally mid-mounted unit, providing a single width of cut. There are models for general purpose or amenity areas as well as more sophisticated fine-turf mowers.

Rotary Mowers
These machines utilize a blade (or blades) rotating at very high speed parallel to the ground. The grass is cut as these blades impact upon it. Optimum cutting performance depends upon a sharp blade meeting upright grass that is turgid and stands up against the blade before it is severed. They are more versatile than cylinder mowers and can cope with a greater range of mowing heights (although they are generally not suitable for cutting below 25mm). The quality of cut improves as the standing height of grass relative to cutting height increases. They are suitable for lawns and amenity areas, and cut all vegetation that they contact, including taller flowers and seed-heads within the sward.

The actual cutting mechanism is usually either a flat metal bar, sharpened at either end on opposite sides to give a cutting edge, or a number of smaller blades attached to a revolving disc. The advantage of the latter system is that the individual blades can swing freely and move away if they happen to hit a stone or other obstacle, which lessens the overall impact and possible damage to the drive mechanism of the machine. On smaller pedestrian mowers, the blade can be attached directly to the drive shaft from the engine but on larger mowers blades will be indirectly driven via belts and pulleys. Belts are the pre-

Greens Triplex Mower. Note the lightweight chassis to reduce mower weight and the smooth tyres to prevent marking of the fine turf surface. (Photo: RansomesJacobsen)

Table 6: Performance of cylinder mowers

Type/size	Hectares per day (8 hours)	Suitable for area (number of hectares)
Pedestrian mowers		
36cm (powered)	0.8	Up to 0.4
41cm (powered)	0.9–1.1	Up to 0.8
51cm (powered)	1.1–1.2	Up to 1.6
61cm (powered)	1.3–1.6	1.6–2.0
76cm (powered)	1.6–1.8	2.0–2.4
91cm (powered)	4.0	2.4–4.0
102cm (powered)	4.9	2.8–4.9
Gang mowers		
Triple (3)*	8	Golf courses, sports grounds, parks
Quintuple (5)	14–16	Golf courses, sports grounds, parks
Septuplet (7)	20–24	Large playing fields/airfields
Nonuple (9)	36–40	Exceptionally large areas/turf farms

*A fine-turf triple mower is normally capable of cutting 18 golf greens in two to four hours.

ferred drive as they have the capacity to slip if necessary, thus lessening any impact damage to the mower. Rotary mowers are, however, more rugged, robust and less prone to damage than cylinder mowers, especially with regard to objects and stones within the sward.

It is critical that cutting blades are sharpened or replaced regularly if cutting quality is not to be compromised. Dull, blunt or damaged blades will result in torn rather than clean-cut grass, which is detrimental both to the grass and to the turf appearance. It is important that cutting edges are ground as necessary, maintaining the recommended relief angle on the blade. Blades can be sharpened with a file or powered-abrasive wheel. Blunt blades not only give poor cutting quality but need more power from the machine to cut through the grass.

Equally important is blade balance. A blade that is not evenly balanced (through being heavier at one end than the other) will cause vibration and strain on drive mechanisms and other machine parts. In the workshop, magnetic blade-balancers hold

Pedestrian rotary mower with grass collection box. (Photo: John Deere)

the centred blade in place, allowing the blade to freely rotate vertically to determine if the blade is balanced or not. At the same time, check that the blades are not distorted, bent or misshapen. Blades that are severely distorted or unbalanced should be replaced.

The mower deck is better situated in front of wheels or rollers, to prevent long grass being flattened prior to cutting. For this very reason, some larger models can now be attached to the front of tractors or other power units. Another factor to consider with rotary-mower deck design is the discharge point for the cut grass. Cut grass is thrown out either at the rear or to the side of the cutting deck. In rear-discharge machines, guards must prevent grass, stones and other objects hitting the operator's legs or the machine's drive mechanisms.

Grass can build up around engines and transmission on such machines, and this can lead to problems. With side-discharge machines, there is less of a problem to the machine and operator but grass and other debris, including stones, can be thrown on to surrounding surfaces. Care must be taken when mowing near people or buildings, and guards must be correctly fitted to minimize the chance of damage or harm being caused to property or people as material is discharged from the mower deck.

In recent years, the development of mulching mowers has helped in the dispersal of grass clippings with rotary mowers. With these machines the design of the cutting blade and mower housing, or deck, keeps the grass suspended so it is repeatedly cut into smaller pieces, which fall readily into the grass sward for quicker decomposition. This technology works best with dry grass. Rotary mowers are generally less effective in wet conditions as the grass is pushed over easily. The grass blades and stems need to be turgid and stand upright against the mower blade if they are to be cut effectively and cleanly. For effective mowing, it is important to keep the mower deck and housing clean. The build-up of grass, dirt and other debris will quickly restrict blade movement, airflow and discharge of cuttings.

Grass collection is possible with rotary mowers, and many models have chutes from the cutting deck through which grass is thrown into collection boxes, usually to the rear of the machine. This collection is aided by the airflow generated by the revolving blade; in some machines fans are fitted to assist grass collection. Again, performance is dramatically affected by moisture, and deteriorates as the grass becomes wetter. Chutes frequently become clogged in such conditions. Reducing ground speed and increasing cutting blade revolution per minute will improve performance in long or wet grass.

Adjustment of the height of cut is not as precise as it is with cylinder machines but it is usually more straightforward and quicker. Common methods for adjusting cutting height include:

• Altering the position of land wheels in relation to the mower deck.
• Moving the cutting mechanism up or down while leaving the machine in the same position.
• Altering the position of spacers around ground wheels.
• Removing or adding spacers above the cutter bar (as with hover-type mowers).

Scalping can occur on uneven terrain or where machines are set too low. To minimize such effects when mowing undulating terrain, it is necessary to have a number of decks, mounted independently of each other, which 'float' over the ground.

Machines up to 500mm wide are often pushed, although there are some that are self-propelled. These machines have only one cutter bar or disc. Machines between 500mm and 760mm wide may have one or two cutters but will be of the self-propelled type. Machines that are wider than 760mm often have three cutters and are of the ride-on type, while machines larger than 1.88m are generally tractor-mounted. The configuration of decks, number of blades or cutters and deck width varies from pedestrian to very large tractor-mounted machines. The relative low cost, ease of operation and

ABOVE: *Ride-on rotary mower with grass-collection facility, which is very useful on many amenity areas. This machine has a box that can be emptied from the operator seat into a trailer. (Photo: John Deere)*

RIGHT *Large ride-on rotary machine with three cutting decks for mowing large areas of grass. (Photo: RansomesJacobsen)*

simple maintenance requirements has made rotary mowers the most popular choice for many who are maintaining general-purpose lawns and amenity grassland areas.

Hover Mowers

This type of mower hovers above the ground. Air drawn in by a fan is pushed out around the edge of the hood that covers the cutting blade. The build-up of pressure under the hood lifts the mower off the ground. If the engine is run too slowly, it will be hard to move the mower about. This type of machine is most often fitted with a two-stroke petrol engine and is popular for use on banks.

Ride-on Rotary Mowers

Various designs of rotary mowers – with front-, mid-, or rear-mounted, mower decks are available for the domestic and professional markets. Cutting blades are powered either via PTO shafts and drive-belts or directly from the engine via a drive-belt. Mowers for the domestic market commonly have mid-mounted cutting decks with a single cutting blade, giving a cutting width of 660–760mm. Grass is discharged from the side. Some have grass-collection chutes to deliver the clippings into a rear-mounted bag. One variant that is very popular for use in large gardens and estates is the lawn tractor.

Lawn tractors are powerful, robust machines with hydrostatic drive, giving an infinite range of forward and reverse speeds. Some have four-wheel steering for enhanced manoeuvrability around trees and other obstacles. The mid-mounted decks usually have two or three blades with cutting widths from 965 to 1170mm. The deck is supported by wheels or small rollers that also serve to adjust the cutting height. Some models have grass-collection systems.

Mid-mounted decks are now also available as attachments for compact tractors. The tractor in effect is converted to a high-output rotary mower capable of cutting relatively long grass and large areas very efficiently. These cutting decks usually have three blades with widths of 1.8m. The tractor PTO shaft

Hover mower – very suitable for banking mowing. Great care must be taken when mowing banking with such equipment. (Photo: Allen Power Equipment)

powers the blades and the deck is raised or lowered by the hydraulic system.

Front-deck rotary mowers are the type most commonly used by professionals. They are highly manoeuvrable and robust machines capable of a high work output, with cutting widths from 1.25/1.8 to 2.25m. Most have hydrostatic transmission, four-wheel drive and power steering.

A hydraulic lift system raises or lowers the cutting deck into position. The deck is designed to follow ground contours. Cutting height is usually adjusted via deck wheels and spacers. Some machines have removable decks that can be replaced with other attachments such as brushes, snowploughs, dozer blades or flail mower heads.

RIGHT: *Garden tractor-type rotary mower with mid-mounted cutting deck – a popular machine for use in large gardens and small park areas. (Photo: John Deere)*

BELOW: *Front-mounted cutting deck with a short chassis base makes these machines highly manoeuvrable. They are sometimes called ZERO turning mowers. (Photo: John Deere)*

Tractor or Mounted Rotary Mowers
These are available for compact and larger tractors and other power units. They can be mounted on the three-point linkage and powered via a PTO shaft. Cutting widths of 1.8 to 2.3m or more are available. Cutting height can be altered by adjusting the land wheels or the rollers on the cutting deck.

LEFT: *Tractor-mounted rotary mower suitable for long grass areas. (Photo: Bomford-Turner)*

BELOW: *The future of banking mowers? A remote-controlled rotary mower designed especially for banking. It has four-wheel drive and a low centre of gravity for enhanced stability and manoeuvrability. (Photo: RansomesJacobsen)*

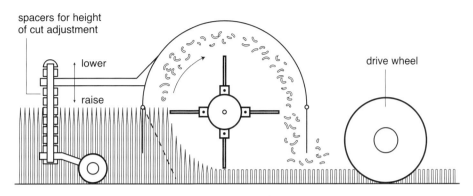

Flail mower layout (height of cut adjustment and rotation of flails contrary to travel).

There are also front-mounted mowers for large tractors. These cut the grass before the tractor wheels pass over the area, thereby overcoming the problem caused by rear-mounted mowers when tractor wheels flatten the grass (particularly in areas of long grass) before the cutting blades reach it.

Flail Mowers

The flail mower is a specialized mower designed to cut rougher areas than either cylinder or rotary mowers can cope with. The grass is cut in the same manner as the rotary mower, with blades, or flails, impacting against and cutting the standing grass or vegetation. The difference with a flail mower is that the blades are hinged to a horizontal shaft that rotates at high speed, up to 2,500rpm. The flails are held outwards by centrifugal force and, as the machine moves forwards, they cut any grass or other vegetation in their path. The flails are free to swing backwards if they hit a stone or other obstacle, thus lessening damage to the machine.

Flail mowers are very robust machines, many being capable of cutting quite heavy vegetation, including woody material. Their strong construction makes them very suitable for cutting long grass and for scrub clearance, and they are less prone to damage from debris in the sward than are other machine types. They can reduce tall vegetation to a finely ground mulch relatively quickly, although overall area-coverage speed can be slow. Because of the small clearance between the flails and the mower hood, debris is re-cut until it is small enough to clear the housing and fall to the ground as mulch. Grass is discharged evenly across the cutting width of the machine (although this can be limited in wet conditions, where clogging and clumps will form). The horizontal rotation of the cutting implement means that these machines are less prone to throwing material away from the path of cutting than are rotary mowers.

A variation on the flail is the Humus cutting deck, which utilizes a rotating shaft fitted with a spirally mounted cutting blade designed to cut and mulch very coarse grass and vegetation. (Photo: Simon Tullet Machinery)

ABOVE: *Ride-on flail mower designed for longer grass areas. Roadside verges and other low maintenance areas are often mown with such machines. (Photo: RansomesJacobsen)*

The blades or flails must be checked regularly for damage and sharpness. Cleanness of cut is not as high as that of cylinder and rotary mowers, and it will be worse if blades are not maintained. Sharpening individual flails is rarely practicable as most will wear at the same rate and the cost of this must be weighed against that of total replacement. It is imperative that the shaft has all its flails fitted or vibration will occur, with possible damage to the machine. Close-cutting is not practicable with flail mowers and height adjustment is more limited than for either cylinder or rotary mower types, although many machines have spacers on land wheels for this purpose. Flail mowers are best suited to cutting areas that require infrequent mowing or for ground clearance operations. In many areas that are cut by flail mowers the vegetation is most commonly cut close to ground level, so it is not always necessary to adjust the height of the cut.

Flail mowers are available in pedestrian, ride-on or tractor-mounted versions. Some are available mounted on hydraulic arms fitted to the rear of a tractor for cutting bankings, ditches or hedges. In recent years, advances in design have greatly improved the quality of

LEFT: *A pedestrian mower fitted with the Humus cutting deck. This is a mower suitable for long grass and scrub areas. (Photo: Simon Tullet Machinery)*

ABOVE: *Tractor-mounted flail mower suitable for long grass areas such as rural roadside verges. (Photo: Bomford-Turner)*

cut available and there are models, particularly larger tractor-drawn machines, with grass-collection facilities.

Grass-collection hoppers are fitted above the modified mower hood and special fan blades at intervals on the rotor shaft help to create draught to blow grass clippings into the hopper. The hopper can be emptied remotely via controls in the tractor cab. These machines are suitable for many amenity grassland areas.

Reciprocating Knife Mowers

This is a highly specialized type of mower that has limited application in turf culture or amenity grassland management. The cutting mechanism usually consists of a series of 'fingers' bolted onto a cutter bar. Each finger has a ledger plate, providing a sharp edge against which a knife consisting of a number of triangular blades reciprocates to cut the grass or other vegetation. Grass is thereby cut by the scissor action and, providing the knife is sharp, it is cut quite cleanly.

Reciprocating knife mowers are ideal for areas where it is necessary to remove the cut

Reciprocating knife cutter bar designed for attachment to a pedestrian tractor power unit. (Photo: Agria Outdoor Power Equipment)

material from site. The grass is left in long swathes on the surface as it is cut close to the ground. This material can then easily be raked up, by hand or by machine, after mowing. This makes this type of mowing

Pedestrian reciprocating knife mower useful for long-grass areas and species-rich swards where cuttings need to be gathered afterwards. (Photo: Agria Outdoor Power Equipment)

MACHINE PURCHASE

Purchasing a new mower is a significant investment. There is a vast array of models for each of the principal mower types, designed to suit all types of surface and conditions. It is well worth looking at several models that fit your specific requirements. Some factors worth scrutiny include:

• Surfaces it is suitable for.
• Operator safety (guards and safety features) and comfort.
• Ease of use and adjustment.
• Quality of cut (clip for cylinder machines).
• Power source and hp or kW rating.
• Manoeuvrability and versatility.
• Productivity (hectares per hour).
• Durability (life expectancy)/ reliability.
• Power steering/four-wheel drive.
• Machine weight.
• Grass-collection system.
• Optional extras/attachments.
• Service and repair costs/parts availability/dealer support.
• Tyres/rollers/skids.

Finally, seek the recommendations of others. Obtain quotes from different manufacturers. Check out the range of procurement options available.

Using Mowing Machines Effectively

• For cylinder mowers it is essential to maintain correct adjustment between the cylinder or reel and the bottom blade. Check this frequently. A good indicator is whether the grass is being cut cleanly or not.
• The cutting height should be set for the particular surface and conditions. Heights should be changed as required to take account of ground and environmental conditions, grass growth and particular surface requirements. When lowering heights of cut, do so in gradual increments.
• Operating speed is important. With pedestrian machines, this is determined by the walking speed of the operator. On cylinder machines, the frequency of clip is determined by forward speed. When using ride-on or tractor-powered cylinder mowers, there is often a tendency to travel forwards too quickly, resulting in areas being uncut or left with a 'ribbed' surface. When cutting long or wet grass, it is often necessary to reduce ground speed if cutting quality is not to be compromised.
• Disengage all cutting units when the machine is stationary or being transported. This is for safety purposes, but also to ensure that cutting units do not run 'dry' – cylinder mowers utilize grass 'juices' to lubricate cutting parts and, when the machine is not cutting, the friction caused by contacting metal parts will generate heat and may cause blade distortion.
• Maintain sharp cutting edges for all mower types. Dull blades mean that grass will not be cut cleanly and this is detrimental to turf health and vigour.
• Mow frequently at a suitable height of cut. If the grass is growing, turf uniformity and density will be sustained better if it is mown. In periods of slow growth, mowing frequency can be reduced and cutting heights raised, but mowing should never be abandoned. Frequent mowing generates fewer clippings for removal or dispersal.

machine the preferred choice for cutting wildflower swards and meadows. There is only a limited number of mowers of this type on the market, most being pedestrian machines used in wildflower meadows or similar grassland areas.

The gap between the fingers on the cutter bar limits the girth of vegetation that can be cut satisfactorily and, in effect, limits it to grass and similar herbaceous material. Also, the height of cut is restricted to ground level. For efficient cutting, the knife must be kept sharp with either a file or angle-grinder. The cutting mechanism should not be lubricated as oil will attract dirt and grit, which will cause wear to moving parts. The cutter bar must be protected with a guard when not in use.

- Avoid mowing in hot, dry weather, in periods of excessive ground or surface moisture or if surfaces are frosted.
- Always check surfaces for debris, stones, and so on, prior to mowing, and remove them. Fine-turf surfaces also benefit from switching or brushing prior to mowing to remove dew.
- Vary the mowing direction, on each occasion where possible, to reduce grain or nap and to minimize wear, compaction and possible travel lines, markings from rollers or wheels on the surface.
- Whenever possible, do not remove clippings unless the surface warrants it or there are particular user requirements.

Mower Maintenance

With any mowing machine, a little care and attention will pay great dividends. Machine life will be increased, cutting quality enhanced and overall running costs reduced. The essential rules of good mower maintenance are as follows:

- Keep the machine clean. Wash it immediately after use. Take care when using high-pressure hoses, especially near any electrical components or switches. Care is also needed with bearings, so as not to blow out grease or oil from load-bearing parts of the machine.
- After washing, lubricate the machine. Apply grease to bearings and other parts as required. Oil any mechanisms requiring lubrication in this way. Apply a corrosion inhibitor to blades/cutting mechanisms.
- Carry out any adjustments necessary, including those to the cutting mechanism and height of cut. Check drive chains and belts and adjust where necessary.
- Service the engine at required intervals. Inspect and maintain air, oil and fuel filters; change oil and check coolant levels regularly. Pay particular attention to engine-cooling systems. Keep airways and intake screens clean and unclogged.

MOWING FAULTS AND REMEDIES

Most problems arise from incorrect machine setting, mowing in inappropriate conditions, or poor operator or management decisions. The cardinal sin is that of mowing too closely and too infrequently, which leaves the cut grass resembling a field of stubble with very poor density or uniformity. Other problems that may be encountered include:

- Scalping. This occurs when the cutting height is set too low for the contours of the area being mown. Change the cutting height or select a machine more appropriate for that terrain.
- Ribbing. The grass has a distinctly ribbed surface following mowing. The grass is too long for the machine setting or, more usually – in the case of a cylinder mower – for the diameter of the reel and the number of blades. Poorly adjusted cylinder mowers can also lead to this condition. Adjust the mower correctly or if necessary use a different mower such as a rotary.
- Washboarding. The surface has a wavy or undulating appearance following mowing, caused by mowing continually in one direction. Vary the cutting direction on each occasion.
- Chewing/torn leaves. The machine is not cutting cleanly. Adjust the cutting action and sharpen the blades or replace them.
- Uneven cutting heights. Poor machine adjustment. Set each side of the mower to the same height on a level surface with a mower gauge.

Check more frequently if you are working in dusty conditions.
- Check tyres for correct pressure and condition. Most mowers have relatively low tyre pressures; take care not to exceed the specified pressure. Incorrect pressure will affect machine height and height of cut.
- Check hydraulic systems and pipes regularly for leaks and damage to hoses. Check

hydraulic oil levels and replenish or change as required.

- Check batteries for condition and charge. Keep the housing clean and remove any corrosion from terminals. If the machine is out of use for an extended period, remove the battery from the machine for storage and give it a top-up charge if required.

- Use only replacement parts or accessories supplied, or approved, by the manufacturer. Using other parts or accessories may infringe any warranty or guarantees for that machine.
- The machine should be stored in a secure, ventilated building and be ready for immediate use.

SOME HEALTH AND SAFETY RULES

- Always wear appropriate personal protective clothing and footwear.
- Follow the manufacturer's guidelines at all times. Read and comply with the instructions and information supplied with the machine by the supplier/manufacturer.
- Ensure that all guards are fitted and all controls are working correctly. Make sure that you know how to stop the mower quickly and safely in an emergency.
- Never try to adjust cutting mechanisms or heights with the engine or power source running. All adjustments should be made whilet the machine is stationary and the power source isolated or switched off.
- Conduct a risk assessment to identify any hazards for the site and the machine. Ensure that you consider: the area to be cut, especially if there are slopes or banking to mow; ground conditions such as surface moisture; the machine controls and safety features.
- Take any appropriate control measures to limit the possibility of an incident or accident occurring.
- Make sure you are familiar with all aspects of the machine as well as its limitations and suitability for the area to be cut.
- If in any doubt, seek the advice of a qualified and competent person.

CHAPTER 3

Irrigation

Water is a vital constituent of all living plants. The growing grass plant requires water in order to sustain its life processes and development. The water content of actively growing grass plants is generally between 75 and 85 per cent by weight. Water content will vary with grass species, environmental conditions and level of cultural intensity. Younger, developing plant tissues are highest in water content, and it is these growing parts of the plant that are also more prone to desiccation in times of water shortage. For most physiological and developmental processes including, crucially, photosynthesis and transpiration, the plant requires water.

Within the plant, the balance between water absorption (via the roots) and transpiration (from the leaves) determines actual water content. For sustained, healthy growth, absorption should exceed transpiration; where this is reversed a water deficit will occur with often serious consequences for the plant. The effects may range from death of plant tissues – or the whole plant – to less severe morphological and physiological adaptations. The internal water balance significantly affects growth rate and plant turgidity. In water-deficit situations the plant may show increased root depth, increased root–shoot ratio, decreased tillering, and a decrease in the number of leaves as well as in leaf area. In some species, there are distinct visual symptoms. For example the grass plant may change colour as well as lose turgidity. The experienced turf or amenity grass manager will get to know these symptoms and use them to schedule irrigation.

Irrigation can be defined as the input of water to supplement or replace rainfall. This chapter will discuss the requirements of the grass plant, the need for irrigation, the methodology of watering grass areas, and the equipment available to do this. Grasses are very resilient plants and will often survive quite dry periods. It should be remembered that the vast majority of turf and amenity grass areas do not receive any irrigation, save that afforded by natural rainfall, and survive relatively well. However, irrigation is sometimes necessary on those areas for which a high degree of surface uniformity is a management requirement or which are subjected to wear or other user factors. This generally means surfaces used for sport, ornamental lawns and other grass areas subjected to intense use or traffic.

The specific reasons for irrigation may include any or all of the following:

- To ensure that there is an adequate supply of water to sustain turfgrass growth and development.
- To ensure successful seed germination or initial turf establishment.
- Where necessary to prevent the death of drought-susceptible species such as Annual Meadow Grass (*Poa annua*).
- To maintain essential turfgrass qualities such as turgidity, verdure and uniformity.
- To wash in fertilizers, pesticides, wetting agents or other materials into the grass surface and flush out accumulated salts.

- To facilitate other turfgrass cultural practices such as aeration, rolling or seedbed preparation.
- To influence or change playing surface characteristics, such as ball bounce and speed on cricket tables.

The costs of irrigation must be considered carefully and the implications evaluated fully before undertaking such expense. Water can be very expensive and is subject to ever-increasing control by water suppliers and, in the UK, by the Environment Agency. An installed irrigation system is also a significant outlay of capital requiring considered justification. The benefits of irrigation are usually obvious and immediate but should only be used where the surfaces or their intended use would be adversely affected without it. The practice of irrigation also needs careful management as it can easily be over-used to the detriment of grass and playing surfaces. It is relatively easy to keep 'green' grass but these overwatered surfaces do not necessarily equate to the best surfaces for play. They will inevitably be slow and soft or spongy and be of no value where ball roll, speed or player traction are important.

The Soil–Water System

When rainfall or irrigation falls onto a soil or turf surface it will soak into the soil profile and displace the soil pore space (the air between soil particles). The rate at which water enters the soil is known as the infiltration rate. If water continues to infiltrate the soil it will eventually displace all the air within the soil pores and the soil will become saturated. If rainfall or irrigation continues a situation will arise in which, depending on the topography of the area, water will remain on the surface (leading to 'pooling') or it will run off onto other areas. This situation is often exacerbated with compacted soils where there is little or no pore space to absorb the water. The key determinant in the behaviour of water in a soil is largely the system of pore space and capillaries. This in turn is

determined by the relative amounts of the various solid constituents (sand, silt and clay particles), described as soil texture or more precisely as the particle size distribution and the way in which these combine as aggregates to form soil structure.

In a natural soil system with good structure, water will drain away though the system of pores and capillary channels. As this occurs, air will be allowed back into the soil and it will revert to an unsaturated state. The water, which drains away, does so under the force of gravity and is termed gravitational water. When all such free water has drained away, the soil is said to be at field capacity – that is, the soil contains only the water that is 'held' against the force of gravity. In a soil or root zone with good structure, there will be a balance of air and water within the pore and capillary system. The water retained in this manner is also known as capillary water. Some water may be held in clay soil particles as their physical structure allows them to absorb water.

After drainage, water is lost from the system principally through two routes. Some water may be lost directly from the soil surface by evaporation, but most water will be taken up by the plant from the soil and used in growth and development processes or lost from the leaves through transpiration. For the purposes of irrigation, these two factors are usually considered together and termed evapotranspiration. The amount of water lost is directly influenced by both grass-growth rates and solar radiation.

As a soil dries out the plants will wilt if no further water is added to the system. This is commonly referred to as the wilting point (WP). The water that is in the soil and available to the plant between the states of field capacity and the wilting point is known as the available water capacity (AWC). The amount of water required to restore a soil to field capacity is known as the soil moisture deficit (SMD).

Available water capacity can be expressed in millimetres (mm) depth of water that is available to the grass plant in each metre (m) depth of soil. (*See* Table 7) The depth of soil

Table 7: Available water capacities (AWC) of the main soil types

Soil	mm (water) per m (soil)
Sand	60
Fine sand	90
Sandy loam	110
Loam	170
Silt loam	170
Clay loam	165
Clay	140

or root zone is critical, as it is this that provides the 'reservoir' of soil water for the plant. One can calculate the actual amount of water available to the plant in mm using the following simple equation.

$$\frac{\text{available water (w)} \times \text{soil depth (R)}}{1000}$$

Irrigation Practice

In determining the quantity or volume of water to apply to a particular area, two methods are most commonly used:

1. Estimating consumptive water use (measuring evapotranspiration).
2. Taking measurements of soil moisture status.

Evaporation Pans

The water lost, via evaporation, from an evaporation pan approximates to that lost from a well-irrigated turf area. The actual loss will depend on environmental factors such as temperature, wind, relative humidity and soil water potential. The pan needs to be maintained in an open unshaded area and protected from high winds. It is often necessary to conduct some local trials to correlate actual losses with local environmental conditions over a set period to arrive at meaningful figures for water loss. Figures can be calculated from turfgrass wilting stage to post irrigation to provide a series of benchmarks against which future irrigation inputs can be determined. Variations in turfgrass rooting depth, thatch levels, soil type and bulk density (degree of soil compaction) will affect evaporation rates whilst other environmental conditions in the vicinity may not change. Therefore, it may often be necessary to make adjustments or recalculate irrigation figures during the actual growing season. This methodology for calculating irrigation need has not been fully developed or utilized in the UK for turfgrass. The weather conditions in the UK are very variable and there is a distinct lack of precise data available for using these instruments for turf and amenity grass areas.

Set up correctly, and calibrated to local conditions, such equipment can provide guidelines or parameters in which to operate, but there is still an essential degree of local knowledge, technical acumen and personal experience in making irrigation decisions.

Soil-moisture Measurement

There are several devices for the measurement of soil moisture status but the most commonly used one is the Tensiometer. This device consists of a porous ceramic cup at the tip of a tube that is connected to a vacuum gauge at the other end. When the soil system is filled with water (to field capacity), the ceramic cup is inserted into the ground so that there is immediate contact between the cup and the soil. As water is removed from the soil and it dries out water is pulled from the tube of the tensiometer via the ceramic cup, causing the gauge to register a higher tension – this equates to lower soil water potential. This measurement is usually expressed in kilopascals (KPa). In the UK, field capacity in turf and grassland soils generally approximates to minus 4KPa. Soils should not be allowed to dry out to less than about minus 15KPa before irrigation is applied. It is important to site the tensiometers correctly and in

Table 8: Typical irrigation demand for turf and amenity grass areas			
Area	**Application (mm)**		
	Day	*Week*	*Season*
Fine turf (greens, and so on)	4	28	280
Sports pitches and lawns	3.6	25.2	252
Amenity areas	2.5	17.5	175
Rough grass and trampled open space	1.8	12.6	126

particular with consideration for the effects of site topography and soil depth.

Many factors will affect exactly how much water an area of turf or grassland requires. These include prevailing weather conditions (including, most importantly, rainfall), soil type, topography, rooting depth and mowing height together with use and wear patterns. In the UK, the average rainfall nationally is around 1,090mm, but this varies quite dramatically around the country. The west side is wetter and may have in excess of 2,030mm (Wales); the east is generally drier, having less than 640mm (East Anglia). When one considers that the potential transpiration loss from turfgrasses is around 60–75mm per month in summer, and that rainfall at this time is often less than 13mm, the need for irrigation is immedi-ately apparent. An important consideration to note when evaluating rainfall figures is that typically most of the UK's annual rainfall occurs in the autumn and winter period. Thus, it is often the case that even in the 'wettest' areas of the country irrigation is needed in the summer to maintain grass growth.

The requirements of turf and grassland areas in terms of their users and management expectations vary quite considerably. Premier sports surfaces require the greatest inputs of irrigation to maintain surface quality and playing standards, whilst many lawns and amenity grassland areas have no such demands and are often not irrigated. The costs of irrigation for these latter areas cannot be justified either economically or environmentally.

THE PROBLEM WITH SPORTS TURF SOILS

Many soils used for the construction of surfaces intended for sport, particularly golf greens, have a very high sand content. This is purposely so. However, this places greater pressure on the soil-water reservoir to sustain desired grass growth. These sand-dominant soils or root zones have a large bulk density and a small total porosity, which makes them very effective in shedding excess water – so much so that little is retained within the soil profile to support grass growth. In some surfaces, the root zone may have as little as 15 per cent of its volume as water. The problem is often exacerbated when there is only a relatively shallow depth of soil over a drainage layer or compacted subsoil. The efficient soil depth for the retention of soil water may be as little as 150mm or less. If the available water capacity were only 15 per cent then such a soil depth would hold only a maximum of 22.5mm of water!

Thus, for these surfaces, irrigation becomes a necessity if any level of cover is to be maintained. Sports surfaces are usually intensely managed and mown closely. Such treatment often favours shallow-rooting grasses, which are then subject to greater stress in times of water shortage as the reduced root system can draw water only from a very limited depth. In effect, such surfaces cannot be maintained satisfactorily without irrigation.

Irrigation Timing and Intensity

It is important that the rate of irrigation or precipitation does not exceed the infiltration rate of the soil, otherwise pooling or water run-off will result. Water infiltration is generally faster as soil texture becomes coarser, and on these soils water can be applied more rapidly.

Coarse soils lose more water to drainage and evapotranspiration than do finer textured soils. Coarser soils therefore require less water per irrigation treatment, although more frequent applications will be needed in the active growth season. Watering in the evening or overnight, in the absence of solar radiation, results in less evaporative loss and more efficient use of water. Watering during the day is both wasteful and, in hot conditions, potentially harmful to grass as it can cause scorch. For sports surfaces, such irrigation timing (evening) is also less disruptive to play as the water applied has time to fully infiltrate the soil prior to play commencing. Wet soils and surfaces are more prone to compaction as the soil structure is wet and liable to collapse when subjected to pressure. Prolonged surface moisture may also favour the growth and development of harmful grass-plant pathogens.

Soils cannot be moistened to a uniform depth when the input of water does not achieve field capacity, as there will be areas within the profile that are not wetted or suf-ficiently moistened. Smaller inputs of water will result in uneven wetting of the soil and whilst grass growth may be maintained, the grasses will often be shallow rooted. For effective irrigation, a better strategy is to soak the soil to saturation point (field capacity) at infrequent intervals and to complement this with lighter applications of 2–4mm either daily or every other day, depending on local weather conditions. Such practice will also help to flush salts from the soil.

Irrigation practice profoundly affects grass root growth and survival. An aim of turf culture is to encourage deep root systems when conditions favour new growth and to preserve this system as much as possible during unfavourable environmental conditions. Grass communities do undergo often quite dramatic changes during the growing season and so irrigation requirements need to be commensurate as well. The strategy outlined above will help to maintain a viable sward when the plants natural tendency is often to shed many of their functional roots during summer drought periods. To achieve greater water infiltration and water penetration to depth that will facilitate deeper root systems, spiking or slitting the area prior to irrigation is beneficial. This will ensure that most of the water applied will penetrate the soil and permeate through the profile to where it is needed most: at the plant's root level. Water infiltration can also be increased if irrigation

Table 9: Infiltration rates for soil-texture types and slopes (mm per hour)

Soil-texture class	Percentage of slope		
	0–4%	*8–12%*	*16%+*
Coarse sand	31.75	19.00	8.00
Fine sand	24.00	14.25	6.00
Sandy loam	19.00	11.50	5.00
Very fine sandy loam	15.00	9.00	3.75
Silt loam	12.75	7.50	3.25
Sandy clay	8.00	5.00	2.00
Silty clay	5.00	2.75	1.25
Clay	3.25	2.00	0.75

is applied in shorter bursts (known as multiple cycling), allowing the water more time to soak into the soil before more is applied. Dry thatch or dry organic soils can be particularly problematic as these materials are difficult to wet (hydrophobic); being water repellent, they tend to shed water and restrict its downward movement. These factors need to be controlled and managed using other cultural techniques such as mechanical scarification. The application of soil-wetting agents may be required for such areas or surfaces.

Irrigation Depth

Irrigation is usually applied and measured as depth of water in mm. The exact amount of water to be applied on any one occasion is obviously dependent upon the amount of water needed to bring the soil back to field capacity. Moderate stress may favour fine turfgrass species, but it is a fine line between this state and that which will lead to loss of turf vigour, uniformity and cover. Adopting such a policy towards irrigation demands careful scrutiny from the experienced turfgrass manager. One guideline is to allow for 50 per cent water depletion from the soil before irrigating. For example if the water holding capacity is 22mm then irrigation might be applied when 11mm of water has been lost through evapotranspiration. In practice, however, you will need to apply more water to allow for probable inefficiency in the distribution system, water movement in the soil profile and possible losses in drift or direct evaporation. As a rule of thumb, allow for 75 per cent additional water to compensate for such losses. Thus, for the example above, 11mm is now 14.7mm, which in effect means 15mm for actual application purposes.

Measuring Water Delivery

It is one thing to turn on a sprinkler but quite another to know when to turn it off. In practice, irrigation does demand that the person applying water to a turf or grass area have some knowledge of local site conditions, prevailing environmental conditions and of grass growth including visual signs of irrigation need or stress. There is really no substitute for such knowledge and experience. Many people rely heavily on such and maintain very good turf surfaces and amenity grassland areas. In recent years, however, there has been more pressure exerted by water suppliers and environmental agencies on those who maintain turf and grass areas to account for and justify the actual quantities of water, which they are using. This requires turf managers to be able to measure the amounts of water that they are using and often even predict the quantities they will require in the future. It is only good practice to measure water use for irrigation purposes and maintain accurate records for future management.

The Water Meter

Take a reading from the water meter prior to starting irrigation; record this figure. Apply irrigation at a pre-determined setting for a fixed period and then turn off. Take another reading from the meter. The difference in these two figures is obviously the amount of water that has been used. Divide the number of litres of water used by the area irrigated in metres square to arrive at a depth of water applied in millimetres (1 litre of water over $1m^2$ of surface will give 1mm depth).

This method gives a useful figure for water use and will probably suffice for most purposes, but it is not wholly accurate. There are inevitably losses of water in the system and factors such as heat and wind will affect exactly how much water actually contacts the ground. It is important to make sure that no water from this same source was used elsewhere during the test period.

The Can Test

This method is most appropriate for installed irrigation systems. In this method, the area to be irrigated is divided up into a grid and cans or jugs of the same size are placed at equal distances over the area to collect the irrigation water. Run the sprinkler system for a set time (one hour) and then record the quantities of water in each container. From these results, one can calculate the average or mean to determine irrigation depth applied. The major benefit of this method is that it enables the operator to determine the efficacy of the irrigation system and calculate a figure known as the coefficient of uniformity (CU).

After calculating the mean application rate (A), determine the difference between this value and all the individual readings. Add all these values together to get a total (T) value. The coefficient of uniformity can then be calculated as follows:

$$CU = \frac{(1 - T)}{(A \times \text{No. of Cans})} \times 100$$

If the result is a figure of 85 per cent or less then it is likely that some improvements are needed to the irrigation system. This can mean adjustments to sprinkler spacing or changing the actual sprinkler heads. Figures lower than 70 per cent for CU mean that a new system is probably required. Too low a figure for CU mean that the irrigation water will not be applied evenly and this will lead to uneven grass growth, waterlogged areas and dry patches in others.

Effects of Under- and Overwatering
Overwatering of turf or grassland is both wasteful and damaging to the sward and surface. Grasses will not develop deep root systems if water is plentiful at the surface. These shallow-rooted grasses will be more prone to damage from wear and from the effects of drought when water reserves are depleted or in short supply. This usually manifests itself through the shedding of roots and aerial tillers leading to a thinning of the sward. Wet conditions will encourage moss and weed invasion and will inhibit thatch breakdown by soil microorganisms, which in turn often means that surfaces are soft and spongy. Such surfaces provide poor playing conditions for sport, or any degree of surface wearing capacity and will often favour the growth and development of several plant pathogens. In fine-turf surfaces these conditions often lead to undesirable grasses such as *Poa annua* (Annual Meadow Grass) dominating the sward.

Underwatering, has a similar effect to those above but most often with the more likely outcome or danger of grass death and total loss of cover. Moderate water stress on fine-turf surfaces generally favours fine-turf species such as fescue and bent grasses (the requisite species for sports surfaces such as golf and bowling greens); such grasses are often the preferred plant species in wildflower swards as they are less invasive or dominant than coarser species, which prefer moist conditions.

Sources of Water

It is imperative for successful irrigation practice that a reliable and sustainable source of water be procured: the source of water must be able to supply all the irrigation water required for a full season. This can often mean quite substantial volumes of water: 10 hectares of turf will need 1 million litres of water to apply 10mm depth of water.

In determining a suitable source, the key factors are likely to be:

- Total volume of water required.
- Security of supply.
- Cost.

There are three principal sources of water for irrigation purposes. These are: mains

---

PORTABLE SPRINKLERS

For those sprinklers attached to a hose-pipe and moved around a site by hand it is useful to know how long to leave such a sprinkler running to achieve a desired depth of water for a particular area. To calculate this, simply turn on the hose, to required flow and pressure, and let the water run into a container such as a water butt or bowser for a set time. Measure this volume of water and then calculate the time needed to apply the required amount of water to the area.

Table 10: Requirements for an 18-hole golf course

Average year	Annual total = 16,000m³
(Irrigation required: 200mm)	Daily maximum = 100m³
Dry year	Annual total = 18,000m³
(Irrigation required: 300mm)	Daily maximum = 100m³

---

supply; surface water abstraction; and ground water abstraction.

Mains Supply

While this may seem to be an obvious source of water – and is indeed used by many to supply their irrigation needs – there are several significant drawbacks that limit its use, especially for the irrigation of large land areas such as parks, golf courses and sports grounds. The major problem is cost. When compared to other sources of water it is very expensive, and the tendency for prices to increase above the rate of inflation is likely to continue in the future. Such water will become increasingly restricted, especially for leisure usage such as watering turf and amenity grassland. Mains supply requires a temporary storage tank facility and pumping equipment to:

• Cater for possible interruptions to supply or restrictions in times of drought.
• Cater for possible low water pressure or fluctuations that would impede effective irrigation application.
• Provide a 'break' in the system to prevent possible back-siphoning and contamination of public water if using liquid feeds or other additives in the irrigation water.

There may also be problems with levels of chemicals in the water, often added in water treatment, such as chlorine and fluorine.

Surface Water Abstraction

Water can be abstracted (under licence from the Environment Agency) from streams, rivers and lakes for use as irrigation water.

The licence will specify the maximum quantity that can be abstracted at an annual, daily or even hourly rate. A minimum flow control will be imposed whereby abstraction must cease in order to protect the water source when water levels fall below this standard. Winter abstraction is generally preferred as water is usually more plentiful. This water will then need to be stored in reservoirs (above or below ground) for use in the summer months. When applying for an abstraction licence the applicant will have to make the case for such abstraction, justifying the need and specifying the quantities required. Surface water is prone to pollution from pesticides, disinfectants, fertilizers, oil, salt and other chemicals and will need to be assessed for such contaminants before it is used to water turf and amenity grassland.

Ground Water Abstraction

The most common form of ground water abstraction is that of the borehole. This is also subject to licensing by the Environment Agency, and licences are granted only when the agency's criteria have been met. The licence will specify the source of supply, location, means and purpose of water abstraction, time period, quality, means of measurement, requirement for records, any special conditions, and the expiry date.

A borehole is established by drilling into water-bearing strata deep underground. Sites that are geologically suitable for boreholes are those containing deposits of limestone, chalk or sandstone. In some areas, boreholes may be artesian but in the majority of cases, a pump and rising main will be required. This means that a supply of electricity, normally

3-phase is needed. This may be available on site, but if not it can prove to be expensive to install. A borehole will usually be 300mm in diameter and can vary in depth from 50m to 120m. Ideally, for the efficiency of water distribution, the borehole should be sited centrally to the area being irrigated. Depending on the local soil type, the borehole may or may not be lined with steel. Boreholes do offer several important advantages in that they are a permanent source of water with little or no variation during the year, running costs are minimal, and usually the water is free from contamination. In some areas, boreholes may reduce the costs of water by over 90 per cent.

The disadvantage of boreholes is that there can be significant costs in initial installation including, not least, those incurred for preliminary extraction testing to locate a viable water source. There are great variations in site hydrology and geology from one area to another and often even within a restricted geographic area. Professional advice must be sought when exploring this possibility as an irrigation source.

Water Quality

Most of the water used to irrigate turf and amenity grassland areas is taken from rivers, streams, ponds, lakes and boreholes. Such water may be contaminated from a variety of physical, chemical or biological impurities. These can cause damage to the grasses and blockages in distribution equipment and sprinklers.

Impurities

Physical Impurities
These include sand and clay particles as well as organic matter and iron in suspension. If not removed they can lead to abrasion and blockages in the irrigation system equipment and can leave deposits on the turfgrass plant. There are a number of different types of filtration systems available to remove these impurities and the types and number required will depend upon the quality of

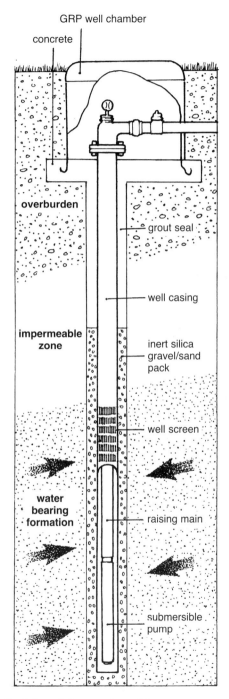

Borehole: typical construction and features.

water required. Filter sizes are defined in terms of the particle sizes they will remove (in micrometres – μm). For most turf and grassland sprinklers, filtration down to 500 μm should be adequate.

Chemical Impurities and pH

Most of the water in the south and east of England is classified as 'hard', that is it contains high levels of calcium and is alkaline. This can lead to calcium carbonate deposits forming in pipe work and distribution equipment, leading to blockages in the system. White deposits may also be evident on turfgrass leaves and tissues, and the pH of the soil or root zone will become more alkaline. It may be necessary to install water treatment equipment to acidify this water. This usually means either ion-exchange units with hydrochloric acid or using concentrated nitric acid.

Water from coastal areas may have high levels of chlorine and sodium, especially where landward seepage of seawater occurs. In industrial areas, copper, zinc, lead and cadmium effluents may find their water into the water supply while in rural areas pesticides and nitrates may be present. If such contaminants are present, it is important that regular chemical analysis is conducted and, where necessary, specialist advice sought.

Biological Impurities

If surface water is being used, there may be a problem caused by algae build-up as well as a risk of plant disease contamination. There are a number of water purification and treatment systems available together with pumps and aquifer equipment to maintain water clarity and purity.

Water Storage

Above ground, tanks constructed from galvanised corrugated steel and lined with butyl rubber provide a useful 24-hour storage facility for irrigation water. These are usually sited adjacent to the pump house and are available in a range of sizes from 15–366m³ capacity. It is critical that such tanks have a rigid cover, both to satisfy health and safety requirements and to prevent algal growth and other contaminants entering the water. Larger storage facilities such as reservoirs may be required for golf courses and other large turf or grassland areas. Reservoirs can be constructed by excavation or by forming embankments to contain the desired volume of water. They can be 'fed' by streams or via pumped water from sources such as a borehole. When constructing large reservoirs, greater than 25,000m³, the advice of a qualified civil engineer should be sought, and this person should oversee the construction on-site. Reservoirs and water storage facilities must be fenced off with appropriate warning signs and safety equipment displayed clearly.

In determining the size of the water storage facility it is necessary to know the volume

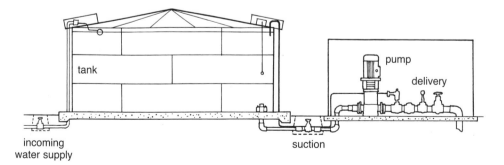

Storage tank above ground and adjacent pumphouse.

of water required for irrigation. A storage tank should hold at least enough water for one day's use at maximum demand, while a reservoir should store at least one week's worth of water, again of maximum demand.

Irrigation Equipment

There is a range of different types of irrigation equipment and systems available for watering turf and amenity grassland areas. These can be broadly divided into two groups or categories:

1. Those that require manual setup and breakdown on a site.
2. Installed permanent systems.

Many factors will determine what equipment will be used for a particular area, but the requirements of the turf or grass must be paramount. To maintain turfgrass uniformity all plants must be watered evenly. The root system of a grass plant draws water from a relatively small lateral area. Root depth is often also limited (often to 100–200mm or less); irrigation depth must be precise when watering to such depths. Grass plants respond rapidly to changes in soil moisture and are readily susceptible to water-deficit stresses.

Portable Irrigation Equipment
In the main, these are either of the sprayline type or the sprinkler type, which may or may not be self-travelling. Spraylines consist of a length of aluminium or plastic piping on which a series of nozzles is mounted through which water is ejected and sprayed over the area being watered. Water is usually supplied via a hosepipe connected to the mains supply or other water source. The pipe will usually be mounted onto a series of wheels or rollers to aid its transportation around a site.

Sprinklers apply water in the form of a jet. Water is commonly dispersed through a hammer-type nozzle that rotates by water pressure and 'throws' the water over the area. Self-travelling sprinklers are available for use on sports and amenity turf areas.

Travelling sprinkler: this is often used for large amenity areas and winter-games areas where no installed system exists. (Photo: Connectomatic)

This type of machine usually consists of a reeling drum mounted on a small irrigator trolley, which pulls itself along on a cable. The cable is pulled out and anchored on the area to be watered and then the water supply is turned on. The reeling drum rotated by the irrigation water gradually rewinds the cable and, in so doing, pulls the trolley along, thereby travelling over the area with the sprinkler watering it at the same time. Most machines can give up to 120m of coverage before being moved to another location. Mobile irrigators operate on a similar principle but have a cable drum operated by a spinner nozzle, which pulls the irrigator along until an automatic stop brings the irrigator to rest and cuts off the water.

Such watering systems afford flexibility in their use but do require greater labour input than do permanent systems. Often problems occur when operatives are off-site attending to other tasks. They are prone to damage caused by frequent movement, set-up and dismantling and vulnerable to theft or vandalism when used on exposed sites without close supervision. They are, however, relatively cheap and easy to operate, making them ideal for small sports grounds or other similar facilities.

Permanent Systems

These are normally installed only for irrigating large areas of high-quality turf or amenity grassland, particularly golf courses and sports grounds. They are very expensive to install but once fitted demand little in the way of labour and, with computer controllers now in common use, they will almost run themselves. They are commonly referred to as 'pop-up sprinkler' systems as they use sprinklers with retractable heads that are lifted up above ground level by the pressure of the irrigating water when the system is activated. They automatically retract below ground so that they are flush with the turf surface when not in use. The sprinklers thereby cause a minimum amount of obstruction and can be safely driven over by maintenance machinery when not in use. A permanent system will consist of a number of component parts, the most significant of which are: the pump; the distribution system (pipe work); a controller; and the sprinklers.

Pumps

Pumps are required to supply the required flow rate at a pressure that will provide optimum operation for each outlet or sprinkler head. The pumps in most common use are usually powered by electricity and either single- or multiple-stage centrifugal type. In the past many irrigation systems have been installed with basic centrifugal pumps driven at a fixed speed. These have proved to be very limited and are now being replaced with variable speed pumps. The former type are inefficient as the required flow rate and pressure conditions of most systems will vary depending upon the system usage; and such pumps are designed to work with one set of operating conditions. Pumps should have a capacity rating to produce 10 per cent in excess of the flow rate and pressure of the system. More than one pump may be required depending upon the size of the installation, the water source, and the size of land to be irrigated.

The Distribution System

The pipes used for irrigation systems will be unplasticized polyvinyl chloride (UVPC) or, much more commonly today, polyethylene. In the past, most irrigation systems used UVPC as it is a cheap material and easy to join with glue. Its major disadvantage is that

The 'heart' of the irrigation system – the pumps. (Photo: Rainbird)

The 'brains' of the irrigation system – the control system. (Photo: Rainbird)

it degrades when exposed to sunlight, turning white and brittle before eventually cracking. Polyethylene is available as blue medium density polyethylene or as black medium or high-density pipe in various classes for particular uses and situations. It is more expensive than UVPC, but most installations now use this material as it is thicker-walled and more durable and flexible. It is commonly available in sizes up to 140mm diameter in either 50m or 100m coils. A wide range of valves and fittings are available to control flow and pressure within the distribution system. Pipe sizes will depend on the length of pipe, the flow required, expected pressure losses due to friction and changes in elevation.

The Controller

A range of mechanical or electro-mechanical timers to electronic and computerized controllers can control the irrigation system. Most new permanent irrigation systems, especially those used for larger areas, are now installed with an electronic or computer control system. Electronic systems provide accurate timing with multi-programme facilities at a relatively low cost, but a computer control system would be most appropriate for a golf course or large sports ground complex. They can retrieve store and process data from weather stations and soil-moisture monitor-

ing equipment and can provide a print-out of data if needed. However, they are obviously more complex to operate and more expensive to install than are electronic systems. In some advanced systems, the central computer controller can be linked to satellite controllers located adjacent to the irrigated area in a more extensive irrigation system. The controller is linked to the electrically operated solenoid valves by a system of wires and cables.

Sprinklers

A wide range of sprinkler heads is available from a host of different manufacturers. For automatic pop-up systems, the main types of rotary sprinkler are characterized by the drive system – whether it is impact-driven, gear-driven, piston-driven, cam-driven or crown head (two-gear-driven control-rotating nozzles). In most modern systems, the gear-driven types are preferred as they are undoubtedly smoother in operation and far quieter than other types of sprinkler. The heads can be full-circle or part-circle sprinklers that reciprocate back and forth across a fixed pre-set arc, or they can be adjustable arc heads. Two-speed sprinklers are also available, which rotate at different speeds during each rotation. Matched precipitation heads rotate through 360 degrees, but a

*Close-up of pop-up sprinkler in operation.
(Photo: Rainbird)*

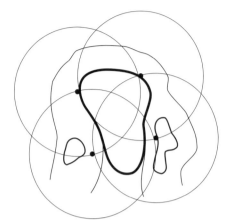

square spacing

blanking plate with a selected arc is inserted in the nozzle so that water is distributed
over part of the circle at the same rate as a
full-circle sprinkler.

A range of nozzle sizes is usually available
for each type of sprinkler head.

Sprinklers can be spaced in different con-
figurations:

- Triangular.
- Rectangular.
- Square.
- In-line.

In order to achieve uniformity of cover,
sprinkler spacing should not exceed 50 per
cent of the diameter for square, rectangular
or in-line spacing, or 55 per cent of the
diameter for triangular spacing. Spacing,
however, will be influenced by wind speed,
direction and the particular requirements of
the irrigated surface as well as changes in
ground elevation and topography. With
installed systems, provision should always be
made for manual watering from hydrant or
take-off points. Mobile irrigators may be
required if the installed system does not
cover the total area of the facility, for example golf-course fairways.

With installed sprinkler systems, it should
be remembered that a consequence of

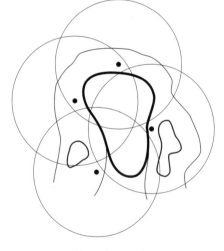

triangular spacing

Sprinkler layout for golf greens.

delivering water in a radial manner is that
the precipitation rate will decrease as the
distance from the sprinkler increases. Overlapping of sprinklers is necessary to ensure
even watering of the whole area. The actual precipitation rate will be influenced by
equipment factors such as nozzle orifice size,
nozzle shape, nozzle number, and the operating pressure. Prevailing weather conditions

ing uniformity, although this will decrease markedly as spacing exceeds 65–70 per cent of the sprinkler-wetted diameter. Fewer sprinklers will reduce installation costs, as there are fewer heads and less distribution pipe work. In golf green situations the distance between heads or sprinklers may be as close as 50 per cent of the wetted diameter and is termed head-to-head. This is generally used only for intensively managed turf areas where turf uniformity is crucial.

System Design

The installation of irrigation systems is a major project requiring significant capital outlay. It is therefore critical to seek the expertise of a professional irrigation designer or consultant before embarking on such a project. The irrigation designer will require some base information on which to design a system. This will include:

- Water use rates and characteristics.
- Soil types and properties.
- Terrain and area requirements.
- Site climate.
- Turf management practices.
- Desired level of provision.

The design process will involve site visits and surveys to collect and assimilate all such necessary information. After determining the irrigation requirements, the position of outlets and sprinklers can be determined with necessary distribution pipe work and controls. Calculation of design hydraulics for pipe work and valves, determination of pumping equipment and control systems will also be needed. Plans and specifications will enable a qualified and competent contractor to install the system as designed.

Careful selection and supervision of contractors installing the system is also critical. There are professional organizations that can assist in the selection of such contractors. Many specialist irrigation companies offer a design and build service. What is most important is that the requirements of the end user and the turf or grass area are fully met.

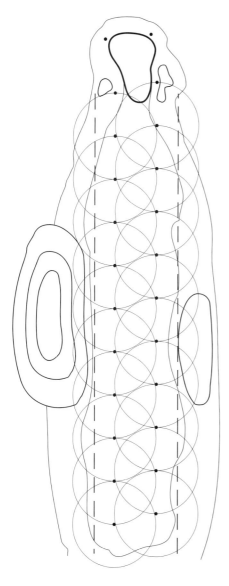

Layout of sprinklers for fairway irrigation.

will also affect water distribution, especially wind and temperature.

Uniformity of coverage is most singularly affected by the layout pattern and spacing of the individual sprinklers. Triangular patterns allow for greater spacing while retain-

---

**KEY POINTS FOR PORTABLE AND
INSTALLED IRRIGATION SYSTEMS**

Portable systems

• Relatively inexpensive.
• Highly manoeuvrable.
• Larger pressure and discharge rates required.
• High precipitation rates susceptible to wind blow.
• Inefficient watering frequently occurs.
• Susceptible to damage with continual set up and break down.
• Labour required for set up, movement and breakdown.
• Generally limited to operative working hours during the day (also the time of maximum evapotranspiration).

Installed (permanent) systems

• High capital cost.
• Potential for high uniformity of application and efficiency.
• Maintenance essential.
• Low labour requirement.
• 24-hour watering capacity.
• Greater water use efficiency.
• Computer controls for data inputs and record keeping.
• Link to weather stations possible.

System Maintenance

Permanent irrigation systems are expensive to install and it is important that they are well maintained and managed to ensure continued effective and trouble free irrigation. It is critical that the system is operational for the peak irrigation period in the summer months. The main period for servicing and maintenance will be during the winter months when the system is shut down. In preparation for the winter, the system must be drained to avoid any possibility of frost damage, particularly in exposed pipe work such as that near to the storage tank. It may be necessary to blow out the system using compressed air to ensure that is no water left in the pipe work. Care must be taken that this process is not executed too quickly to avoid damaging surges of water. During this closed season attention to maintenance and repairs will help to avoid problems during the irrigation season.

During the winter, solenoid valves should be operated occasionally to ensure that the plungers and springs are free. Setting the controller to syringe will operate the valves. Check all sprinkler heads to ascertain their condition and establish any maintenance required. Check the arc, speed of rotation of each sprinkler and that they pop-up, and retract fully from their housings.

It will pay to start up the system prior to the season to allow time for final repairs before full use is required. Reconnect and check the pumps, replacing all drain plugs, and check the seals. Check all pressure switches, valves and reservoir float switches and adjust if necessary. The system should be filled slowly by operating the pump manually with purge valves open. It often takes a few days to clear all the air from the system and up to 8 hours to refill the system on a large complex such as golf course. Close the purge valves and check air release and pressure relief valves, as well as pressure vessels and gauges. Check that the sprinkler heads attain the correct working height and that there is sufficient clearance around the head itself. Check the controller and make sure that the sprinklers are adjusted and working correctly to cover the required area. Finally make sure there are no leaks or drops in pressure in the system.

These guidelines are only for general illustration and there will be variations with different systems and installations. The important point to remember is that irrigation systems must be maintained and serviced in accordance with the guidelines of the manufacturer or supplier. These should have been provided at the time of installation. If in any doubt, seek the advice of a qualified irrigation engineer or the manufacturer.

Water Conversation

Water is an expensive commodity subject to ever-increasing control and restriction. It is

Sprinklers in operation on a golf course. Most golf courses have installed pop-up sprinkler systems for at least the greens and teeing-ground areas. (Photo: Rainbird)

Testing is essential to ensure that the quality of the water is suitable for irrigation and that no contamination of the environment will result from its use. Rainwater collection systems are also a possibility for facilities with major buildings from which it can be collected, such as those found in football and other sports stadia.

Water conservation should be a priority for all turf and amenity grassland managers. The irrigation system must be well designed and engineered to maximize efficient watering. Good management of this equipment should ensure that the potential for irrigation optimization is achieved. In recent years, there have been several developments in irrigation technology that can assist with water conservation. These have included improvements to flow rate and control devices; better sprinkler distribution

only sound economic policy and better for the environment that it is used judiciously and frugally. Many turf and amenity areas do not receive irrigation; but for those intensively managed surfaces that do there are a few guidelines that can be used to ensure efficient irrigation whilst minimizing water usage.

Grass Selection
It may be possible to use warm-season grasses. These grasses have a lower water demand than cool-season grasses, and some grass-breeding companies are currently investigating their use in climates typical of northern Europe and the UK.

Water Sourcing
The use of 'grey water' is now being utilized for irrigation purposes. This is non-potable water unsuitable for public use but sometimes very suitable for irrigation. Large sports complexes, golf courses and other amenity facilities are now investigating reusing wastewater from buildings. Reed-bed systems can be established to filter and clean the water of toxic impurities before its application to the grass areas.

MANAGING TURF TO CONSERVE

- Raise the cutting height – grasses will develop deeper root systems.
- Water infrequently and to depth – to promote deep root systems.
- Maintain good soil condition and structure. Relieve compaction.
- Avoid mowing on hot sunny days – it increases transpiration losses.
- Keep mower blades sharp – limits grass damage and assists rapid healing.
- Apply Nitrogen sparingly – N increases leaf growth and the greater surface area have more transpiration losses.
- In times of water shortage – reduce N, supply more K and Fe.
- Only water those areas it is necessary to do so.
- On hot days – 'syringing' cool season grasses will help them overcome wilting.
- Monitor water usage and where it is actually going. System efficacy.
- Invest in sensor control systems.
- Consider system redesign or other improvements.
- Shaded areas need less water – so give them less!

For scheduling irrigation, a weather station is a very valuable tool for monitoring environmental conditions. (Photo: Rainbird)

patterns; low precipitation rate sprinklers for low infiltration rate soils; sensors for system, soil and environment monitoring; improved control systems; and improvements to communication and remote monitoring equipment. The emphasis has been on improving uniformity of application and greater precision of the operating system.

CHAPTER 4

Nutrition and Fertilizer Application

The growing grass plant requires certain elements or nutrients that are obtained from the atmosphere or the soil. In turf management, soil nutrient levels are supplemented through the well-established practice of fertilizer application. This chapter will discuss the requirements of the grass plant, the need for different plant nutrients, and the methodology of applying fertilizer to turf and grass areas and the equipment available to do this. It should be remembered that the vast majority of turf and amenity grass areas do not receive such treatment, and survive perfectly well without fertilizer input. There has also been an increase in the use of alternative grass seed mixtures containing plants such as clover for large, low-maintenance amenity grass areas. Where clippings are returned to the sward in such areas, they are largely self-sustaining in terms of nutrients. Fertilizer input is usually required on those areas for which a high degree of surface uniformity is a management requirement and those areas that are subjected to wear or other user factors. This generally means surfaces used for sport, high-quality ornamental lawns and other grass areas that must tolerate intense use or traffic.

The costs of fertilizer application must be considered carefully and the implications evaluated fully before undertaking such expense. Fertilizer application usually brings obvious and immediate benefits, but it should be carried out only where the surfaces or their intended use would be adversely affected without it. Fertilizer application also needs careful management as it can easily be overdone – to the detriment of grass and playing surfaces. It is relatively easy to keep 'green' grass, but overfed surfaces are not necessarily the best surfaces for play and, in other areas, overfeeding can lead to the dominance of coarse invasive species that are often not desired.

Soil Chemistry

Plants derive the nutrients they require for growth and physiological responses primarily from the soil, specifically from solution within the soil. The soil water contains a weak solution of various chemical elements that are present in the form of electrically charged particles called ions. Chemical symbols show the type and number of electrical charges present. Within the soil, it is the clay and organic matter fractions that are of greatest significance in the supply of plant nutrients. Clay particles and organic matter have a negative surface charge, which attracts positively charged ions known as cations. These are held by a relatively weak electrostatic force in an exchangeable state. This is referred to as cation exchange capacity (CEC).

The most important cations are calcium (Ca^+), potassium (K^+), magnesium (Mg^{2+}), sodium (Na^+), ammonium (NH_4^+), iron (Fe^{2+}, Fe^{3+}), aluminium (Al^{3+}) and hydrogen

(H$^+$). Many of these cations form the main components of the soils nutrient reservoir. They are readily available for plant uptake or for exchange with each other and with other elements. Cation exchange capacity is very important in determining the potential of a soil or root zone for storing plant nutrients. CEC is determined by soil texture, type of clay particles present, percentage of organic matter and possibly soil pH. Cations resist leaching but can be replaced by other cations due to mass action and the preferential adsorption of some cations over others. When cations such as ammonium (NH$_4^+$), potassium (K$^+$) and calcium (Ca$^+$) are supplied to the soil in fertilizers and lime, these ions replace other cations already adsorbed on exchange sites on the surfaces of soil or organic matter and/or plant roots.

As well as providing a reservoir of nutrients for plant uptake, the presence of different cations has a major impact on the physical properties of soil, specifically its structure. Saturation of exchange sites by sodium (Na$^+$) and/or hydrogen (H$^+$) causes clay particles to disperse, with a consequent loss of structure. Such soils frequently become severely compacted and subsequently impermeable to water. When calcium (Ca$^+$) or other cations are applied to the soil these improve flocculation of clay particles and overall soil structure.

Several important anions (negatively charged ions) also present in the soil do not attach to soil colloids and are thus easily lost from the soil in drainage water. The most significant anions are chloride (Cl-), sulphate (SO$_4^{2-}$), nitrate (NO$_3^-$), hydroxyl (OH$^-$), bicarbonate (HCO$_3^-$), silicate (S$_1$O$_3$) and phosphate (H$_2$PO^{+-}, HPO$_4^{2-}$).

Fine textured soils generally have higher clay content and therefore a higher CEC value than coarse-textured or sandy soils. CEC is expressed as the amount of exchangeable cations per unit dry weight of soil (usually milliequivalents per 100g). Many soils or root zones used for sport turf surfaces contain a high percentage of sand and have a very low CEC capacity, and so they require more frequent fertilizer application. The managers of such surfaces may have to con-

Table 11: Soils and cation exchange capacity (CEC) values

Soil type	CEC value
Sand	1–6
Sand and peat	1–14
Clay loam	25–30
Clay	80–120
Organic matter	150–500

sider whether to incorporate organic matter to such areas to improve nutrient retention.

Organic matter is important in soils as not only does it have a high CEC but it is the major contributor to soil nitrogen levels. Nitrogen is the only major plant nutrient that is dependent upon soil organic matter for its storage and release. Levels of soil organic matter are a good indicator of how much nitrogen is stored in this form for eventual release to the plant. Nitrogen is not found on soil analysis reports because its levels are subject to decomposition of organic matter, and this is highly variable. Nitrogen is also highly prone to leaching as nitrate (NO3-). In addition, organic matter contains phosphorus, sulphur and trace elements, particularly copper, zinc and boron. Many of these are released by soil microbial activity. The soil solution also contains organic compounds as well as dissolved oxygen and carbon dioxide. Many ions are held in the soil solid particles by chemical reactions such as that of phosphate with iron and aluminium to produce insoluble compounds.

The uptake of nutrients from soil solution by plants is most often determined by their concentration and is affected by several factors, including the following:

1. Fertilizer input.
2. Nutrients in irrigation water.
3. Deposition from the air.
4. Amounts and chemical forms of nutrients.
5. Soil processes that affect the relationships between solid and solution.

Soil pH

Soil pH is a measure of soil acidity or alkalinity. It is actually a measurement of the hydrogen ion concentration (more correctly activity) in the soil solution and on negative exchange sites. It is measured using a negatively logarithmic scale ranging from 0 to 14. On this scale pH decreases as the hydrogen ion concentration increases and a change in acidity from 5 to 4 is a far greater change than that from 6 to 5. A pH value of 7.0 is neutral; values below this are acid and those above it are alkaline. In temperate soils containing a substantial proportion of organic matter, pH values are not normally found below 4.0 or above 8.0.

Soil pH is important as it has several significant influences on plant growth:

1. Plant species have different optimum pH ranges.
2. It affects the availability and amounts of nutrients held in the soil.
3. It affects toxicity levels for nutrients and other elements.

4. It affects micro-organisms and their activity.

Over time, there is a tendency for most soils to become more acid. This is attributed to:

- Leaching of calcium from the soil;
- The effects of carbonic acid and dilute sulphuric acid in rainwater; or
- The effects of acidifying fertilizers – particularly those containing ammonium salts.

The rate at which this acidification takes place depends upon the soil type and its buffering capacity. Soils with a high clay content and/or organic matter have a high buffering capacity due to the presence of a large number of negatively charged exchange sites – these maintain the ability to resist changes in pH. On sandy soils, the reverse is true and pH changes can be rapid.

pH and Grass Species
Soil pH has a significant effect upon the botanical composition of the sward, or the actual species of grasses and other plants that

Soil pH and tolerances of some of the main turfgrass species.

| Species |
| Perennial Ryegrass |
| Creeping Bent |
| Hard and Sheep's fescues |
| Smooth-stalked Meadow Grass |
| Annual Meadow Grass |
| Browntop Bent |
| Red Fescue |

4.0   5.0   6.0   7.0   8.0   Soil pH

acid — mildly acid — neutral — mildly alkaline — alkaline

will grow or persist in a particular soil. Most of the common grasses used for sports turf and amenity areas grow best under slightly acidic conditions (pH 6.2–6.5) because this is the pH where most soil nutrients are available to the plant. On fine turf surfaces (greens and ornamental lawns), it is recommended that a pH of 4.8–5.5 be maintained so as to retain the desirable Red Fescue and Brown-top Bent grasses. At this pH, these grasses will grow satisfactorily, but weed grasses such as Annual Meadow Grass will be discouraged. Another desirable outcome for these surfaces is that earthworm activity will also be reduced. On areas containing Perennial Ryegrass it is important to maintain a soil pH above 5.5, or around 6.0–6.5 if they are subject to wear. Soil pH below 5.5 will often lead to an accumulation of fibre and increased thatch layers, making surfaces soft and prone to other problems such as disease ingress.

pH and Nutrient Availability

Nutrient form and availability change in the soil as pH fluctuates. With increasing acidity, the availability to plants of nitrogen, phosphorus, potassium, calcium and magnesium decreases. In acid soils, hydrogen, aluminium, iron, manganese and zinc will be plentiful. At high pH levels, calcium dominates and phosphorus, again, becomes unavailable, as do most of the micronutrients except for molybdenum.

pH and Toxicities in Soils

Plants can be poisoned in acid soils below pH 5.5. In these conditions toxic amounts of soluble manganese can be released into soil water, and with increasing acidity (< 5.0) toxic levels of aluminium are also released. Manganese present in large quantities destroys root and leaf cells. Aluminium can have the same effect, but root damage caused by phosphorus deficiency is amore likely outcome.

pH and Soil Micro-organisms

Many beneficial micro-organisms occupy the soil or root zone. Of particular significance for soil nutrients are those that decompose

Soil pH and nutrient availability.

organic matter and/or convert ammonium to nitrate. Bacteria such as those in the actinomycetes group that decompose organic matter become less numerous as pH declines, their preferred pH range being 5.0–9.0. Fungi, which are slow decomposers of organic matter, dominate at low soil pH. Bacteria that convert ammonia to nitrate prefer a pH below 6.0. Some bacteria are beneficial to grasses in that they attack pathogenic fungi occurring in the soil; these are most prevalent and effective at pH range 6.5–7.5 or near neutrality. Pathogenic fungi harmful to turf include Rhizoctonia (pH <6.0), Ophiobolus and Fusarium (more virulent in neutral to alkaline soils).

Soil pH Testing

The testing of soils for pH is best done in a laboratory where standardized conditions can be maintained and more accurate results determined. Samples must be taken at random over the area for which a pH measurement is required. Sufficient samples should be taken to ensure a representative bulked quantity is available, from which a sub-sample can be tested. Soil cores can be taken with a range of different soil augers and corers. Uniformity of depth is important, and for most turf surfaces a depth of 100mm will be sufficient. In the laboratory, a sub-sample for testing is mixed with distilled water or calcium chloride solution and the pH is measured by electrometry. There are a number of soil-testing kits available, including soil probes for use in the field. These may be useful for a rough check but the effectiveness of the probe types is limited, as pH results will show significant changes with variation in soil water content. The frequency of testing is dependent upon such factors as soil type, particular surface, user requirements and maintenance standards and practices. For turf and grassland on loam-based soils, testing every four to five years may be sufficient, while it will be more appropriate to test those on sandy soils every one to two years.

Soil pH Amendment

Raising Soil pH
In most circumstances soil pH increases or becomes more acidic with time, especially those soils subject to intensive management, and therefore the requirement is usually to raise pH so that the soil is less acidic. Any material that will soak up hydrogen ions will raise pH. Not all materials are suitable however, as some (for example, caustic soda) have potentially damaging side effects. The most commonly used material is limestone, or calcium carbonate ($CaCO_3$). It is never pure, as it will usually contain magnesium carbonate, silicate and other materials, and is normally applied in the form of ground limestone or ground chalk. Burnt lime or slaked lime ($Ca(OH)_2$) will cause scorching if applied to established turf.

The minimum amount of lime to obtain the desired soil pH should be used, as overapplication will lead to a weedy, disease-

Table 12: Guideline quantities for calcium carbonate application (g/sq m)		
Soil texture	pH 4.5–5.5	pH 5.5–6.5
Sand/loamy sand	85	110
Sandy loam	130	195
Loam	195	240
Silty loam	280	320
Clay loam	320	410
Organic soil	680	790

prone turf with increased worm casting. The actual amount of lime to apply will depend on the soil pH value and the physical nature of the soil (*see* Table 12). The final pH required and the timing of application is also important. On fine turf, the consequences of overapplication of lime can be particularly serious, especially with regard to disease. However, in circumstances where the pH has become extremely acidic it will still be necessary to apply some lime. The actual rate of application can be determined by soil analysis. As a general rule of thumb, do not apply more than 2,500kg per ha to actively growing grass. For greater quantities, it will be necessary to split the application into several treatments over a number of months or years. Higher rates than this can be tilled into the soil prior to turf establishment.

Liming changes pH most rapidly under the following conditions:

- The particles of the liming material become smaller.
- Temperature increases.
- Soil moisture content increases (up to field capacity).
- The liming material is thoroughly mixed with the soil.
- The magnesium content of the material decreases.

This means in effect that pH change is most rapid when very finely ground, high-calcium limestone is mixed thoroughly through moist, warm soil. Treatment is most effective if the dressing is mixed with the full topsoil depth as part of seed- or turfbed preparation. If lime is being applied to established turf, it should be done so in early winter so that it is washed into the soil before the growing season begins. Spiking, slitting or coring the turf prior to application will help to ensure that the material quickly enters the soil.

The necessity for lime is obviously dependent upon soil type, turf use and management practices, and the decision to apply it should always be based on soil analysis. No precise guidelines can be given but, as an indicator, fine turf surfaces (such as golf and bowling greens) may need pH amendment every three to five years. For these high-maintenance surfaces, soils should be tested for pH at least annually. For other areas on loam-based soils or clay, applications less frequent than every five years will probably be the norm, but again requirements are subject to grass growth, changes in soil pH and the desired management objectives. On winter sports areas, for example, lime application may be required at least every five to six years in order to maintain the optimum pH of 6.0–6.5

Lowering Soil pH
The process of reducing pH is known as acidification. Sulphur applied to the soil will be converted to sulphuric acid (H_2SO_4) by soil microbes and the pH will decrease when this reaches a high enough concentration. The use of sulphate fertilizers (for example, ammonium sulphate) will also reduce soil pH. This can be supplemented by application of ferrous sulphate in repeated doses every seven to eight weeks throughout the growing season. Overuse must be avoided, however, as it can impair the drought tolerance of the turf.

Calcareous soils that have a pH greater than 8.2 because of the presence of excessive calcium carbonate ($CaCO_3$) are nearly impossible to acidify. As long as lime remains in the soil, it is not possible to decrease pH. If soil tests indicate that the soil is highly buffered with calcium carbonate, then do not expect to increase nutrient availability by reducing soil pH through acidification with sulphur. Instead, apply nutrients in a form that will be quickly available to the plant, such as foliar feeds. Iron chlorotic grass growing on calcareous soils can be rapidly returned to a green colour by treatment with chelated iron.

Use of Topdressing
Soil pH for turf and grass areas can be gradually adjusted by using topdressing materials of the desired pH. Topdressing materials such as sands, loams and compost materials build up in the soil profile over years of application and can have a significant effect on soil pH. A neutral or alkaline topdressing material can be used to balance the effects of acidifying fertilizers where further acidification is undesirable.

Nutrients for Grass Plant Growth

Actively growing grass plants contain 75–85 per cent water, with the remaining fraction composed primarily of organic compounds frequently referred to as dry matter. Such compounds are the result of photosynthesis and the fixation of carbon (C), hydrogen (H) and oxygen (O) drawn from atmospheric carbon dioxide (CO_2) and water H_2O. Carbohydrates are then subsequently used to synthesize complex organic compounds containing not only carbon, hydrogen and oxygen, but also several additional elements derived from the soil. Thirteen mineral elements are recognized as being important for grass plant growth. These are the macronutrients nitrogen (N), phosphorus (P), potassium (K), sulphur (S), calcium (Ca) and magnesium (Mg); and the micronutrients, or trace elements, copper (Cu), manganese (Mn), iron (Fe), molybdenum (Mo), boron (B), chlorine (Cl) and zinc (Zn)

Sulphur, calcium and magnesium are also sometimes referred to as secondary nutrients, as they are intermediate in importance

Table 13: Nutrients important to plants

Nutrient name	Chemical symbol	Form available to plant
Nitrogen	N	NH_4^+, NO_3^-
Phosphorus	P	HPO_4^{2-}, $H_2PO_4^-$
Potassium	K	K^+
Sulphur	S	SO_4^{2-}
Calcium	Ca	Ca^{2+}
Magnesium	Mg	Mg^{2+}
Copper	Cu	Cu^{2+}
Manganese	Mn	Mn^{2+}
Iron	Fe	Fe^{2+}, Fe^{3+}
Molybdenum	Mo	MoO_4^{2-}
Boron	B	$B(OH)_4^-$
Chlorine	Cl	Cl^-
Zinc	Zn	Zn^{2+}

between the other major nutrients (N, P and K) and the micronutrients. These secondary nutrients are important for grass plant growth but they rarely feature in planned fertilizer programmes, as they are seldom deficient in most natural soils.

In addition to the above, grass plants also take up other mineral elements that they do not appear to need for their metabolic functions or whose precise role is unknown. Grasses take up larger quantities of silicon, which may be present at up to 3 per cent in dry leaf matter. Other elements that have been found in grasses include aluminium, arsenic, cobalt, fluorine, iodine, lead, selenium, sodium, strontium and vanadium. Although they may be found in only small quantities, occasionally the presence of these elements may interfere with the take-up of other minerals or have a toxic effect on plant growth.

Nitrogen

Nitrogen is the nutrient required in the greatest quantities by the growing grass plant and differs from the other major plant nutrients in that it is not a mineral derived from soil mineral matter but from organic matter. Principally, soil micro-organisms carry out the transformation of organic matter and the different forms of nitrogen. The process by which soil organic matter is broken down to release ammonium ions is known as mineralization. The rate of ammonium release increases as soil temperature rises. Rather than being a one-way process, mineralization is in fact a net consequence of two opposing microbiological processes – mineralization and immobilization. Micro-organisms utilizing nitrogen-rich materials such as fresh grass clippings will release some nitrogen as ammonium ions, but other micro-organisms breaking down low nitrogen materials (such as peat or woody material) will use ammonium present within the soil in direct competition with green plants. In some cases, this can actually lead to nitrogen deficiency in the plant.

Bacteria convert ammonium ions to nitrate (NO_3^-) by a process known as nitrification, which is also dependent upon soil temperature. Nitrate, unlike ammonium, is not held to any extent on soil exchange sites and is quickly lost from the soil in drainage water if not taken up by plant roots. Nitrogen can also be lost by the conversion of nitrate to nitrous oxide (N_2O) or nitrogen gases (N_2) by soil bacteria under conditions of poor soil aeration and waterlogging. This is known as denitrification. The compacted, organic matter-rich soils of many turf areas provide highly favourable conditions for denitrification as they are often wet and denitrifying bacteria are most active when readily decomposable organic matter is present. The injudicious use of irrigation, giving rise to alternating periods of good soil aeration and waterlogging, results in substantial losses of nitrate through denitrification. Gaseous loss of ammonia (NH_3) can also take place in alkaline soils through a chemical conversion of ammonium ions (NH_4^+).

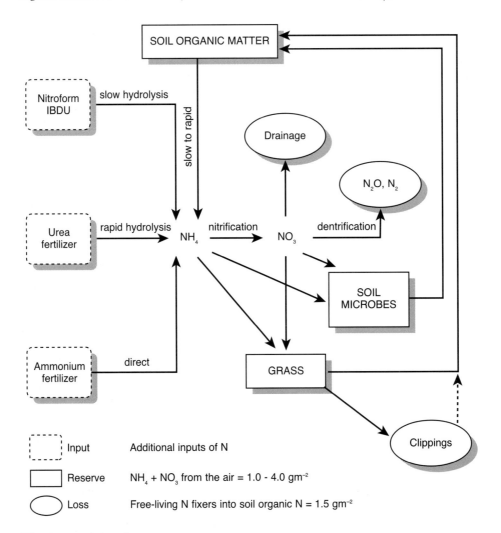

The nitrogen cycle in turfgrass systems.

There is, in fact, little loss of nitrogen from non-intensively used turf or other amenity grass areas where grass clippings are returned to the sward. Grass clippings constitute an important resource in the recycling of nitrogen within grassland systems, and their removal is a major drain on nitrogen reserves. It has been estimated that the removal of grass clippings from fine turfgrass species can be as much as 80kg/ha of nitrogen. For ryegrass swards that receive fertilizer input, this can be as much as 300kg/ha of nitrogen. Thus, it is immediately apparent that for these low-maintenance swards nitrogen fertilizer application is not normally necessary to maintain a healthy sward. As soil nitrogen supply is directly related to organic matter levels, those soils inherently low in organic matter are often very low or even inadequate in nitrogen. This is why sports turf surfaces on sand-based soils require greater nitrogen fertilizer input. The nitrogen content of organic matter is generally constant at 4 to 5 per cent and changes in levels in the soil reflect changes in soil organic matter levels.

Nitrogen is an essential component of chlorophyll, amino acids, proteins, nucleic acids, enzymes and other plant substances. Adequate nitrogen is therefore vital for healthy plant growth. In contast, too much nitrogen will lead to excessive aerial shoot growth, poor root and lateral shoot growth, higher disease incidence, reduced carbohydrate reserves, poor tolerance to heat, cold and drought, and wear. It will also lead to dramatic shifts in those species growing in that sward, favouring coarser invasive grasses that will then dominate. Some turfgrass diseases such as severe infestations of Red Thread and Dollar Spot are most often symptomatic of low nitrogen levels and can often be eradicated with an application of nitrogen fertilizer. Too much nitrogen is not easily remedied and the adverse effects must be weathered until the nitrogen levels in the soil have diminished.

Potassium

Potassium is second only to nitrogen in terms of the quantities required by the actively growing grass plant. It is a major constituent of some soil minerals, micaceous clays and potash feldspar. It is from these materials that potassium is released to exchange sites on soil colloids. Plant roots can access this potassium from soil solution. Soil minerals release potassium very slowly, but where clippings are not removed and the soil is loam- or clay-based they are released at a sufficient rate to maintain grass growth. Very sandy soils are usually dominated by quartz and contain insignificant amounts of micaceous material; even when such minerals are present they will not normally release sufficient potassium to satisfy the demands of sports turf or areas subject to intensive wear. Sand-dominated soils also have a low CEC value and so retain little potassium on exchange sites and what they do retain is readily leached in drainage water. The potassium ion is almost identical in size and behaviour to the ammonium ion and both these cations compete equally for exchange sites. The rate of leaching for

---

FACTORS AFFECTING SOIL NITROGEN LEVELS

Factors that decrease the available pool of nitrogen in the soil:

- Microbial immobilization during organic matter decomposition.
- Leaching (principally as nitrate).
- Clipping removal.
- Gaseous loss due to volatilization of ammonia.
- Denitrification to N_2 and N_2O.
- Possible chemical or physical fixation in the soil.

Factors that increase the available pool of nitrogen in the soil:

- Fertilizer application.
- Deposition of nitrogen from the atmosphere.
- Return of organic matter to the soil (plant residues).
- Mineralization of organic nitrogen by microbial activity.

potassium approaches that of nitrogen in sandy soils.

Potassium can be fixed more stably by some clay minerals where potassium ions occupy the cavities between silica sheets in adjacent clay mineral layers. This fixed potassium can exchange slowly with the soil solution and forms a reserve in the soil.

Potassium is not a constituent of living cells but it is important in the synthesis of numerous plant components and for regulating or catalyzing many physiological processes. Potassium is needed by plants to control water movement between cells, for stem lengthening and thickening of cell walls, and it helps in disease resistance. As potassium concentration within the plant increases, tissue water content decreases and plants become more turgid. Potassium fertilizer is often applied to improve grass wear tolerance as well as survival during periods of cold, heat or drought stress.

Phosphorus

Phosphorus is taken up by plants as anions but the ionic form present within the soil varies with soil pH. At around pH 5.0, 90 per cent of the phosphate may be present as H_2PO^+, but as pH increases to 7.0, or neutral, this phosphate dissociates to HPO_4^{2-} and roughly equal amounts of the two forms are present in the soil. Many turf soils have received liberal quantities of phosphate-containing fertilizers in the past and are high in total phosphorus. However, phosphorus has a tendency to precipitate in solid forms, leaving relatively low concentrations of available phosphate. That said, grass plants are very efficient scavengers of phosphate owing to their extensive root systems and root infection by endotrophic mycorrhiza whose hyphae ramify within the soil to contribute to root exploitation of phosphate.

Phosphate reserves in the soil are present in both organic and inorganic forms. Organic forms are often dominant in semi-natural and natural areas of grassland where little or no fertilizer is applied. The release of phosphate from soil organic matter depends upon microbial activity. This process of mineralization is affected by soil temperature, pH and aeration. In areas where phosphorus fertilizer has been applied, inorganic forms of phosphate predominate. Phosphorus reacts with iron and aluminium at acid pH to form relatively insoluble compounds and with calcium at alkaline pH; it is most soluble in neutral soils. Phosphate can also be absorbed or precipitated onto existing solid particles.

In many situations, the amount of available phosphorus in the soil is surprisingly low compared to the amount removed by actively growing grass plants. This is apparently due to the dynamic equilibrium between soluble and insoluble forms of phosphorus. As the reserve of available phosphorus is depleted by plant uptake, some of the insoluble phosphorus becomes soluble at a sufficient rate to sustain grass growth requirements. On areas where grass clippings are not removed, this may be adequate and no fertilizer input is required. Phosphorus immobilization can be beneficial in that grasses can be expected to utilize a small proportion of fertilizer phosphate in the year of application and some of the subsequently immobilized phosphate will be available to the plant for several years.

Phosphorus provides the plant with a means of holding and transferring energy for metabolic processes. It is a constituent of adenosine triphosphate (ATP), an inorganic compound containing high energy bonds that, when broken, can transfer energy for use in the synthesis and decomposition of various organic compounds. Because of its mobility in the plant, phosphorus is conserved and used repeatedly where needed. Maximum concentrations of phosphorus occur in meristematic tissues where new cell production takes place. Phosphorus is also essential to photosynthesis, in the making of protein and new cell walls, and in promoting rapid extension of shoots and roots.

Calcium

Calcium is most often the principal nutrient absorbed onto exchange sites, and in neutral soils it takes up the majority of negative exchange sites on soil colloids. Soils formed from limestone and chalks contain large quantities of calcium carbonate (Ca^{2+}). Calcium minerals are soluble and with adequate moisture are easily leached from the soil, which has the effect of reducing soil pH. Calcium minerals are very prevalent and deficiencies are rare except on very sandy soils or where strong acidity has resulted in calcium leaching. Plants need calcium in high quantities. It is required in meristematic regions for cell production and is an important constituent of cell walls. Calcium also influences the adsorption of other nutrients, particularly potassium and magnesium; it is used by Rhizobium bacteria in forming nodules on the roots of legumes that fix atmospheric nitrogen; it influences soil structure because its electrical attraction to negatively charged colloids allows flocculation of clay and organic matter; and as a chemical constituent of lime it increases pH and thus influences the availability of other nutrients.

Magnesium

Magnesium ions (Mg^{2+}) are readily absorbed onto exchange sites in the soil and made available for plant uptake. They are susceptible to leaching in sandy soils, although this is not usually as rapid as for calcium owing to the ions' relatively low solubility. Deficiency is uncommon but is most likely on sandy soils with acid pH; high concentrations of potassium, calcium and ammonium in the soil can also restrict plant uptake of magnesium. Magnesium is a central constituent of the chlorophyll molecule and is essential for photosynthesis. It also assists in the adsorption of phosphorus and serves as an important catalyst in enzymatic reactions.

Sulphur

The sulphate ion (SO_4^{2-}) is readily leached from the soil. Despite this deficiency is rare, due in part to the use of sulphate-containing fertilizers, which ensure adequate levels of sulphate for grass growth requirements. The other factor contributing to soil sulphate levels is the deposition of atmospheric sulphur dioxide from the burning of fossil fuels. In industrial areas, sulphur emissions into the atmosphere are washed into the soil with rainfall or absorbed by plant leaves. Naturally, sulphur occurs in relatively large amounts in most soils and is contained within the organic fraction, from which decomposition releases sulphate into the soil solution. Deficiency may, therefore, occur in soils of low organic matter content and where grass clippings are removed. Sulphur is a constituent of amino acids required for protein synthesis, and is an essential component of several plant vitamins.

Micronutrients, or Trace Elements

Plants require these nutrients in only trace amounts; they are found at concentrations around 0.0001–0.02 per cent in dry leaf matter. The availability of micronutrients is dependent upon soil physical conditions and deficiencies are most often a consequence of these conditions as opposed to an actual lack of a specific nutrient. The stability of many such nutrients is affected particularly by changes in soil pH and aeration. Except for molybdenum, all micronutrients required by plants are more readily available at lower pH levels. Despite the occurrence of soil conditions that reduce the availability of trace elements, deficiencies are very rare in turf and amenity grassland, even on sandy soils. On rare occasions, copper or boron deficiency may be evident – copper levels are very low in sandy soils and boron is easily leached out. Iron fertilizers are often applied to high-quality surfaces in order to toughen plants and promote green colour but iron deficiency is not common itself. The role of all micronutrients within the plant is not fully known but many are important as activators for plant enzymes (*see* Table 14).

Fertilizers for Turf and Amenity Grass Areas

Fertilizers sold in the UK are labelled and generally contain the major plant nutrients nitrogen (N), phosphorus (P) and potassium (K), and sometimes micronutrients and other additives. The N-P-K content is expressed by percentage weight, and as

Table 14: The major nutrients for grasses

Nutrient	Nitrogen	Phosphorus	Potassium	Calcium	Magnesium	Sulphur
Normal concentration in topsoil	0.05–2%	0.02–0.1%	0.1–3%	0.1–2%	0.1–1.5%	0.02–0.2%
Major forms in the soil	N compounds in organic matter. Ammonium ions (NH_4^+). Nitrate ions (NO_3^-). Soluble organic compounds	Within soil organic matter. Phosphate ions $H_2PO_4^-$ and HPO_4^{2-}. As insoluble calcium phosphates in alkaline soils, and aluminium phosphates in acid soils; as phosphate absorbed on iron and aluminium oxide material	Part of silicate materials. Potassium ions (K^+). Fixed as potassium ions within clay mineral particles	Calcium sulphate ($CaSO_4$). On exchange sites and in soil solution as ionic form Ca^{2+}. In alkaline soil present as calcium carbonate ($CaCO_3$)	Part of silicate materials. Magnesium ion Mg^{2+} on exchange sites and in soil solution	Within soil organic matter. Metal sulphides, especially iron sulphide. Calcium sulphate. Sulphate ion (SO_4^{2-}) in soil solution
Forms taken up by the plant	Mainly as NO_3^- but also as NH_4^+	Mainly as $H_2PO_4^-$ but also as HPO_4^{2-}	K^+	Ca^{2+}	Mg^{2+}	Principally as SO_4^{2-}. Sulphate and sulphur dioxide (SO^2) absorbed directly from the atmosphere by plant leaves
Concentration in plants	3% of leaf dry matter	0.3% of leaf dry matter	2% of leaf dry matter	0.5–5% of leaf dry matter	0.05–1.5% of leaf dry matter	0.1–1% of leaf dry matter

Role within the plant	Part of the molecular structure of amino acids and Found in chlorophyll and nucleic acid proteins.	Part of the energy-rich ATP molecule. Forms part of nucleic acid compounds	Required as enzyme cofactor, particularly for protein synthesis. Associated with the control of leaf stomata opening and closing. Required for photosynthesis process	Required for the integrity of cell membranes. Important for cell division, especially in roots	Enzyme activator, especially for enzymes associated with photosynthesis. Part of chlorophyll molecule. Associated with ribosomes, which function in plant cells to produce proteins and amino acids	Part of the two essential amino acids methionine and cysteine, which are components of most proteins
Deficiency symptoms in turf	Leaves lose overall green colour and turn yellow.* Growth rate is significantly lowered	Dark blue-green coloration of leaves followed by purple coloration along leaf edges	Leaves droop and interveinal areas turn yellow	Reddish-brown discoloration along leaf margin, which develops to light red. Root growth is severely restricted	Similar to those of calcium except visual symptoms begin in the older leaves	Similar to those of N deficiency
Causes of deficiency	Clipping removal. Losses by leaching. Low levels of soil organic matter. Denitrification	Too little phosphorus in soil (unlikely!). Too little phosphorus in available form	Too little potassium in soil – especially common with quartz sands and calcareous soils. Clipping removal. Leaching in sandy soils	Very low pH. Excessive application of ammonium and/or potassium fertilizers	Low pH. Heavy application of fertilizers containing potassium	Leaching in sandy soils. Soils with low organic matter levels

---

COMMON TERMS APPLIED TO FERTILIZERS

Organic

A product of animal or plant origin, for example, dried blood, bonemeal.

Inorganic

Minerals mined from the ground or the products of industrial manufacture, for example, ammonium nitrate.

Straight fertilizer

Those fertilizers containing only one plant nutrient.

Compound fertilizer

Those fertilizers that contain two or more plant nutrients.

Slow release

Fertilizers that release small amounts of nutrients over a long period.

Quick release

Fertilizers in readily soluble form that release nutrients very rapidly.

---

percentage N for nitrogen, percentage P_2O_5 (phosphorus pentoxide) for phosphorus and percentage K_2O (potassium oxide) for potassium. Magnesium (where present) is expressed as MgO (magnesium oxide). A bag of fertilizer labelled as 20-10-10 will therefore contain 20 per cent N, 10 per cent P_2O_5 and 10 per cent K_2O.

The nutrient content of fertilizers can also be expressed in terms of the pure element that is N, P, K and Mg. To convert P to P_2O_5, multiply by 2.29; to convert K to K_2O, multiply by 1.20; and to convert Mg to MgO, multiply by 1.20.

For phosphorus, the proportions soluble in water and in citrate solution indicate its solubility. Sometimes fertilizers are also expressed by the ratio of nutrients present, so that, for example, a 20-10-10 fertilizer would be expressed as a 2-1-1.

Nitrogen Fertilizers

Inorganic Sources of Nitrogen
- Ammonium sulphate (21 per cent N). This is the preferred inorganic fertilizer for fine turf. In powder form, it is easy to spread uniformly and is not picked up by the mower. It has an acidifying effect on the soil as a by-product of the nitrification process. It is also available in granular form and provides quick grass growth response.
- Ammonium nitrate (35 per cent N). A soluble quick-release inorganic fertilizer that supplies nitrogen direct to the plant roots. Normally available in granular form, it has a lower acidifying effect than ammonium sulphate. Granulated forms are not suitable for fine turf as they are likely to be picked up by the mower, but they are very suitable where grass is longer. Pure ammonium nitrate is a potential fire and explosive hazard and must be stored with care.
- Sodium nitrate (16 per cent N). Being in nitrate form this is very quick-acting fertilizer in a granular form. It has no ammonium and little acidifying effect.
- Potassium nitrate (13 per cent N). A soluble source of nitrate nitrogen with a high concentration of potassium (46 per cent K_2O).
- Urea (46 per cent N). This material is very soluble in water, which has made it a popular choice in liquid feeds. In the soil it is quickly converted to ammonium carbonate and then to nitrate. The acidifying effect is reduced owing to the carbonate content. When it is applied to the soil surface, nitrogen loss can occur through ammonia gas (NH_3), especially on sandy soils and in warm conditions. Because of this ammonia release, it is not a suitable material to use with germinating seeds and young seedling turf.

Organic Sources of Nitrogen
- Dried blood (10–14 per cent N). Dried blood is quickly mineralized to ammonium by soil micro-organisms and in warm conditions it can provide a rapid response in grass growth; it is non-acidifying.

Table 15: Common sources of nutrients for turf and amenity grassland				
NITROGEN	Inorganic	Ammonium sulphate	21% N	$(NH_4)_2SO_4$
		Ammonium nitrate	35% N	NH_4NO_4
		Sodium nitrate	16% N	$NaNO_3$
		Potassium nitrate	13% N	KNO_3
		Urea	46% N	$(NH_2)_2CO$
	Organic	Dried blood	10–14% N	
		Hoof and horn meal	13% N	
	Synthetic	IBDU	32% N	
		CDU	32% N	
		Ureaform	40% N	
POTASSIUM	Inorganic	Potassium chloride	60% K_2O	KCl
		Potassium sulphate	50% K_2O	K_2SO_4
PHOSPHORUS	Inorganic	Superphosphate	19% P_2O_5	
		Triple superphosphate	47% P_2O_5	
		Ammonium phosphate	50% P_2O_5	
	Organic	Bonemeal	22% P_2O_5	
		Steamed bone flour	28% P_2O_5	
MAGNESIUM	Inorganic	Kieserite	27% MgO	$MgSO_4.H_2O$
		Epsom salts	17% MgO	$MgSO_4.7H_2O$

• Hoof and horn (13 per cent N). Mineralization is lower than for dried blood and hoof and horn provides a longer lasting grass growth response. The finer the material the quicker breakdown occurs in the soil. Non-acidifying.

Slow-release Nitrogen Fertilizers
Some natural organic sources of nitrogen have noticeable long-term nitrogen-release characteristics but their properties tend to be rather unpredictable. Many synthetic slow-release nitrogen fertilizers have been developed for turf and grass areas with more predictable outcomes and grass growth patterns. The specific benefits of slow-release nitrogen fertilizers include:

• A steady grass growth rate from eight to sixteen weeks.
• Reduced leaching.

• Fewer applications each year, saving on labour costs.
• Some products release nitrogen during warm winter spells.

There are three main groups of slow-release nitrogen fertilizers:

1. Synthetic organic nitrogen compounds.
2. Inorganic fertilizers treated to decease their solubility.
3. Products containing nitrification inhibitors.

Synthetic organic nitrogen compounds The slow-release properties of these products depend largely on the fact that they are only slightly soluble in water. They include isobutylidene diurea (IBDU), crotonylidene diurea (CDU) and ureaformaldehyde (Ureaform).

81

- Isobutylidene diurea (IBDU) (32 per cent N). This material is broken down in the soil by micro-organisms to release soluble urea. Its rate of breakdown increases with soil temperature and moisture. This rate is also dependent upon particle size – smaller particles are quicker to release their nitrogen. The urea is converted to ammonium carbonate and there is little or no acidifying effect. Grass growth response may take up to four weeks but can last for up to 16 weeks depending upon environmental conditions. IBDU is widely available in proprietary fertilizers.
- Crotonylidene diurea (CDU) (32 per cent N). This material breaks down to release soluble urea into the soil. The rate of decomposition is influenced by the same factors as for IBDU, although there is little release until the soil temperature rises above 10°C. Very little nitrogen is released in the first six weeks after application at pH 6.0 or lower.
- Ureaformaldehyde (methylene urea) (40 per cent N). This is the oldest of the synthetic organic fertilizer materials. It is actually composed of a range of chemical compounds that vary in their solubility and break down in conditions as for CDU and IBDU. Particle size is again influential in determining release rate and it is not very effective below 10°C. Release rate slows over time to a gradual trickle and the fertilizer may even provide a slow feed months or years after application.

Inorganic Fertilizers with Restricted Solubility
These are either coated or are dependent on a chemical reaction in order to be broken down. This group also contains materials that have a low inherent limited solubility, such as magnesium ammonium phosphate.

- Resin-coated fertilizers (usually 26–34 per cent N). Various products are available that are coated with a water-soluble plastic resin that gradually breaks down to allow diffusion of nutrients into the soil. Nutrients other than nitrogen are sometimes coated in this same way. These fertilizers have a major advantage over other fertilizer products in that all nutrients can be gradually made available to the grass plant. The permeability of the coating is sensitive to temperature and increases in hotter conditions. These fertilizers require careful handling as they can easily be damaged, which can lead to more rapid nutrient release, scorching or uneven grass growth. The large prill size of many of these products makes them unsuitable for very fine turf surfaces. Most products give effects and growth that may be sustained for up to six months.
- Sulphur-coated urea (32 per cent N). This is urea coated with elemental sulphur that greatly reduces its solubility. The rate of release is determined by the thickness of the sulphur coating and by particle size. Urea gradually enters the soil by diffusion through the coating or as this decomposes in warmer conditions. The sulphur coating is converted to sulphate (SO_4^{2-}) by soil bacteria, which then increases soil acidity. Sulphur content can vary from 12 to 22 per cent. The particles can easily be damaged in handling as with resin-coated materials, and the same problems can result. The large prill size also makes this material unsuitable for fine turf. Grass growth response generally lasts for eight to ten weeks and initial growth is better than with other synthetic organic nitrogen products.
- Magnesium ammonium phosphate (10 per cent N). The chemical nature of this material makes it very slightly soluble in water. Nitrogen as ammonium is released by chemical reactions and this is not dependent on soil temperature. It is sometimes used in compound fertilizers but its high phosphate content makes it unsuitable for fine turf surfaces.

Addition of Nitrification Inhibitors
Nitrate, the primary form in which nitrogen is taken up by the plant, is highly soluble and therefore liable to leaching from the soil. Soil bacteria undertake the process of nitrification. If an ammonium fertilizer is,

therefore, applied to the turf with a material that restricts the activity of these bacteria, then smaller amounts of nitrate will be available to the plant over a longer period. The two most common such products included in proprietary fertilizers are dicyandiamide (DIDIN) and nitrapyrin.

Potassium Fertilizers

All sources of potassium commonly used in fertilizers are inorganic and highly soluble in water.

- Potassium chloride (60 per cent K_2O). This is also known by its more traditional name of muriate of potash. It is the most common source of potassium in commercial granular fertilizers. As a straight fertilizer, it is susceptible to water absorption and forms lumps.
- Potassium sulphate (50 per cent K_2O). This is a more expensive form of potassium but is more suitable for mixing as it does not settle in damp conditions, unlike potassium chloride.

Phosphorus Fertilizers

Inorganic and natural organic forms of phosphorus are both used in fertilizers for turf and amenity grass areas. The inorganic phosphates tend to be more soluble and therefore available for quicker plant uptake.

Inorganic Sources of Phosphorus
- Superphosphate (19 per cent P_2O_5). This is a widely used source of soluble phosphate that is present in the form of mono-calcium phosphate. It also contains a large proportion of calcium sulphate (gypsum). Both powder and granular forms are produced; the powder form tends to settle in damp conditions.
- TripleSuperphosphate (47 per cent P_2O_5). Because of its lower calcium sulphate content, this material has a higher phosphate level. It reacts in the soil in a similar way to superphosphate.
- Ammonium phosphate (50 per cent P_2O_5). This is used as part of high-analysis compound fertilizers, not being readily

available on its own. It also contains 11 per cent nitrogen. The phosphate present is water-soluble and so this fertilizer is often used as a phosphate source in liquid feeds.

Organic Sources of Phosphorus
These materials are based on preparations of bones. Phosphate is present as tri-calcium phosphate and is highly insoluble, being released only slowly into the soil.

- Bonemeal (22 per cent P_2O_5). This is produced from crushed bones. It contains around 4 per cent nitrogen and is often used as a conditioner to stop settling of other powder fertilizers contained in mixtures.
- Steamed bone flour (28 per cent P_2O_5). Very similar in composition and effect to bonemeal and used as a conditioner in fertilizer mixes.

Magnesium Fertilizers

Two materials are commonly available: kieserite (27 per cent MgO) and Epsom salts (17 per cent MgO). On acid soils to which lime is being added, dolomitic limestone can be used; this contains 17–18 per cent MgO.

Micronutrient/Trace Element Fertilizers

There are many proprietary compound fertilizers containing one or more micronutrients along with the major plant nutrients. Products containing micronutrients are also available in powder form, in solution or fused with glass frits, which release elements slowly into the soil solution. Many organic nitrogen sources and seaweed products also have significant micronutrient contents.

Iron
This micronutrient is sometimes included in fertilizer mixes, in proprietary compounds and in liquid feeds. Often it is applied on its own as a tonic to green up the grass. This has a rapid effect, as the plant leaf will absorb much iron. Iron is also applied as calcined ferrous sulphate ($FeSO_4.3H_2O$; also known

as sulphate of iron) in order to control broadleaved weeds, moss and algal growth. It is most often spread with a sand carrier, when it is known as lawn sand. Calcined ferrous sulphate has been subjected to a heating process that reduces its water content and increases the iron content to around 25 per cent Fe within a fine powder.

Liquid Fertilizers

These are commonly derived from highly soluble inorganic materials such as urea, ammonium, sulphate and potassium nitrate. Proprietary products are also available and have a wide range of nutrient contents. Liquid fertilizers are usually quick-acting, as the leaf takes up a proportion directly, and they are therefore useful for rapid results or for applying small amounts of nutrient evenly. Ferrous sulphate can be added again to green up the grass.

Products derived from seaweed extract and farm slurries usually contain little in the way of major plant nutrients for grass plant use and must be reinforced with inorganic sources of major nutrients if they are to be of real value. Many of these products are, however, useful for micronutrient feeds if these are required.

Fertilizer Programmes

The objectives of applying fertilizer to turf or any area of amenity grass will vary depending upon the specific situation and criteria for that surface or area. In general terms, fertilizer programmes should result in the following:

- A vigorous sward that is dense and tolerant to wear.
- Resistance to diseases.
- Few undesirable species present.
- Tolerance to adverse environmental conditions.
- Good colour and aesthetic appearance.

Nitrogen is by far the most important nutrient for grass as it is this that has the greatest effects on growth. Notwithstanding this fact, it is still important that grass plants obtain all necessary nutrients, as a deficiency in any one will be detrimental to growth. It is a fact, however, that the majority of soils contain adequate concentrations of calcium, magnesium, sulphur and the micronutrients; only nitrogen, potassium and possibly phosphorus are likely to be deficient in turf and amenity grass surfaces and need supplementing with fertilizer application. Factors that affect the need for fertilizer application or the amounts required include grass species, soil type, fate of mowing clippings, age of turf and soil and plant nutrient status. These are dealt with in more detail below.

Grass Species

Fine turfgrass species, such as Red Fescue and Browntop Bent, are found naturally on soils of low fertility and therefore require little nutrient input; when maintained in a near natural state, the invasion of weed and coarser grass species such as Annual Meadow Grass is reduced. Coarser, broadleaved species such as Perennial Ryegrass and Smooth-stalked Meadow Grass are found on heavier soils and are more nutrient demanding.

Soil Type

Owing to its low organic matter content and lack of electrical charge, sand does not retain nutrients as do clays and loams, whose greater cation exchange capacity allows them to hold nutrients applied to the soil. This is particularly important for nitrogen and potassium, which would otherwise be leached from the soil.

Grass Clippings

Grass clippings contain 3 per cent nitrogen, 0.7 per cent phosphorus and 2 per cent potassium in dry leaf material. Grass clippings play an important part in the recycling of nutrients, particularly nitrogen, and so when they are removed, especially continually, this has the effect of depleting the soil nutrient reserve. Grass clippings are broken down by soil organisms to release nutrients. Areas where clippings are not removed or that are not subjected to intensive wear can be sustained perfectly well without the application of fertilizers.

Newly Seeded or Turfed Areas

Seedlings and newly laid turf need nutrient input to promote rapid establishment. Phosphate will aid rooting of seedlings and the extension of roots in turves into the soil. Potassium is also valuable for disease resistance and drought tolerance at this stage. When established, young swards benefit from higher nitrogen application than more mature areas in order to promote vigorous growth and rapid density of coverage.

Soil Nutrient Status

Soils can be analysed for major plant nutrients, particularly phosphorus, potassium, magnesium and many of the micronutrients, although no reliable analytical test for predicting the concentration of plant-available nitrogen in outdoor soils is available. This is partly due to the rate at which nitrogen is mineralized from organic matter, which is variable and compounded by the fact that nitrogen is highly mobile and readily leached from soils, thus making any analysis redundant in practical terms. Soil analysis is an important tool in the formulation of fertilizer programmes but it is not precise. This lack of precision is not that critical, as good turf management should not be wholly dependent on soil analysis results. Observation of the surface, grass growth and assessment of performance factors should be used in conjunction with soil analysis to arrive at a given fertilizer programme.

Soil sampling Care must be exercised to ensure that soil samples taken will give meaningful results for interpretation and formulation of subsequent fertilizer regimes. Errors incurred in assessing the availability of nutrients using an extractant are small compared with differences caused by sampling errors in the field. Soils supporting grass swards are not cultivated as are other soils and they remain largely static in profile, which often leads to nutrients settling and concentrating at different levels in the soil or root zone. Nutrients such as phosphorus can differ in concentration by as much as twofold over 20mm depth. It is therefore important that turf soils be sampled at a precise and constant depth to obtain true results; for most situations, 100mm will be satisfactory. Shallower depths may be appropriate where grass is not deep-rooted, as often occurs on golf and bowling greens.

As with pH testing, several soil samples are taken in the field, bulked together and then a sub-sample of about 50g is subjected to testing. As a guide, a minimum of five samples and a maximum of 20 should be collected on site in a W pattern over the area concerned. In many situations where soils are relatively stable and predictable, testing every three years and the subsequent adjustment of fertilizer programmes will be sufficient. On sandy soils and sand-based root zones, annual testing is recommended.

Following soil sampling, the amounts of nutrient extracted from soil samples can be converted into an index of availability. On this index scale, the preferred value for turf and grass areas is 2 or 3, and fertilizer programmes should aim to maintain these levels in the soil. A value of less than 2 means that fertilizer input is required, whilst values greater than 4 mean that a decrease or cessation in fertilizer input is necessary.

Tissue Testing and Plant Nutrient Status

Testing a soil does not supply information about actual nutrient status in the plant itself, an accurate estimate of which can only be

Table 16: Soil nutrient index scale

Index value	mg/l P	mg/l	mg/l mg
0	0–9	0–60	0–25
1	10–15	61–120	26–50
2	16–25	121–240	51–100
3	26–45	241–400	101–175
4	46–70	401–600	176–250
5	71–100	601–900	251–350

Table 17: Target ranges for major plant nutrients		
Nutrient	**Tissue target range (%)**	**Soil target range (ppm)**
Nitrogen	2.8–5.5	—
Phosphorus	0.3–0.6	15–30
Potassium	1.0–3.5	100–250
Magnesium	0.2–0.6	—

obtained through plant analysis. Using information from both soil and plant analysis gives the most complete picture about nutrient levels but in reality few situations require this depth of analysis. Plant and tissue testing are most commonly used when deficiency of a nutrient is suspected and accurate analysis is required. This is most often only carried out for high-profile areas such as premier sports turf surfaces.

Tissue testing and plant analysis are two different techniques that have both been used to assess the nutrient status of grasses. Tissue testing involves field analysis of extracted cellular sap using reagents and test kits. Plant analysis is a more accurate estimate of the tissues' elemental content and involves submitting plant samples to the laboratory. Plant samples must be collected fresh, with the youngest leaves being the best source for testing. Clippings from mowing can be collected when fresh and bagged in permeable plastic bags before prompt dispatch to the laboratory and subsequent analysis. As with the soil nutrient index scale, a similar concept is applied to maintaining plant nutrient levels within prescribed target ranges (*see* Table 17).

Fertilizer Programme Strategies

Each area of turf or amenity grassland should receive fertilizer according to plant requirements, local conditions and the objectives of management. One strategy is to supply nutrients based on plant level ratios. In grasses, the nutrient ratio of N, P and K is 4-1-3. Simplistically, supplying fertilizers with this same ratio during periods of growth will maintain a supply to the plants of all the major required nutrients. However, although

this approach has a sounder basis than simply using the proprietary spring/summer and autumn/winter fertilizers promoted by many commercial companies, the major flaw is that it does not consider the levels of nutrients actually in the soil or plant. An alternative strategy, which has more scientific basis, is to supply a high phosphorus fertilizer occasionally (once a year or less), with more frequent applications of nitrogen and potassium. This strategy is supported by the fact that phosphorus is retained in the soil and phosphorus fertilizers have a high residual effect, whilst nitrogen and potassium, being more mobile in the soil, are readily leached and need more regular replenishment.

It is unwise to allow a major nutrient other than nitrogen to restrict grass growth. Instead, keep other nutrients supplied as required and use nitrogen as a controller. Nitrogen has the most immediate and dramatic effects on grass growth and applications can be made when necessary to maintain the sward. This strategy should be supported by soil analysis, and potassium in particular should be managed to maintain the N-K balance. Another strategy is to follow the guidelines or recommendations of professional agronomists or advisory organizations. The Sports Turf Research Institute (STRI) is one such organization and has issued guideline nutrient requirements for different turf surfaces used for sport in particular.

Fertilizer Application

Application Timings
If fertilizers are applied when weather conditions do not favour grass growth, their

Table 18: STRI fertilizer recommendations for different sports turf areas

Area	Nutrient	Rate per annum
Golf greens and tees, bowling greens, ornamental lawns	Nitrogen	8–20g/sq m
	Phosphorus	2 g/sq m
	Potassium	6–15g/sq m
Cricket tables, tennis courts	Nitrogen	8–12g/sq m
	Phosphorus	2g/sq m
	Potassium	4–10g/m^2
Cricket outfields	Nitrogen	4–12g/sq m
	Phosphorus	0–6g/sq m
	Potassium	0–6g/sq m
Hockey pitches	Nitrogen	40–200kg/ha
	Phosphorus	0–20kg/ha
	Potassium	0–150kg/ha
Football and rugby pitches	Nitrogen	80–200kg/ha
	Phosphorus	20–100kg/ha
	Potassium	20–100kg/ha
Racecourses	Nitrogen	80–100kg/ha
	Phosphorus	20–50kg/ha
	Potassium	20–50kg/ha
Newly seeded areas	Nitrogen	16–20g/sq m
	Phosphorus	8–10g/sq m
	Potassium	8–10g/sq m
Seeding/turfing (spring)	Nitrogen	4–8g/sq m
	Phosphorus	6–12g/sq m
	Potassium	4–8g/sq m
Seeding/turfing (autumn)	Nitrogen	1–3g/sq m
	Phosphorus	6–12g/sq m
	Potassium	4–8g/sq m

use will be inefficient: nutrients will be leached when not taken up by plants, held on exchange sites or immobilized. The experienced turf or amenity manager decides when spring growth is commencing as air and soil temperatures increase. Experience and careful observation of growth are invaluable aids in determining when to commence fertilizer application. Soluble fertilizers should not be applied when soil or air temperatures are below 5°C, and many applications of autumn/winter fertilizers are often inappropriate.

The first application of fertilizer in spring is valuable in aiding grass recovery from winter and in improving turf colour and appearance. During the growing season, applications to fine turf in particular will normally take place every four to six weeks. Applications in late summer (late August) must be low in nitrogen, as high nitrogen levels at this time will favour disease ingress, especially Fusarium. Potassium fertilizers can be used at this time to increase disease resistance. On heavily used turf such as football pitches, which receive most damage during the winter period, light dressings of compound fertilizers in late autumn (mid-October) and early spring (mid-March), when growth is minimal, have been known to aid turf recovery.

The availability of synthetic slow-release products now means that fertilizer applications need not be restricted to periods of active growth. The low solubility and diminished leaching of these materials allows them to be applied from December to February, so that during periods of mild weather sufficient nutrient will be available, and during spring there is no check to growth. It is important to avoid applications of any fertilizer during hot spells of weather or drought, as scorching of the turf will result.

Preparation of Site-made Mixes
Many turf professionals now apply solely proprietary compound fertilizers because of their ease of use and convenience. However, these commercial fertilizers have a fixed nutrient ratio that may not always be the most suitable for the area concerned and, furthermore, significant savings (up to 60 per cent) can be made when fertilizers are mixed on site from straight materials. The preparation of such mixes requires a storage building and a clean floor surface on which to mix the materials. Protective clothing, including a face mask and goggles, should be worn and Control of Substances Hazardous to Health (COSHH) requirements followed fully. Mixtures should be applied within two or three days of mixing as they are prone to setting. The inclusion of a conditioner such as steamed bone flour at a rate of 10 per cent of the total weight will help to reduce setting. The mix is bulked up with dry sand for application and passed through a 3mm mesh to remove any coarse stones or grit.

Nitrogen Application
Nitrogen increases grass biomass, particularly shoots and leaves. In many situations, such as sports turf surfaces, this may be desirable as it creates a cushion or protective surface for play. Loss of grass cover is followed, inevitably, by loss of soil structure, increased compaction and subsequently wetter surfaces unsuitable for play or other use. Nitrogen also promotes green coloration, which is often desired in many situations. It must be remembered, however, that a green turf is not necessarily the best, especially on surfaces used for sport. The turf manager's skill, knowledge and experience are key determinants in deciding upon nitrogen application.

No single application of nitrogen should exceed 5g/sq m, otherwise turf quality and growth performance will be adversely affected, and in any case much nitrogen will be lost in leachate. Excessive use of nitrogen fertilizer will have a number of adverse effects upon the sward and the environment:

1. A change in botanical composition of the sward.
2. Increased lush grass growth.
3. Greater susceptibility to, or incidence of, disease.
4. Poorly developed grass root systems.
5. Build-up of organic matter and thatch.
6. Reduced plant tolerance to heat and drought.
7. Decreased turf strength.
8. Loss of nitrogen through leaching and subsequent pollution of groundwater.
9. Rapid decrease in soil pH.
10. Excessive leaching of calcium through repeated use of ammonium.

Areas Not Requiring Nitrogen Many mixed grassland areas – that is those areas containing both grasses and broadleaved plant species, especially legumes such as clover – will grow perfectly well year after year without any nitrogen application. Legumes have the ability to fix atmospheric nitrogen to support their nutrient requirements. There are many commercial seed mixtures for use in amenity situations that contain clover and other broadleaved plant species, and many of these are suitable for low-maintenance areas such as roadside verges. Many areas of amenity grassland do not need fertilizer input, particularly where they do not receive artificial irrigation, where weed species invasion is not important, where turf quality is not

Table 19: Common turfgrass species and their nitrogen requirements

Grass species	N requirement per month of growing season (g/sq m)
Chewing's Fescue	0.75–1.5
Perennial Ryegrass	1.3–1.9
Browntop Bent	1.3–1.9
Tall Fescue	1.3–1.9
Annual Meadow Grass	1.3–1.9
Smooth-stalked Meadow Grass	1.5–2.5
Creeping Bent	1.5–2.5

NITROGEN SHOULD NOT BE APPLIED WHEN:

- The turf cannot be irrigated if rainfall fails to wash in the fertilizer.
- The weather is hot and dry.

---

important and where more than minimal growth is a nuisance.

Areas Requiring Nitrogen Turf subjected to intensive wear must receive fertilizer if acceptable cover and appearance are to be maintained. The grass itself will be a good guide regarding timing and rates of nitrogen to apply. Factors such as turf density, ground cover and root growth should be considered rather than colour. Apply only the minimum needed and do not use nitrogen solely to compensate for other maintenance shortcomings or problems.

Phosphorus Application
Many soils have levels of phosphorus above the optimum required by grass plants. This is due to overapplication in the past and the fact that much phosphorus is readily immobilized. Increasingly, a range of zero-phosphate fertilizers has become available

whose use in more recent years may now be positively affecting this situation. High phosphorus application is wasteful, aggravates iron deficiency and encourages Annual Meadow Grass. Even though phosphorus may often be immobile in the soil, grass plants are very effective in scavenging for it sufficiently well to sustain their needs.

New installations benefit from phosphorus fertilizer as it promotes root growth in seedlings and recently laid turves. An initial application, if needed, followed by annual or less frequent applications, will generally more than suffice. There is some loss of phosphorus from the soil in grass clippings where these are removed but this is minimal.

Potassium Application
Optimum levels of potassium will ensure maximum root growth. In recent years the role and significance of potassium for grasses has increased and more high-potassium fertilizer products are now available. Deficiency symptoms are rare and only very occasionally seen on sand-based sports turf surfaces. Where grass clippings are removed, potassium must be replaced and should be balanced with nitrogen. On sandy soils, light and frequent applications may be required as potassium is leached from such soils. On sports turf surfaces, potassium applications may be heavier as these areas are subjected to intensive wear and stress, which the nutrient will help to alleviate. The key factors for potassium application are soil nutrient levels, clipping fate, amount of nitrogen applied, time of year and turf use.

Fertilizer Calculations
A manager of turf or amenity grass must know the areas of the land he/she is responsible for in order that appropriate amounts of fertilizer (and other maintenance materials) can be sourced and applied. Areas that are treated differently (for example, greens, tees and fairways on golf courses) must be measured and their precise requirements calculated individually. When applying fertilizer, it is normal practice to use rates of grams per square metre (g/sq m) for smaller areas and

kilograms per hectare (kg/ha) for larger ones. The conversion for these is simple, as 1g/sq m is equivalent to 10kg/ha. Fertilizer recommendations are usually expressed as amounts of nutrient per unit area and not the amount of fertilizer to apply. This is because fertilizers vary in their nutrient concentration and several fertilizers of different concentration may be suitable for any given area. Following area measurement it is then important to calculate the actual amount of a particular fertilizer to apply in order to achieve a particular nutrient supply level. Below are given examples of calculations for the application of straight and compound fertilizers, as well as liquid products.

Straight fertilizers In this first example, the nitrogen requirement is for 5g/sq m and the fertilizer to be used is ammonium sulphate, which contains 21 per cent nitrogen. The amount of fertilizer to apply is calculated as follows:

21 per cent = 21 ÷ 100 = 0.21

So, for 5g/sq m N you will need:

5 ÷ 0.21 = 24g/sq m of ammonium
           sulphate

An alternative method takes as its start point the fact that 21 per cent N in ammonium sulphate equates to 0.21kg of N per 1kg of product. Therefore, to work out how much ammonium sulphate is required to apply 50kg/ha of N, the following calculation is used:

50 ÷ 0.21 = 238kg/ha

When applying straights, especially nitrogen materials, it is good practice to apply them with a sand carrier. This helps to ensure even distribution of the product and minimize any possible scorching of the turf. Normally, sand carrier is used a rate of 140g/sq m for this purpose. For mixing purposes, it is easiest to work in kg/ha. For the first example above, the weight of product was 24g/sq

m (using ammonium sulphate at 5g/sq m) and therefore:

(140 ÷ 24) × 1kg = 5.83kg of carrier
                   needs to be added to
                   the fertilizer

Compound fertilizers In many situations compound fertilizers are used that contain more than one plant nutrient. Obviously, it is not possible to apply one material at different rates for the different nutrients that that fertilizer contains. In these situations, the nitrogen value should be taken for the basis of calculating an application rate for the material. This is because nitrogen has the most dramatic and immediate effects on turf, and overapplication will have adverse effects for the sward as well as being potentially damaging to the environment. A good strategy is to find a fertilizer that matches the nutrient recommendations. If the recommendation is for 20g/sq m of N and 15g/sq m of K2O, then a fertilizer with a nutrient ratio of 20-0-15 or 4-0-3 would be most appropriate. As previously stated, grasses utilize nutrients in the ratio 4-1-3 and some products are available with this ratio of nutrients.

If using a compound that is not in the exact ratio required to match the nutrient recommendation for application, it is useful to calculate how much of the other nutrients is actually being applied. In this example, the nitrogen requirement is for 5g/sq m, the fertilizer to be used is a 20-10-10 compound product and the area for treatment is 1,000sq m. In order that sufficient product can be obtained, it is necessary to know how much fertilizer is needed for the total area. The calculation for this is as follows:

The total N required =
1,000sq m × 5g/sq m = 5,000g

The amount of fertilizer needed =
5,000 × (100 ÷ 20) = 25,000g = 25kg

At this rate of application it will also supply:

$(10 \times 5) \div 25 = 2g/sq$ m each of phosphorus and potassium

To conclude, the application rate of 25kg per 1,000sq m delivers 5g/sq m N and 2g/sq m of P and K.

Liquid products In this example, a liquid product contains 20 per cent N, which equates to 20g of N per 100ml of liquid. The product must be diluted, as it would otherwise scorch the grass on application, and this is normally done by adding at least two volumes of water to one of fertilizer. In this case, the diluted material would now contain 6.66g N per 100ml. If the diluted product is applied at 75 litres per 1,000sq m (75ml per sq m), this equates to:

$(6.66 \div 100ml) \times 75ml = 4.995g/sq$ m N

Fertilizer Costs
Fertilizer is the lowest cost maintenance resource for the return on investment that can be put into turf. Fertilizers contain different concentrations of plant nutrients and assessment of their value is best determined by calculating the cost per unit amount of nutrient contained. When using compounds, the N value should be used again for the basis of cost calculations.

In this example of cost comparison, 20-10-10 fertilizer at £6.00 per 25kg bag is compared with 9-7-7 fertilizer at £5.50 per 25kg bag. First, looking at the costs to achieve an application rate of 5g/sq m N (50kg/ha N):

(a) $20\text{-}10\text{-}10 = 5 \times (100 \div 20) = 25g/sq$ m
$\qquad = 25kg/ha$ product

(b) $9\text{-}7\text{-}7 \quad = 5 \times (100 \div 9) = 56g/sq$ m
$\qquad = 56kg/ha$ product

Second, looking at the cost to achieve an application rate of 50kg/ha N from 25kg bags:

(a) $20\text{-}10\text{-}10 = (25 \div 25) \times £6.00$
$\qquad = £6.00$

(b) $9\text{-}7\text{-}7 \quad = (56 \div 25) \times £5.50$
$\qquad = £12.32$

The cost of applying nutrients from the 20-10-10 product is therefore lower.

Obviously, there are other factors to consider in arriving at full costs of fertilizer application, including handling, storage and labour costs. For most products, bulk purchase will often mean cheaper prices can be obtained. Slow-release products reduce the number of applications per year but are more expensive.

Fertilizer Distribution
Correct application rates and even distribution are essential in the management of quality turf surfaces. Uneven distribution of fertilizer will cause variation in grass growth patterns and possibly scorched or damaged areas. Fertilizer can be applied by hand to small or irregular-shaped areas where equipment use may be impractical but great care must be taken to ensure even distribution. A constant walking speed and a steady rhythmic

---

KEY POINTS FOR FERTILIZER PROGRAMMES

- Maintain sufficient levels of all nutrients to ensure unimpeded growth.
- Use soil analysis together with visual observation of growth and environmental conditions to determine fertilizer application.
- Use nitrogen as the control for grass growth.
- Measure areas for fertilizer application and calculate requirements.
- Monitor turf/grass performance and apply fertilizer accordingly.
- Time applications to grass growth and appropriate weather conditions.
- Do not use fertilizer to replace other essential maintenance operations.
- Remember that green grass is not always the best!
- Trial products on test areas and keep records of application.

DESIRABLE FEATURES OF A FERTILIZER DISTRIBUTOR

Ideally, a fertilizer spreader for use on turf should:

• Be capable of handling a range of products and materials.
• Be capable of spreading both small and large amounts so that a wide range of application rates is possible.
• Have the facility to change application rate easily.
• Be easy to calibrate.
• Be easy to clean and maintain.
• Be constructed from corrosion-free materials.

Fixed-width and spinning-disc pedestrian fertilizer spreaders. (Photo: Scotts Company UK)

MATERIALS REQUIRING DISTRIBUTION

Fertilizer spreaders or distributors will often have to apply a diverse range of products and materials. When choosing fertilizers it is important to consider the type of surface and the use of the area being treated.

Granular products are generally more suitable for use on long-grass areas, whereas fine-turf mini-granular or mini-crumb products are better suited to shorter grass as they are less prone to being picked up by the mower or by other objects such as balls used in sports.

Fertilizers in various formulations

• Granules – particles mainly in the 2.5mm range. Most granular products are irregular in shape but some may be spherical.
• Prills – fertilizer particles that are generally smaller and more spherical than granules.
• Powders – products whose median particle size is less than around 0.5mm and can be in the range of a micrometre.

Seed

• Grass seed can be distributed effectively with a fertilizer spreader. Small quantities may be diluted with sand to aid distribution.

Sand

• Either on its own as topdressing or as a carrier for fertilizer.

Salt

• For distribution onto paths and other hard surfaces in winter.

Pesticides

• Usually those in granular or pellet form.

distribution technique are necessary for uniform application of the product. On most turf, a pedestrian mechanical spreader is used to distribute fertilizer. Many large areas of turf or amenity grassland do not receive fertilizer but for those that do there are larger distributors, including tractor-mounted machines. Most of these are simply larger versions on their pedestrian counterparts.

Product Handling
Always wear appropriate protective clothing and personal protective equipment (PPE) when handling fertilizer products as directed by the manufacturer and in accordance with relevant legislation such as the COSHH regulations. A facemask, goggles, overalls and gloves should be worn to protect against irritants or injury. Take care when lifting and moving fertilizer bags – most weigh 25kg.

Fertilizer Storage
Fertilizers must be stored under cover in a secure ventilated building. Keep bags dry and off the floor, preferably on pallets, to avoid condensation spoiling the product. Bags should be stored in a convenient, accessible location to avoid excess manual handling. Lay the bags in a criss-cross arrangement for secure stacking.

Types of Fertilizer Distributor
The three main types of distributor used in professional turf and grass care are the belt conveyor (drop or fixed-width) spreader, the spinning disc (rotary or centrifugal) spreader and the oscillating spout (pendulum) spreader. These are dealt with in more detail below.

Belt conveyor spreaders This type of machine has a rubber belt in the base of the hopper that carries the material out and deposits it on the ground across the full width of the machine. The endless rubber belt is rotated by a shaft, which forms the axle between the two land wheels. This design is not affected by the speed at which it travels. The width of spread is fixed and care must be taken to ensure that there is a correct lining up of the machine between bouts, otherwise a gap

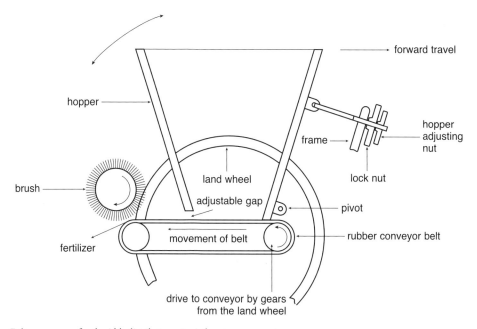

Belt conveyor or fixed-width distributor – typical main components.

or double application will occur. Some machines have a marker, which scratches the ground, and the wheel is pushed over this mark. The application rate is altered by moving the hopper to increase or decrease the gap between the belt and the hopper. To obtain a better distribution, some models (particularly those with an engine or attached to a power unit) are fitted with a rotating brush at the end of the belt that flicks the material off the belt rather than it simply falling off.

Dividing the material into two equal quantities and applying it at half-rate in two opposing directions minimizes missed areas or double application. These types of spreader are well suited to the application of bulky materials such as fertilizers with a sand carrier or topdressings. The distance that the material falls from the hopper is quite small on hand-pushed pedestrian machines and so application is not normally affected by wind. Most pedestrian materials are between 600mm and 1,000mm in width. Larger models mounted onto utility vehicles or compact tractors are also available.

Spinning disc spreaders This type of machine consists of a hopper with an adjustable-size hole in the base. The material falls out of the hopper under gravity, even when the machine is stationary, so the hole at the bottom of the hopper must be closed when the machine stops or the material will continue

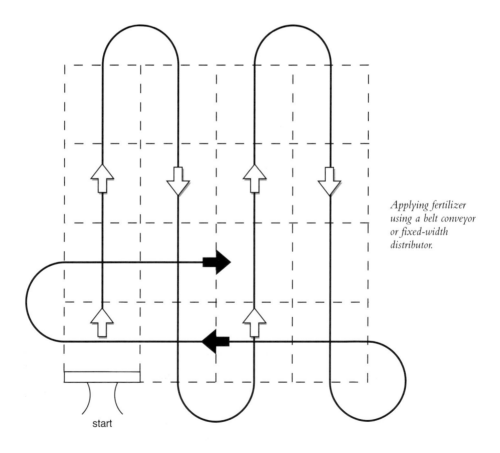

Applying fertilizer using a belt conveyor or fixed-width distributor.

start

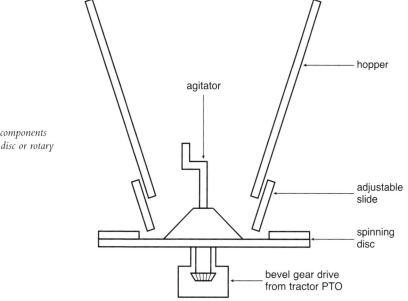

*Typical main components
of a spinning-disc or rotary
distributor.*

agitator

hopper

adjustable
slide

spinning
disc

bevel gear drive
from tractor PTO

to flow out and onto the ground. The rate of flow will depend on the size of the hole and type of material being used. Those materials that flow rapidly (such as prill-type fertilizers) will have a higher application rate than those that are much slower flowing (such as coarse organic fertilizers). To take account of this, the size of the hole will have to be adjusted to suit all the different types and makes of materials.

The material falls down onto a spinning disc, which is powered by the land wheels, and the material is then thrown out off the disc by centrifugal force. The speed of travel is very important: if the forward speed is doubled then the application rate is halved; if the speed is halved then the application rate is doubled. As a result, the forward speed must be kept constant. A higher disc speed will impart more centrifugal force to the material and will thus increase the spreading width of the machine.

Application of various particle sizes further reduces the uniformity of coverage. The majority of larger, heavier granules will travel further and so be distributed furthest

out from the spreader. Smaller, lighter material is first to drop to the ground. On large tractor-mounted machines, PTO often drives the disc, which is independent of ground speed.

Wind has a greater influence on product distribution from these spreaders because of the velocity of the product as it leaves the machine and the greater distance above the turf at which it is released. Overlap of product is necessary when using a spinning disc spreader. Adjacent bouts or passes should be overlapped by 30–50 per cent of the diameter of product application. For a spreader that applies a product at a width of 3m, for example, there should be a distance of 2.1–1.5m between passes to provide 30–50 per cent overlap of the diameter respectively.

Oscillating-spout spreaders These distributors are either trailed or, more usually, tractor-mounted machines that are mostly suitable for use over larger areas. They are really an alternative design to the spinning disc machine. The hopper has an oscillating (swinging) spout that distributes the fertilizer

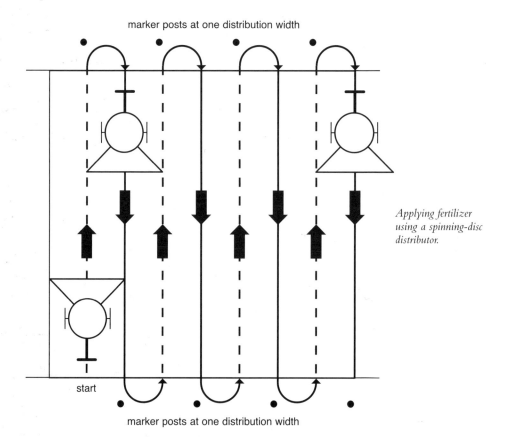

marker posts at one distribution width

Applying fertilizer using a spinning-disc distributor.

start

marker posts at one distribution width

Oscillating spout- or pendulum-type fertilizer distributor mounted on a turf utility vehicle. (Photo: RansomesJacobsen)

through an adjustable outlet. The spout moves backwards and forwards at high speed, driven by the tractor PTO, and provides a rectangular distribution pattern. An adjustable disc with holes at the bottom of the hopper regulates how much material enters the oscillating spout. A larger hole size releases more material and thereby increases application rate. The hole opening can be controlled from the tractor seat, thus enabling flow to be stopped for turning and manoeuvring the machine and when application is complete. As with spinning disc spreaders, care is needed to ensure that sufficient overlap is given so that even application is obtained. There are various sizes of machine available, with hoppers ranging

Agrostis capillaris
(Browntop Bent),
a major grass of
fine-turf surfaces.
(Photo: Barenbrug)

BELOW: Agrostis
stolonifera
(Creeping Bent),
a fine-turf species
that requires careful
and intensive
management.
(Photo: Barenbrug)

THIS PAGE:
ABOVE: Festuca rubra
commutata *(Chewing's
Fescue), a major grass
of fine-turf surfaces.*
(Photo: Barenbrug)

LEFT: Festuca rubra
rubra *(Strong Creeping
Red Fescue), found in
many mixtures for both
sports turf and amenity
use. (Photo: Barenbrug)*

OPPOSITE PAGE:
TOP: Festuca ovina
*(Sheep's Fescue), sometimes
used with other fescues
in amenity mixtures.*
(Photo: Barenbrug)

BOTTOM: Lolium perenne
*(Perennial Ryegrass), the
dominant turfgrass for all
but the finest surfaces, such
as greens. (Photo: Barenbrug)*

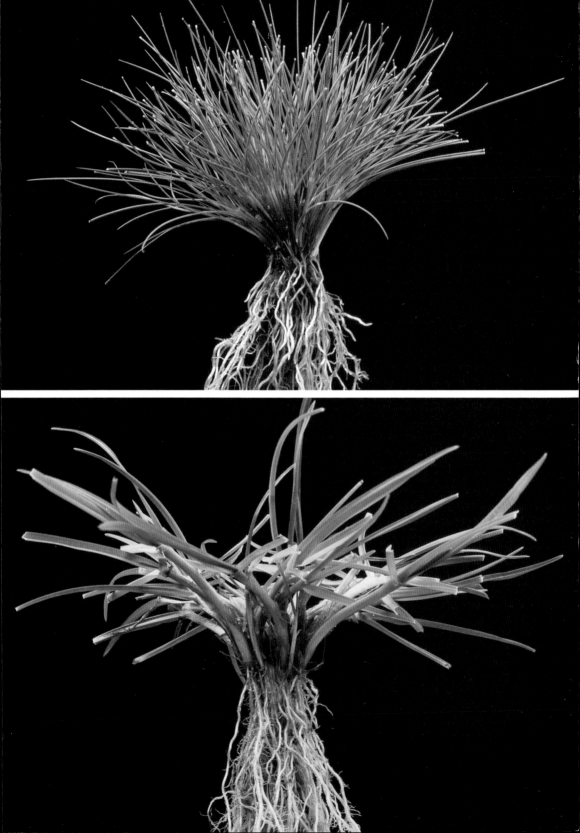

Poa pratensis
*(Smooth-stalked Meadow Grass),
often used for
hardwearing surfaces
such as winter
games areas.
(Photo: Barenbrug)*

BELOW:
Poa annua
*(Annual Meadow
Grass), the most
common weed-grass
of turf. (Photo:
Barenbrug)*

Deschampsia caespitosa *(Tufted Hair Grass), a grass suitable for shade areas. (Photo: Barenbrug)*

BELOW:
Festuca arundinacea *(Tall Fescue), suitable for use in areas that receive wear but are not mown closely. (Photo: Barenbrug)*

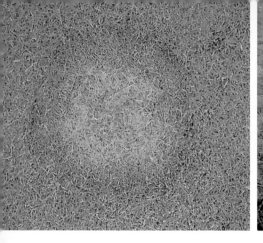

Fusarium patch: orange-brown curricular spots increasing in size. (Photo: SCOTTS)

Type 1 fairy ring: ring of dead grass or bare soil between stimulated areas. (Photo: SCOTTS)

Red thread: patches in turf, 5–20cm in diameter; 'red needles' on affected leaves. (Photo: SCOTTS)

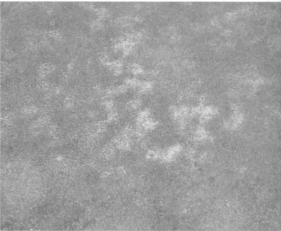

Dollar spot: small white to yellow (dry) spots, 10–20mm. (Photo: SCOTTS)

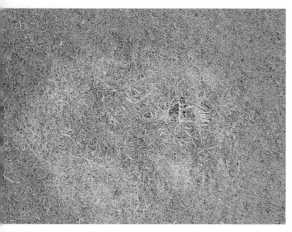

Take-all patch: small patches of failing grass with rotted roots. (Photo: SCOTTS)

Thatch fungus: fungal activity in thatch layer; characteristic musty smell. (Photo: SCOTTS)

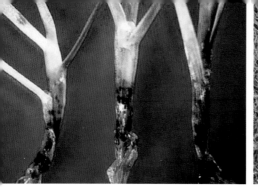

Anthracnose: yellowing of the plants; bases rotten. (Photo: SCOTTS)

Damping-off: patches of dead grass; rotten seed; thin grass. (Photo: SCOTTS)

Leatherjacket grubs are 20–40mm long, brown or greyish in colour, and found in the turf surface layers. (Photo: Bayer)

The adult leatherjacket or crane fly. (Photo: SCOTTS)

Chafer grubs: fat, pale, waxy bodies with a characteristic brown head. (Photo: Bayer)

The adult chafer beetle. (Photo: SCOTTS)

Many areas of grassland can be left to grow as species-rich swards. (Photo: Barenbrug)

BELOW: Species-rich swards are often very appropriate for low-maintenance areas. (Photo: Barenbrug)

from 250kg to 2.5 tonnes capacity and giving spreading widths of 6–12m.

Calibration of Fertilizer Distributors

The on-site calibration of fertilizer distributors is essential for efficient distribution and correct application rate. Equipment manuals should be consulted for proper use of the machine and calibration, although the settings advised in such literature should be used as a guide only and are no substitute for proper on-site calibration. The adjustments on many models are often quite crude and basic, which results in variation in application rates. Machines should be calibrated both for specific products and for desired application rate. Weather conditions and storage can affect the physical nature of materials, so the rate of application at a particular setting may vary even when using the same fertilizer. Variables that affect application of fertilizers include hopper opening size, swath width and ground speed. The opening gate of the hopper can be precisely adjusted and changed to allow more or less fertilizer through the opening. Swath width and ground speed should remain constant for accurate calibration. For hand-pushed spreaders, speed is dependent upon the operator and swath width on the type of spreader being used. Remember to keep records of calibration results for future use.

Belt conveyor spreaders Operate the machine with the appropriate material in the hopper over a board or tray of a known size and weigh the collected material (a 0.5sq m tray works well for this). A number of attempts should be made and an average calculated. Adjust the hopper gap as necessary until the desired application rate has been achieved.

Spinning disc spreaders These machines are more difficult to calibrate compared to belt conveyor types because the width of spread varies for each material used. Most instruction manuals give guidelines for hole setting position and width of spread, but for accurate distribution a little effort spent calibrating the machine is worthwhile.

The first task is to determine the effective spreading width of the machine for a given material. This measurement is needed so that when the spreader is being operated each pass can be properly spaced; it will also be required for calculating coverage area during calibration. To work out spreading width, place a row of collection containers, of the same size, in a straight line 30cm apart and perpendicular to the spreader's direction of travel. Conduct this test on a flat, firm, level surface. Partially fill the hopper and set the gate control to midway. Operate the spreader across the containers at normal walking speed. Several passes may be needed to collect enough material in each container for weighing purposes. The weights for each container and their position on the line will enable the effective distribution to be calculated. This test will also reveal how evenly the material is being spread on each side of the run.

After determining the effective width, the spreader can be calibrated by measuring the amount of material applied to a given area at a specific spreader setting. Select a test area, again on a flat, dry, clean surface such as a smooth concrete floor (a 100sq m area works well for calculation purposes). Calculate forward distance required with the effective spreading width arrived at earlier. For example, for a spreader with a spreading width of 3m, the forward distance to travel to cover 100sq m will be 33.3m (100sq m ÷ 3m). The spreader should be operated over this distance and the distributed material collected and weighed. Several passes should be made and a mean, or average, determined from the results. Repeat this process several times whilst changing the gate setting in increments until the desired application rate is achieved.

Another method is to place a measured quantity of material into the hopper, then operate the spreader over the test area and weigh the material remaining in the hopper. This volume is subtracted from the original to arrive at the amount of material used over the test area and thus give the application rate. Calibration will be required at different spreader settings to obtain a range of application rates for that material if required.

Oscillating spout spreaders The procedure for calibrating this type of machine is similar to that used for the spinning disc distributor. Another method is to remove the spout, run the machine with the tractor stationary, and collect the fertilizer in a bucket. If this is done over a period and the fertilizer weighed, the application rate can be calculated by referring to the manufacturer's instruction book.

Spreader Maintenance
Maintenance should be carried out immediately after machine use and in accordance with the manufacturer's instructions. Machines must be cleaned out and all traces of fertilizer removed as it will corrode metal parts and fittings. After cleaning, the machine should be lubricated as required, especially drive mechanisms and bearings. The integrity of all controls should be checked and any screws and nuts tightened. Finally, it should be ensured that the disc or belt is free from debris before it is stored inside a dry building with the hopper covered.

Biological Turf Products

While fertilizers are added to a soil to improve its nutrient content, there is now also a wide range of biological products available to the turf manager. These are referred to as biostimulants, bio-solubles, microbial inocula and bacterial liquids, and most are promoted as agents to improve soil microbial populations, soil health and turf vigour. Soil microbes are essential for soil nutrient levels (especially nitrogen) and for organic matter breakdown, and many are antagonistic towards pathogenic fungi that cause turf disease. Biostimulants are usually made up from seaweed or humic acid and are said to enhance plant growth and development. Many formulations contain a range of microbes (bacteria and fungi), as well as fertilizer materials.

Biological products maybe useful for a range of situations in both new and established turf. In newly constructed surfaces, especially sand-based surfaces, the populations of soil microbes are often very low. Without adequate levels of these microorganisms, such soils are prone to nutrient leaching, thatch build-up and turf diseases. Endomycorrhizae are fungi that have been shown to improve grass establishment on new root zones. These fungi attach themselves to plant roots and form a symbiotic relationship with the host plant that is mutually beneficial. The fungal hyphae extend throughout the soil and channel water and nutrients back to the fungi and hence into the plant. In turn, the fungi benefit from the relationship as they obtain sugars from the grass plant.

The use of biological agents on established turf is less certain. In most such situations, there should already be a good population of soil microbes present. It may be that where such populations have become depleted through, for example, overuse of pesticides, such products help to boost them and thus improve turf health and vigour. However, what is more important is that environmental conditions such as poor drainage or aeration are identified and remedied, as biological agents cannot rectify these problems. There are two ways to increase the bacterial populations in turf:

1. Apply a bacterial feed product to encourage beneficial bacteria to multiply. This is a consistent method of increasing bacterial populations.
2. Apply a bacterial amendment product that will supply extra bacteria to the soil. These products work best if they are compatible with the bacterial population found in your turf root zone.

While biological products undoubtably bring benefits, it should be remembered that no single agent is a panacea for all microbial problems or soil conditions. It is only by following good turf husbandry and environmental and management practices that turf health and vigour will be improved over time, although biological products may play a useful role in a balanced, integrated turf management programme.

CHAPTER 5

Aeration, Thatch Control and Topdressing

This chapter describes several aspects of turf maintenance that are sometimes referred to as secondary, or supplementary, practices. This is because their significance for the grass plant and for most amenity grassland areas is far less than those of mowing, irrigation and nutrition. This is not implying that they are not important maintenance activities but, when considered in terms of grassland management generally, they are not practised on many areas of amenity grass because they are expensive and in some cases unnecessary.

The need for and the intensity of these operations are significantly affected by mowing, irrigation and fertilizer application, but they are necessary on turf that receives intensive wear or where the highest standards of presentation are desired, such as sports turf surfaces. Thatch control and aeration are essential for surfaces subjected to wear and compression forces such as those imparted by players (or sometimes maintenance vehicles) to maintain free draining, disease-free turf surfaces. Topdressing is beneficial in maintaining playing surfaces as well as assisting in maintaining a root zone that is well aerated and free-draining. Rolling is often incorrectly practised and often not required, but for some surfaces, notably cricket pitches, it is an essential part of surface preparation and maintenance. Switching and brushing, covered at the end of this chapter, are mainly tasks undertaken for presentation purposes.

Soil Aeration and Compaction

Soil is composed of physical particles or solids that in a healthy soil are arranged into a system of larger aggregates interspersed with spaces. These spaces are referred to as pores. The size and volume of pore space is dependent upon the type and size of solid particles present and the degree of soil compaction. Pore spaces are essential for plant growth as it is here that the roots extend and take up both oxygen and water. The system of pores also facilitates water drainage and gaseous exchange with the atmosphere. Of greatest significance are pores larger than 75µ, which are known as macropores and which ideally will extend beyond the rooting depth of the grass plant. Soils that have not been subjected to intensive traffic from vehicles or people generally manage to maintain a moderate volume of macropores. Ideally, the soil should have an even distribution of water and air in its pore spaces.

The air-filled pores of the soil are essential for healthy root growth and for the many soil micro-organisms that have beneficial effects for the plant and soil ecosystem. There is no precise value for this, as many factors such as plant growth and soil type will have an effect, but it is generally considered that for grass growth the air-filled pore space in a soil by volume should not be less than 10–15 per cent. Grass plants take up oxygen from the soil as part of their respiration, and the significance of the air in the pore space is that oxygen diffuses through air ten times faster than through water. Thus when the soil air supply is depleted, oxygen availability is greatly reduced, with subsequent detrimental effects to the plant and other soil organisms. In a well-drained and aerated soil that has an extensive and continuous network of macropores, gaseous exchange will be adequate to maintain soil oxygen levels and sufficient to ensure that excessive concentrations of harmful gases do not accumulate.

To achieve a healthy the balance of water and air in the soil, it must have a system of pores to allow for efficient drainage. Effective water uptake by plants is dependent upon the flow of water through the soil. Saturation is not good for healthy plants as the resulting stagnation and anaerobic conditions are inhospitable for growth. Microbial activity is suppressed in such conditions, with often adverse effects on organic matter breakdown and nitrogen release. Under such conditions of restricted aeration, organic residues provide an ideal environment for anaerobic microbial activity, leading to such phenomena as black layer formation within the organic layer or at the interface between this layer and the soil mineral layer. In a healthy soil pore system, water drains from macropores and so allows air into the soil, while smaller pores retain water because it is held at tensions greater than the force of gravity. The smaller the pore's size, the greater the tension at which water is held.

The system of macropores also allows for grass root development and, more importantly, root extension. Grass roots range in diameter from 60μ to 250μ and thus it is imperative that the soil macropores are present to enable root extension and expansion. When such pores are restricted, root growth is physically impeded with, again, detrimental effects on plant growth.

Compaction has the effect of reducing macropore (and micropore) space to the extent that soil air supply is restricted, drainage is reduced and root growth is physically impeded. The degree of soil compaction can be measured as bulk density:

$$\text{Bulk density} = \frac{\text{weight of soil (g)}}{\text{volume of soil (cu cm)}}$$

When a soil is compacted, the proportion of solids to pore space increases in a given soil volume and bulk density increases. The particles of coarse-textured soils (sands) are heavier than those of fine-textured soils (silts and clays) and so, when not compacted, their bulk density will be higher. However, fine-textured soils are compacted more easily and so the potential increases in bulk density are greater in these soils.

Soil compaction affects turfgrass growth in many ways, most of which are detrimental to plant growth. Shoot growth, rooting, carbohydrate levels and water use rates are all influenced by soil compaction. Compaction can occur at different depths and is affected by turf use, wear and particular particle size distribution. Even though sands, because of their larger particle size, are less prone to compaction, if the particle size distribution is too wide interpacking can occur, leading to compaction and its adverse effects. Sports turf root zones are often prescribed with a narrow particle size range distribution in order to avoid this situation in the field.

It is important to understand the causes and depths of compaction if the most appropriate remedy is to be found. In some circumstances compaction is uniform to a particular depth as a result of deliberate management practices, such as those for the preparation of cricket wickets. For most

Table 20: Estimates of minimum soil bulk densities at which root growth becomes restricted	
Soil type	**Bulk density (g/cu cm)**
Coarse, medium, fine and loamy sands	1.8
Sandy loams	1.75
Silt loams	1.55
Clay	1.4

surfaces compaction will occur to different depths depending on the type of wear and the compacting force. On winter sports pitches, one of the worst problems is that caused by the smearing and kneading of the top 30mm of soil during play. Compaction is most severe with loss of surface grass cover as there is then no protective layer for the soil. In many situations, the top 20mm or so of soil may retain its macroporosity levels because of the presence of grass stems and roots, but compression forces above result in compaction lower down in the soil profile at depths of 80–120mm. With grass cover, some air will enter the soil profile near to the surface and so severely anaerobic conditions are most likely in the 15–60mm depth range. Those surfaces that receive shearing-type wear as well as compression forces to the turf are more readily compacted. Problems of compaction are often exacerbated by play or management practices in inappropriate weather conditions.

Improving Soil Aeration and Decompaction

For all areas of turf, but especially those used for sport, aeration is a necessary maintenance practice and is required for a number of reasons:

1. To improve surface drainage – channels or fissures are created through the soil profile to allow water infiltration and movement.
2. To improve soil air supply – grass roots need a good supply of oxygen for healthy normal growth and functioning.
3. To improve root growth – roots will grow well in the macropores created by aeration tines and will benefit from increased oxygen supply as well as better drainage.
4. To relieve compaction – soil compaction has a detrimental effect on roots, not only by causing anaerobic conditions but also by creating mechanical impedance to root growth (roots need macropore spaces greater than 60μ in order to grow). Compaction also impedes surface drainage and thus causes problems for play.

Aeration of turf will also have the following indirect effects:

- Soil structure and texture will be improved, especially when aeration is used in conjunction with topdressing, whereby materials can be incorporated to ameliorate the topsoil.
- Increased drought resistance of the sward will result because of greater and deeper grass root growth.
- Breakdown of thatch and mat will occur because of increased microbial activity resulting from better aerated soil. Aerated soil is also better drained and potentially warmer.
- A longer growing season, primarily because improved drainage leads to a warmer soil that will stay warmer for longer and stimulate grass root growth.
- Release of unwanted chemicals and gases from the soil by both infiltration and evaporation from the surface.

By virtue of all or most of the above factors aeration will often mean that the playing season or period is prolonged and/or the area is fit for playing on in what may often be undesirable conditions. To alleviate soil compaction and improve aeration it is necessary to create new macropore space. In simple terms, this can realistically be achieved in only two ways. For a given mass of soil, if you remove some of it (for instance, by extracting cores) the remaining soil will have a greater volume to occupy, thus increasing the pore spaces between the solid particles. The other method is to raise the surface (for example, by causing upheaval with mechanical tines), this again leading to a given mass of soil occupying a greater volume as well as causing physical fissuring to create macropores.

Aeration of turf is best carried out when the soil is moist in order to ensure that tine penetration into the soil is at its maximum. In conditions that are too wet, soil structure may be adversely affected; if conditions are too dry, tine penetration will be difficult. Turf aeration can be exercised by manual or mechanical means utilizing a range of

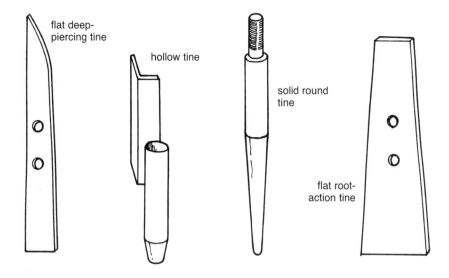

The main types of aeration tine.

different tines, each of which is designed for a specific purpose and has its own effects on the turf sward.

Aeration Equipment

The three basic types of tine used for aerating turf are slit or knife tines, solid or spike tines, and hollow or coring tines.

Slit or Knife Tines

These tines are basically blades that cut vertically into the turf surface. They come in a variety of shapes and sizes, and are also known as diamond tines, chisel tines and root pruners, depending upon their exact shape, size and/or depth of operation. The working depth or penetration of such tines varies from 75mm to 150mm for those on pedestrian machines or hand-held forks, and up to 300mm on the larger tractor-mounted models.

The use of such tines (slitting) is probably the most frequent aeration treatment for most turf areas in the UK as it introduces air into the soil and aids water infiltration with the minimum of surface disturbance. The frequency of such treatment must relate to the quality of the soil and the needs of the site, and may be anything from weekly to monthly. In some areas, slitting is practised more frequently in the autumn and winter to aid surface drainage; the problem of slits gaping in dry conditions generally prohibit their use on heavy soils in spring and summer.

Some tractor-mounted machines have pressure frames or are controlled by downward pressure from the tractor to give variable depth of penetration and to facilitate full depth when needed. Machines for fine turf often have a pressure roller following the tines to smooth down any surface lifting caused by the action of the tines. Slitting can be overdone and marks that are too close create an uneven sward surface. This is especially prevalent on heavy saturated soils or during frosty conditions. The depth of slitting (as with any aeration treatment) should be varied in order to prevent the formation of pans within the soil profile.

Solid Tines or Spikes

Solid tines or spikes enter the ground vertically and punch a hole into the turf surface. They are used in the main to increase air and water infiltration into the sward but do not

Mounted slitter, fitted with knife-type tines, in operation on a winter-games pitch. (Photo: SISIS)

relieve compaction; indeed, they may actually cause localized compaction around the hole left by the tine. Most solid tines are designed for the top 100mm of the soil profile and work to this depth. Solid tining provides a safer alternative to slitting during spring and summer months, especially on heavy soils, as the holes do not gape open.

Solid tining is most frequently used on localized areas to relieve specific problems, such as dry patch on greens, worn rink and wicket ends, and so on. When used to relieve dry patch, solid tining is carried out before application of water and wetting agents. It can be useful for allowing water penetration on worn soccer pitch goal mouths and when executed with a hand fork can relieve compaction in those areas because of the heaving action it is possible to obtain. Frequency of treatment varies with the intensity of wear and environmental conditions, and may be anything from fortnightly to monthly. Machines with cam action punch cleaner holes, while drum types, if not used carefully, can rip the turf and even roll up weak-rooted grass.

Hollow (Coring) Tines

These tines physically remove a core of soil from the turf/soil profile and leave a comparatively large hole. They have a number of beneficial effects, including:

1. Thatch removal – hollow tining at 50mm centres can remove 5 per cent of the thatch from an area of turf.
2. Soil exchange and amelioration – poor soil is removed and replaced with topdressing of the desired material.
3. Relief of soil compaction by removing soil.
4. Introduction of air into the soil profile and hence also increased water infiltration.

Hollow tines mainly work to depths of 75–100mm but come in a range of diameter sizes from 6mm to 25mm. This size influences the spacing used, suggested spacings being as follows:

- Narrow tines (6mm): 25mm spacing.
- 12mm-diameter tines: 50mm spacing.
- Large-diameter (25mm) tines: 100mm spacing.

Obviously, using large-diameter tines at too close a spacing will result in too much of the turf/soil being removed. It is normal practice to topdress with a suitable material after hollow coring, but it is not unknown for areas to be left open over the winter to allow greater drainage during wet weather. Overdoing hollow coring and topdressing can lead to problems with layering, especially if topdressing materials are inconsistent, as

Pedestrian hollow-core aerator in operation on a golf green where coring is a common practice. (Photo: John Deere)

Core collection can be a time-consuming operation unless you have a core harvester such as this machine. (Photo: RansomesJacobsen)

well as the creation of a 'soft' surface – compact soil is removed and the holes filled with unfirmed material. The problem will also be exacerbated by using too close a tine spacing. Hollow coring is sometimes used as an aid to improving surface levels, mainly by removing cores from high spots and then leaving these areas to settle down again.

A variation of the hollow core tine is the spoon tine, which is curved and half-round in shape and removes a plug from the sur-

face. A spring on the tine is fitted to minimize any ripping of the surface that would occur otherwise. Such tines are limited in their application and are probably best used on larger areas with light sandy soils.

In the past, hollow coring could be a time-consuming operation, but today's machines are faster in operation. Both drum and punch types are available; some drum types collect the cores inside a hollow drum, while the punch-action types generally leave cleaner holes at the surface. There is a wide range of machines available, including pedestrian, ride-on and tractor-mounted varieties, while core harvesters can be purchased to clean up the cores from the surface. Hollow coring is most frequently carried out in the autumn as part of the end-of-season renovation, particularly on fine turf areas.

The three basic types of tine covered above can be fitted in various sizes to a wide range of equipment and machines for turf aeration.

Hand Forks

These are purpose-designed frames onto which are bolted the desired tines. They are time-consuming and laborious to use, but are handy for smaller areas. The traditional garden fork can be used and can be very effective for relieving localized compaction

Hand-pushed Aerators

These are useful labour savers as a pedestrian progression from hand forks but are still of limited value. Some are relatively fast in operation and are commonly used on confined areas such as bowling greens and cricket squares.

Self-propelled Aerators

These pedestrian machines come in both drum and cam-action types, and there are even mini-mole plough machines available. They are used extensively for lawns and smaller sport areas or for localized treatment on larger areas.

Ride-on Machines

Mostly of the cam-action type, although drum varieties are available. They are fast in operation and highly manoeuvrable, and are used where transport from site to site is needed quickly – for example, greens on a golf course.

Tractor-mounted and Trailed Types

These are used for treating large, extensive areas of grassland or where more power is needed to achieve soil penetration. A wide range of sites for both compact and conventional tractors is available.

Aeration machines can be further categorized into two groups depending upon their type of action. These are dealt with below.

Fixed-knife Aerators

With this type of machine the tines are mounted onto a series of discs, the diameter of which can vary from machine to machine. The tines may have a flat or half-rounded end, and are pulled through the ground to cut a semi-circular slit. This type of machine can lift stones out of the ground and rip poorly rooted turf. The discs are either steel (lightweight) or cast iron (heavyweight), the steel disc is usually limited to about 1,200mm in width, and the discs are mounted on a full-width shaft. The lightweight discs may require some extra weight to achieve full penetration. Care must be taken not to overload the machine or the shaft will bend as it tries to follow the contours of the ground. Heavyweight discs are usually mounted in pairs so that they can follow the contours of the ground, and because of their weight they are usually mounted on the three-point linkage of a tractor or have a special trailer for transporting them from site to site.

The majority of models are pulled at fairly high speed, although one very common model is driven forward by rotating the shaft with the tines on it and so travels at a much slower speed. The spoon tine is also fitted to a disc and is used to remove soil. It does not remove a clean core or plug and can rip the surface, so a spring is mounted around the tine to press the turf down. Because of its speed, it can cause fissuring of the soil. The spiker slitter consists of a series of steel discs along whose edge are a large number of spikes. This type will relieve compaction at the surface and enable water to penetrate the surface, and so is most frequently used before irrigation or rain.

Vertical-tine Aerators

With this type of machine the tines go into and out of the ground vertically, so that it cannot lift stones and does not rip turf. There are two different types of machine: drum type and cam type.

Drum types are the simplest and consist of two wheels that are joined together with a number of tine bars to form the shape of a drum. The tines are attached to these tine bars. To enable the tines to enter or leave the ground vertically, the tine bars rotate through 180 degrees. The bars rotate as the drum moves, but they are spring-loaded so that the tines are reset to the correct entry angle after they leave the ground. The speed of operation is slow. The machines might be self-propelled for transport and perhaps fitted with a hydraulic lift system. If the machine is fitted with hollow core tines then the cores are left on the turf surface. A slight variation to this design consists of a drum, fitted with short hollow core tines. The cores are collected inside the drum and then emptied through a hinged section when it is full. This particular type of drum spiker is used for thatch control on sand-based constructions. The area will need topdressing with sand afterwards.

Cam types are often expensive machines. The tines are pushed into the ground by means of a cam or crankshaft. Although there are a number of tines (frequently eight), they do not go into the ground at the same time but are mounted in pairs and are staggered so that they enter it in a continuous cycle. The tines must go into the ground and out before the machine moves forward or the tines will become bent. The tines can move slightly during this part of the operation and there is often a spring above them to prevent damage should a tine hit stone – the tine retracts into its mounting if this happens. This type of machine must be at least self-propelled and might have a hydraulic lift system.

Specialist Methods for Soil Aeration and Decompaction

There are several machines available that relieve compaction of soil by fracturing or loosening it. Currently, the techniques employed include fracturing by injection of air or water, and mechanical fracturing or loosening through the use of tines, blades or drills. All of these specialist systems have their merits and particular uses for localized or severe problems. On heavily trafficked areas many turf managers are now using machines such as verti-drains up to two or three times a year as part of routine maintenance.

Water Injection
This machine introduces a high-velocity jet of water into the soil profile to create pore space. Highly pressurized water (380 bar) is injected in ten-millisecond pulses at speeds of up to 1,000kph. Varying the pressure allows for different depths to be achieved from 100mm to 500mm without disturbance to the turf surface. The machine is manually operated and needs to be connected to a water source, limiting its use to relatively small areas such as golf greens, for which it is most suitable. It is reputed to work faster than conventional hollow-tine aerators and obviously there is no spoil to remove from the surface. Water injection has shown some beneficial effects in reducing dry patch problems on areas or turf. It has been noted, however, that such treatment can have the undesirable effect of separating fine and coarse particles in the soil, which may actually lead to further compaction problems.

Air Injection
The basic principle of such machines is that air is injected under pressure into the soil, causing soil heave and fissuring. Theoretically, such air can follow lines of least resistance to escape from the soil profile and may therefore be ineffective in breaking up compacted soil evenly. The SISIS machine has air-injection tines mounted alongside conventional solid tines on a tractor-mounted and tractor-powered machine. Working at 150mm spacing, air is injected into the soil at 88 litres per minute from carbide-tipped 10mm-diameter tines up to a depth of 127mm. This machine is faster than other aeration machines as it has multiple aeration tines and a working width of 1.8m. It is claimed that the machine can aerate a football pitch in two hours and a golf green in 20–25 minutes. The machine can be fitted with a range of different tines, including hollow coring for use as a conventional aerator.

There are other machines that can penetrate to deeper depths, up to 900mm, but these have only one or two probes and are relatively slow in operation, thereby limiting their use to smaller areas where such extreme treatment may be necessary. There is no value in using these machines that penetrate deeply, on surfaces with gravel drainage carpets, as the air would simply dissipate through this drainage layer. The air-injection machines can cause significant surface heave, which often settles to leave irregular surface levels. Their application on surfaces used for sport, especially where surface levels are important, therefore needs careful consideration.

Mechanical Fracturing
Of the mechanical fracturing systems, the verti-drain is currently the most popular. Tines can penetrate up to 400mm (larger tractor machines) and as they are removed they have a heaving action that lifts and causes fissuring in the soil. Such tines also leave holes to depth in the soil profile for entry of air and water. Speed of operation is relatively fast and machines are available in all sizes from pedestrian ones to tractor-mounted varieties. Verti-draining is best carried out when surfaces are not in play, and when a period of time can be set aside for light rolling and topdressing to counteract any surface disruption. Where turf areas are in use year-round, timing is critical and needs to be considered carefully. Autumn is the best time as full penetration can be achieved, helping to improve drainage in the winter months.

If the soil is too wet and heavy, a system of mini-wells will be created as the holes fill with water. Care must be taken to avoid buried cables and pipework, such as those for irrigation systems. Verti-drain machines have been used on a variety of turf surfaces to great effect and are now a common machine in the turf manager's fleet.

Rotary decompactors These are a recent introduction to the UK and are being used more commonly for the aeration and decompaction of turf surfaces, particularly those used for sport. The machines have a number of blades that rotate vertically on a shaft powered by a tractor PTO and penetrate the turf surface. The action of the curved rotating blades creates an open slit in the turf surface, and with forward movement of the machine causes a shattering effect on the soil. The blades are set on flanges in a staggered arrangement so that they enter the soil at different times. Decompaction and soil loosening is achieved by the sideways displacement of soil blocks, when the blades from one flange cut into a slot made by the blade from an adjacent flange, and by associated soil fissuring.

Rotary decompactors are available from widths of 1.0–2.5m and with between 12 and 27 blades. Blades are available in thicknesses of 10–25mm, and the working depth of such machines also varies, with different models available with working depths of up to 550mm. Thus there are different model options for use on different surfaces, from

The Aer-Aid aerator machine, which injects compressed air into the soil to relieve compaction and improve soil aeration. (Photo: SISIS)

greens to winter sports pitches and amenity grass areas. The machine is mounted on skids, which have the effect of settling the disturbed turf surface as the decompactor moves forward.

Drill aerators Drill aerators relieve severe compaction through the use of a series of drills that physically drill holes up to 450mm deep into the compacted soil. The drill diameter can be varied from 10mm to 30mm depending upon the situation, and hole spacing can range from 110mm to 160mm. The drills are able to penetrate through severely compacted soils, and the holes can be back-filled with sand or other ameliorant to improve water and air penetration into the soil. This in effect creates a series of vertical drainage channels and relieves compaction by virtue of soil removal. This technique can be particularly effective in improving drainage on poorly constructed surfaces but does not relieve compaction in the soil between the drilled holes.

Aeration and Decompaction Practice
Aeration is one of the most vital maintenance operations on any area of sports turf or other intensively used turf. Its primary purpose is to increase water and air infiltration

ABOVE: *View of the Earthquake machine's blades (or tines), which revolve and cut through the soil. (Photo: Earthquake Turfcare)*

LFET: *The 'new breed' of turf-aeration machines: a rotary decompaction machine operated from a tractor. (Photo: Earthquake Turfcare)*

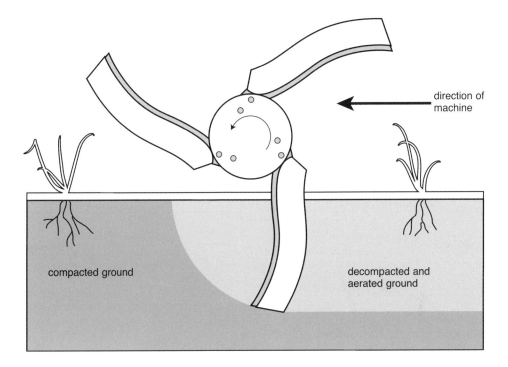

direction of
machine

compacted ground

decompacted and
aerated ground

ABOVE: *The effect
and action of rotary
decompactors.*

RIGHT: *A deep drill
machine suitable for use
on local areas of severe
or deep compaction.
(Photo: Ecosolve)*

into the soil profile and throughout the turfgrass root zone. Aeration will improve surface drainage and is of benefit in improving the efficiency of irrigation and restoring surface levels. There is a tremendous variety of machines to choose from to complete what are essentially the same tasks, each of which should be selected according to particular circumstances so that the desired results are achieved. For areas receiving intensive use, it is important that aeration is both frequent and regular. A variety of tines and/or machines should be used to ensure that pans do not occur in the soil through

109

continuous treatment to the same depth. Aerate when soil conditions are not too wet and the grass is actively growing or has sufficient time to recover before the onset of adverse environmental conditions. Examine the soil profile, monitor grass growth and choose the most appropriate method for the particular site and situation. For all machines, check tines for wear or damage before use and replace where necessary, and ensure that all appropriate guards and safety mechanisms are in place and functioning correctly. For effective use and longevity, tines must be kept clean and lubricated.

Thatch

Thatch is the general term used to describe the layers of organic fibrous material found in turf. Thatch accumulation is a natural phenomenon of turf development and cannot ever be entirely prevented. It is, in fact, desirable to have some thatch within the turf as it improves resilience and shock-absorption characteristics, which for some activities (such as horse racing) is vital. A turf surface with no underlying fibre would lack such resiliency and would easily become muddy in wet weather.

Problems arise when thatch layers build up to an excessive degree, especially if the turf is to be used for sport or other demanding activity. In fine turf, a 15mm layer of matted material would be acceptable, whereas a layer exceeding 25mm in depth would be troublesome. It is not unknown to find layers of 100–150mm, which greatly reduce the quality of any turf surface for sport.

There are many problems that are directly caused by thatch or at least exacerbated by its presence within the turf. These include:

- Increased disease problems, such as thatch fungus.
- Localized dry spots.
- Leaf chlorosis.
- Proneness to scalping.
- Creation of a soft, spongy surface that 'footprints' easily, affects ball roll/bounce, and holds water.
- Decreased heat, cold and drought tolerances of grasses.

Types of Thatch
The three main types of thatch are litter, fibre and thatch (or mat).

Litter
This consists of a loose and fluffy accumulation of grass clippings and decaying grass plant shoots and leaves, which collect in amongst the grass plants at their base. Such litter is most often a feature of old and neglected lawn areas that receive little treatment other than mowing and do not have the

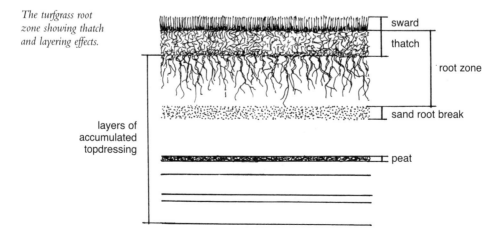

The turfgrass root zone showing thatch and layering effects.

clippings removed. It is not normal to see such litter on intensively managed turf.

Fibre
Fibre resembles coconut matting, being tough, wiry in texture and brown in colour. It consists of old roots and other decaying plant debris. It is usually associated with acidic conditions and often overlies dry soil, making it difficult to re-wet after drought conditions.

Thatch, or Mat
Thatch, or mat as it is sometimes referred to, remains waterlogged throughout most of the year and smells strongly of decay and stagnation. It is yellow/brown in colour with black streaks, showing the activity of anaerobic bacteria. The underlying soil is wet, compacted and usually consists of clay, with restricted drainage. Annual Meadow Grass (Poa annua) tends to dominate the sward, with little surviving bent or fescue. Such thatch layers can accumulate to form layers several inches thick, especially in water-collecting hollows on heavily used turf.

Causes of Thatch
Thatch will develop when the accumulation rate of dead organic material in the turf exceeds the natural rate of decomposition. Any cultural or environmental factor that stimulates excessive shoot growth or impairs the decomposition process increases the thatch accumulation rate. The major cultural factors contributing to thatch accumulation are:

• Vigorous-growing turfgrass species and cultivars.
• Acidic soil conditions.
• Poor soil aeration.
• Excessively high plant nitrogen nutritional levels.
• Infrequent or excessively high mowing.

Different grasses tend to produce thatch at different rates. The desirable fescue grasses, for example, tend to have leaf bases that are resistant to decomposition and are therefore prone to encourage fibre. Annual Meadow Grass, the common weed grass, also tends to produce thatch, probably because of its fast growth under moist, fertile conditions. Where there are low populations of soil macro-organisms such as earthworms, as occurs in many sand-based sports turf surfaces, thatch has a propensity to build up more rapidly. This is because earthworms and other soil organisms assist in the incorporation and breakdown of organic material in the soil or root zone.

Thatch Control
There are a number of cultural methods that may be used by the turfgrass manager to minimize or reduce the incidence or effects of thatch:

• Minimize use of fungicides – these restrict the naturally occurring bacteria and fungi within the soil that ordinarily break down organic matter.
• Use aeration equipment, particularly hollow-coring types, which as well as improving soil air content also physically remove the thatch.
• Topdress with sand to improve surface drainage and prevent anaerobic conditions.
• Minimize Annual Meadow Grass as this is very thatch productive.
• Use correct fertilizer regime – not too excessive, especially in relation to nitrogen as this encourages lush growth.
• Apply lime if soil is too acidic.
• Improve sub-aeration.
• Improve sub-drainage.
• Minimize use of irrigation.
• Box off clippings whenever possible.
• Maintain earthworm and soil microbial populations where possible.
• Physically remove thatch through mechanical or manual means. This is commonly referred to as scarification, vertical mowing, power-raking or de-thatching

Scarification Machines
Verti-cutting on a regular basis will minimize thatch accumulation, but even so, on intensively used turf more severe measures

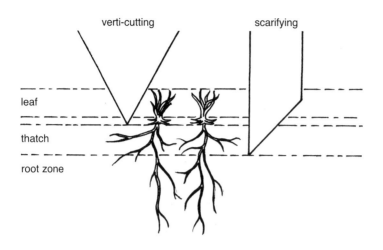

Verti-cutting and scarification – depth of tine penetration.

will also be needed from time to time. Specialist scarification machines are available to remove thatch and fibre layers that accumulate in the turf.

Such machines are available in a range of sizes from pedestrian varieties to tractor-mounted and trailed types for large areas of grassland. There is also a range of exchangeable units with scarification and other turf management reels that can be fitted to ride-on and pedestrian cylinder machines to replace the grass-cutting cylinder. The machine becomes a power unit (like a tractor) and can then perform a range of turf maintenance tasks. The pedestrian mower units are popular with small sports clubs that have limited financial resources. Some larger sports grounds and golf courses are now retaining old ride-on mowers solely for use with these turf management reels or cassettes.

At its simplest, scarification can be achieved on small areas with a wire rake (springbok type) or on larger areas with grassland chain harrows. For scarification to be effective, it is necessary to collect and remove the arisings. Many machines have such a collection facility, but often (especially with larger models) separate collection later with a leaf sweeper or similar machine is necessary.

The most important feature of all scarification machines is the type of tine (or blade) with which they are fitted. There are several basic types of tine, each designed for a specific purpose.

Heavy-duty fixed-knife tine This type of tine is relatively thick and usually has two or three work faces. The tines are commonly made of hardened and tempered steel and mounted onto a shaft. They are capable of entering the soil and are most suited for use on old neglected lawn areas in need of renovation and removal of large quantities of thatch or mat. They are normally used during the autumn, so that the grass can be left to recover over winter. Units fitted with such tines are sometimes referred to as thatch removal reels. They should be used in at least three directions, each at a slight angle to the other, across the area being scarified.

Light-duty fixed-knife tine This type of tine is relatively thick and usually has three or more working faces. The tines have sharp cutting edges that are not designed to enter the soil (if they do so they will wear very rapidly). They are often called verti-cut tines and are commonly triangular. Such tines are mounted onto a shaft so that the points of each blade are offset; one is straight, one is set to the left and the third is set to the right. The action of machines fitted with these tines is much lighter and is often carried out during the growing season many times. They are sometimes known as thatch control reels and are best used little and often throughout the growing season to reduce thatch accumulation, to lift trailing growth and to control weeds and coarse grasses. These tines can also be used for autumnal renovation works and again should be used in slightly varying directions over the area.

Flail-type tine This type of tine is mounted in a similar way to a flail mower. The tines are mounted closely together and are free to swing about the fixing position. Like the flail mower, they swing out to their working position by means of centrifugal force. Many machines fitted with this type of tine are not self-propelled but must be pushed manually. The machine must be pushed forward very slowly if you are to achieve its full effect. The tine is not designed to penetrate

The innovative Thatch-Away system, which uses different cassettes on triplex turf machines. There are a variety of cassettes for different applications. (Photo: GreenTek)

the ground. This type of machine is invariably cheap and often limited to small-scale or amateur use only.

Wire-type tine This type of tine is rather similar to the flail type, but the tine, instead of being a flat piece of metal, consists of a piece of wire. The tine is therefore much lighter and does not have the same momentum as the flail type. It has more of a lifting than a cutting action and is therefore sometimes used before mowing to lift grasses and trailing weeds for a more efficient cut by the mower. The best results are achieved if, again, forward speed of travel is slow and the tines do not penetrate the ground. Normally the tines will swing freely to minimize the risk of breakage if they hit an obstruction.

Brush-type tine This is a series of nylon brushes fitted to a rotor or shaft that make up a rotating brush head unit. It is used primarily for removal of surface debris, including leaf litter, and is commonly utilized on such specialized areas as cricket wickets. The tine's action is light and it is used for lifting horizontal growth prior to mowing.

For most scarification machines, it is possible to change heads or units for different circumstances and particular uses. Most machines employ a method of contra-rotation, whereby the reels rotate in the opposite direction to that of the machine's forward travel. The blades therefore have a lifting action and actually tease the thatch or fibre out of the turfgrass sward. For most machines, it is also possible to change the depth of action of the tines depending on the specific circumstances of use. The different types of scarification machine are looked at below.

Pedestrian scarifiers Pedestrian scarification machines may be hand-pushed or self-propelled. The hand-pushed type consists of a rotor, to which the tines are fitted, its main frame supported on wheels or rollers, and with the engine on top and a clutch and drive connected to the rotor. It is common for this type of machine to be capable of having

Pedestrian scarifier in operation. A box can be used with this machine to collect the arisings (this is the normal method). This picture clearly shows the amount of plant material that can be removed in the scarification process. (Photo: SISIS)

different tines fitted. The usual tines attached are light-duty fixed-knife types, wire types or flail types. Where the tines are free to swing it is important that the machine is pushed very slowly to achieve its full action. The material it removes can be thrown out in front or to the rear of the machine. A better action is achieved when the material is thrown out in front, but unless there is a collecting box the removed material keeps passing through the machine. The front wheels or roller controls the depth of tine penetration. It is important that the rotor does not continue turning when the machine is stationary or else damage can occur to the turf. These machines are fitted with a clutch for this purpose.

Larger machines are usually self-propelled and have some form of box to collect the arisings. Such machines travel at a reasonable speed because the blades or tines are fixed and do not swing out of the way when they hit the turf surface. Heavy-duty versions have larger engines and tines that are more robust. A front roller or wheels that adjust in a similar manner to that found on cylinder mowing machines usually control depth. The tines usually have a square centre hole that fits over a square centre shaft running the full width of the machine. A

rubber spacer that allows the blade to flex when the tines hit a stone or other physical impediment often separates the tines. Machine width is generally around 500mm so that it can follow the contours or turf surface more readily. It is desirable that the rotor be disengaged for transport. The drive to the rotor is usually via belts or chains and normally there is only one forward gear.

Tractor-drawn or tractor-mounted scarifiers These machines are similar in configuration and operation to gang mowers but the usual cutting cylinders are replaced with scarifying reels. Most commonly, they will have three, or possibly five, units mounted on a frame that is attached to the tractor's three-point linkage system. Hydraulic motors, belts or chains connected via the tractor's PTO shaft may power the reels. These machines are suited to larger areas and can remove considerable quantities of material. A major disadvantage of the gang-type scarifier is that it does not collect the debris, which means that some other machine, such as a leaf collector, has to pass over the surface afterwards to carry out the job. Other machines scarify grassland with flail-type tines and have grass-collection hoppers, and so are suitable for any large sports field or amenity grass areas.

Tractor-mounted scarifier for use on large areas. After scarification a trailed leaf sweeper or similar machine could be used to collect the arisings. (Photo: RansomesJacobsen)

Scarification Practice and Timing

As well as removing thatch, scarification machines are also useful in removing or controlling moss, creeping weeds such as Creeping Buttercup, and stoloniferous grass growth. Scarification machines also assist in air and water infiltration into the surface of the sward. Additionally, they are useful in breaking up soil cores following the use of hollow-tine aerators; these can then be incorporated back into the sward with drag-mats and brushes. It is important that the correct type of machine be used to achieve the desired result.

Scarification must only be carried out when there is active grass growth in order that it can recover from what can be quite a damaging operation, and the directions of each pass of the machine must be varied but never at right angles to one another. The surface should be dry, but hot weather conditions should be avoided as they will stress the grass plant too severely. Scarification is often practised as a part of autumnal renovation for many turf surfaces, along with aeration, topdressing and over-seeding. Where surfaces are in continual use, such as golf greens, there should be more regular but less intensive scarification in order to control excessive thatch build-up.

Scarification machines can be very effective in creating a seedbed for over-seeding, as they create grooves in the surface into which seeds fall and provide a good environment for germination. For best results, mow the grass prior to scarification to remove excess top growth and allow the scarifier to penetrate the thatch layer effectively. Set the appropriate depth depending upon the ground conditions and particular surface – the aim is to remove thatch and other organic material but not to allow the tines to penetrate the soil as this wears them excessively and damages the turf surface. Prior to use, check machines for worn, bent or distorted tines or blades, and check that guards and safety equipment are correct and in place.

Topdressing

In turf culture, topdressing is the application of a bulky material to the surface of the sward. Topdressing usually has none or only minor nutritional valve, but is carried out for the following reasons:

1. To restore a level surface – in this respect it is more efficient than rolling in improving surface trueness.
2. To improve the nature of the soil, usually by ameliorating it to change the particle size distribution.

It also has the following indirect effects:

- It increases soil aeration.
- It increases drought resistance.
- It assists surface water movement. (drainage).
- It affects playing surface characteristics.
- It controls (usually reduces) the organic matter (thatch) content of the surface soil.
- On newly turfed areas it can fill joints, and on newly seeded areas it can help protect fragile seedlings

Because of the quantities involved, topdressing is more commonly used on limited areas such as golf and bowling greens, tennis courts, cricket tables, high-quality winter sports pitches and good ornamental lawns.

Hollow coring followed by the reincorporation of the removed soil has similar effects to topdressing. If the soil is suitable for that surface then such practice may be just as effective as, or better than, topdressing with a foreign material. The volume of material returned will obviously depend upon core size and spacing, which in itself is dependent upon the amount of disruption that can be allowed for that surface.

Topdressing Materials

Sand
Sand is used as a major component for most topdressing mixes as well as being used extensively on its own; this is due in the main to its natural porosity and resistance to compaction. Pure sand dressings are useful for their stabilizing and drainage properties, and on sand-only constructions the policy must be to apply the same material to ensure uniformity through the profile. The type of sand used is important – it should have a narrow particle range size (generally 0.125–0.5mm). It is best to avoid sands from coastal areas owing to their lime (shell) content.

Soil profile showing a recent core that has been back-filled with sand in order to improve soil aeration and drainage. (Photo: Ecosolve)

The use of sand alone continually may lead to problems in the future, and the long-term consequences should be considered. These may include:

- Increased wear of mower cylinders and bottom blades.
- Increased incidence of dry patch.
- Reduced microbial activity within the superficial sand/thatch layers.
- Lower nutrient and moisture retention.
- Greater vulnerability to turf wear over the winter.

Sand should never be used on tennis courts and cricket squares as it creates a crumbling surface unsuitable for play.

Topsoil
Topsoil is used in composts for topdressing and in some instances on its own, if of sufficient sand content, for fine turf areas. It is, however, rare to find natural topsoil readily available and suitable for direct application without ameliorating it with sand. On cricket and tennis courts, heavy clay loams are the most suitable materials for topdressing.

Peat
Peat is used as a component for some topdressing composts. It improves the moisture-holding capacity of a root zone whilst being relatively inert and sterile. Fine ground peat must be used for fine turf areas while coarser grades can be used on other areas of grass when mixed with compost. Sedge or sphagnum peat can both be used, although the latter is preferred as it is more fibrous. Some peats extracted from fenland areas can be alkaline and are best avoided.

Compost
Compost is a valuable material for topdressing but is in short supply. Home-made compost should be formed in heaps from compostible organic material and left for sufficient time to decay before screening and use. It is particularly rich in trace elements. Continuity of supply is essential and a regular production programme should be followed.

Substitute Composts

After sand, these are the most popular materials for topdressing. Various mixes are possible, of which the following is a common example:

6 parts sand
3 parts screened sandy loam
1 part granulated peat

The proportions can be changed and peat is often omitted altogether. Compost comprising 60/40 or 70/30 sand/soil mix is commonly prescribed for use on fine turf areas.

Topdressing for Fine Turf Areas

Materials used for such areas should in general:

1. Be free of stones and gravel, having been screened through a 5mm mesh.
2. Have a majority (75 per cent) of mineral particles within the size range 0.25–1.0mm.
3. Contain no more than 10 per cent fines (very fine sand, silt and clay).
4. Contain 4–6 per cent organic matter.
5. Have less than 0.2 per cent lime content.
6. Have a pH reaction of between 5.0 and 6.0.
7. Be sterile (free of pests, diseases and weeds).

Golf Greens

The best approach to topdressing of golf greens is based on very light applications (approximately 0.5–1.0kg/sq m) spread at regular intervals through the growing season, up to an amount of 5–6kg/sq m per annum. Normally sand alone or, more commonly, a substitute compost material is used. An 18-hole golf course may use between 80 and 100 tonnes of topdressing per annum for greens, tees and surrounds.

Bowling Greens

On bowling greens, topdressing is usually applied as part of the end-of-season renovation in the autumn. It is usual to apply all of the topdressing in one application although, it is sometimes split into two applications in autumn and spring. For a standard 42 × 42yd green, 4 tonnes of topdressing will be needed every autumn as a minimum after hollow coring, although where levels need substantial correction up to 6 tonnes may often be required. The most common mixes used are:

6 parts (by bulk) suitable sand
2 parts screened sandy loam topsoil
1 part fine peat

Or:

Trailed topdressing machine applying topdressing to a golf green. Such machines allow large areas to be treated quickly and effectively. (Photo: Campey Turfcare).

3–4 parts (by bulk) suitable sand
1 part screened sandy loam topsoil

Such mixes and application rates would also be suitable for high-quality ornamental lawns if so desired.

Cricket Squares
For the game of cricket a consolidated surface that will provide both pace and reliable ball bounce is required. Clay loams have been found to be the best materials for providing such surfaces. Topdressing is probably the single most important practice in cricket square maintenance and the choice of which particular material to use is not always straightforward. It is important that the surface is scarified to leave no more than 20 per cent grass cover prior to topdressing, and the material must be compatible with the existing soil. Topdressing of any quality for cricket must have the following characteristics:

- It should be a natural topsoil and not artificially concocted.
- It should be sterile.
- It should have a clay content of 24–30 per cent for club level and 28–39 per cent for test and county cricket.
- Particles exceeding 2mm should make up less than 1 per cent of the total.
- ASSB test figures of no less than 40kg at club level and 55kg for county standard.
- It should contain 4–12 per cent organic matter.
- It should have a pH no lower than 5.5.

Topdressing is carried out as part of the end-of-season renovation in the autumn. An application rate of around 2.0kg/sq m would be suitable for most cricket squares.

Tennis needs similar surface performance characteristics to cricket and therefore similar topdressing may be used. Normally, a clay loam with lower clay content, say 20–25 per cent, is preferred.

Winter Games Pitches
The major use of sand in the maintenance of winter sports areas is to dilute accumulations of fine material and organic matter at the surface so that the permeability of the pitch is retained and a firm surface provided in wet conditions. With this in mind, pure sand with no soil amendment is the obvious choice for a topdressing material. Sand or sand loam is also valuable in repairing divots kicked out during play, thereby restoring surface levels.

Sand topdressing is critical for those pitches with slit drainage systems where applications are needed to retain the open top of the slits. Slits tend to be smeared over with soil during play and thus become ineffective; if they are not kept open with sand dressings, water cannot enter them from the surface.

The amount of sand required will vary according to particular construction type, standard of game catered for and available finance. Typically, it will be within the range of 25–100 tonnes per annum, applied at the end of the playing season as part of renovation.

Topdressing Equipment
Traditionally, topdressing has been applied manually with shovels and then incorporated with hand drag-mats, brushes and tru-lutes. This method is still practised on small areas but it is time-consuming and laborious, and it demands great skill to spread the material uniformly. With the increasing demand for the more regular topdressing of larger areas, a range of machines is now available for the job. They can be found as dedicated units or as attachments to utility vehicles or tractors. Smaller pedestrian machines are self-propelled and controlled by an operator walking with the machine.

Topdressing machines are essentially the same design as fixed-width fertilizer distributors, although they are larger in order to handle the more bulky material. The basic design is a hopper that holds the topdressing material, under which runs a conveyor belt. This moving continuous belt picks up the material and moves it towards an opening, through which it passes before being directed downwards to the turf by a rotating brush. The rate of application is dependent upon forward speed and the size of the

Pedestrian topdresser suitable for small areas, such as a bowling green. (Photo: SISIS)

opening at the base of the hopper. The machine can be calibrated by filling the hopper with a known volume of topdressing material, setting the opening of the hopper and belt, and then running the machine until the hopper is empty. After measuring the distance travelled and the width of spread, the area of spread can be calculated and the application rate determined. The ground speed is normally a constant and adjustments are made to the hopper opening to apply more or less material as required.

When evaluating topdressing machines, the following factors should be considered:

- Hopper volume – a larger hopper will mean less frequent filling, but large hoppers filled with topdressing will be heavy and may compact the soil.
- Hopper dimensions – ideally, the hopper will be wider than the filling loader so as to avoid spillage and allow efficient filling.
- Conveyor belt – ribbed belts are more efficient at picking up the material in the hopper.
- Machine weight (especially when full) – the compacting pressure will be affected by the number and width of tyres.

After use, it is important that the machine is cleaned. Special attention should be given to

drive mechanisms, gears and bearings where sand or sandy topdressings have been used. Sand is abrasive and can cause severe wear on moving parts and mechanisms.

Successful Topdressing Practice

Topdressing is an important maintenance practice for turf and can significantly affect a sward's development and performance in play. It is worth the effort paying attention to some important considerations if the desired result is to be achieved:

1. Use only quality materials supplied by a reputable dealer or extracted from a known source of quality. Such materials must be sterile and free of coarse particles, having been passed through at least a 5mm mesh. Thorough mixing is required if you are preparing your own topdressing, but you will still need good-quality ingredients.
2. Topdressing is best applied when both it and the surface are dry. It must be thoroughly incorporated into the turf using drag-mats and tru-lutes as appropriate. It should only be applied during the growing season so that the grass has a chance to grow through it, and it should never be applied so heavily that it smoothers the grass. Topdressing machines used for application should be adjusted correctly and calibrated to ensure uniform distribution; it may be necessary to split the material and apply it in opposing directions to achieve this.

TOPDRESSING STORAGE

- Topdressing must be kept dry and clean.
- For loose topdressing, purpose-built bays with a sloping roof and a concrete floor are required.
- A tarpaulin cover will keep the topdressing free from contamination by weed seeds or diseases.
- Bagged topdressing should be stored under cover and stacked on pallets.

---

3. Topdressing is easier to work into the sward if the areas have been mown and scarified prior to application. If it is being carried out as part of autumn renovation work, it may be possible to mow the area closer than normal.
4. The single most important factor is that of consistency. The use of different materials over any period will invariably lead to layering within the soil/root zone profiles. This in turn causes problems with surface drainage, aeration, root growth and playing characteristics such a ball bounce. It is critical that the same material (as far as is practically possible) is used consistently for topdressing. This policy should only change where there is evidence and sound agronomic reasons for doing so. Of equal importance is that the material used is compatible with the existing site topsoil. In most situations when dealing with a purpose-made or constructed surface, the best material to use for topdressing is that which was used for the root zone itself.

Rolling

Rolling is practised in an effort to obtain a smooth, flat and level surface. However, it is frequently overdone and leads to excessive soil compaction and loss of structure, resulting in poor drainage, aeration and root growth. For some sports, surface rolling is a critical part of preparation and maintenance, especially where ball bounce is important, such as for cricket and tennis. Other areas such as golf and bowling greens require a resilient surface and need rolling only to restore the surface after winter frost heave; thereafter, the roller on the mower will be sufficient to maintain the surface. Winter games pitches sometimes need a light roll after play to refirm divots or after frosty weather to smooth the surface.

Rolling should be avoided during wet conditions, as it will cause soil particles to squash together, reducing the air spaces between them and so restricting drainage,

aeration and root growth. For healthy turfgrass growth you should aim to maintain at least 10–15 per cent of the total soil volume as air space, or else root growth and soil bacterial action will suffer. Rolling is especially useful in preparing seedbeds and consolidating newly seeded or turfed areas. Excessive rolling may also lead to invasion by moss and Annual Meadow Grass as the desirable grasses within the sward decline.

Types of Roller
Rollers for turf are flat, have rounded edges and are in section to facilitate turning with minimal damage to the turf. A wide range of hand-pulled, powered pedestrian, ride-on and tractor-drawn rollers are available for different situations. Smaller rollers will usually be between 600mm and 1m wide, while larger tractor-drawn ones are usually at least 2m in width. There are now rollers that can be fitted to triple mowers in place of the cutting units. These rollers are obviously heavier than the cutting cylinders and care must be exercised so that they do not overload and

Ride-on fine-turf roller (turf iron) used on golf greens in tournament preparation. (Photo: RansomesJacobsen)

damage the machine frame or hydraulics. Depending upon their weight, the tractor models will either be mounted on the three-point linkage or towed by the tow hitch. Weights vary from 250kg for smaller hand rollers to 6,000kg for tractor units.

Some larger rollers are mounted on a tool frame for ease of transport. One example has the rollers pivoted centrally under a tool frame, with pneumatic-tyred wheels at the rear that are raised and lowered with a hydraulic ram. When the wheels are lowered for transport, the roll is lifted clear of the ground and hydraulically turned through 90 degrees to allow it to pass through narrow openings. Many rollers are of the ballast type and the weight can be varied by filling the hollow roll with materials such as sand or water. Adjustable ballast rollers allow the weight to be changed for different purposes and different ground conditions.

The Rolling Factor

The effect of a roller on turf is dependent on its diameter and width as well as its weight. Weight of the roller is important, although sheer weight means little in terms of compacting effect. Other factors must be taken into consideration to determine how the weight is spread over the turf, ground pressure being the important figure. A formula to determine this is used to compare the compacting effect of different rollers and is known as the rolling factor:

Rolling factor = gross weight of roller (kg) ÷ [width (cm) × diameter (cm)]

For winter games and general grassland areas, aim for a maximum rolling factor of 0.03. Rollers should be chosen carefully for their smoothing action and not for compaction effect.

Switching and Brushing

Switching or brushing is carried out on areas of fine (mainly sports) turf to remove surface dew and to disperse worm casts,

Ride-on greens triplex machine fitted with rollers. (Photo: RansomesJacobsen)

grass clippings and other debris on the surface. Switching disperses dew and dries the surface, thus making it easier to obtain a clean cut with the mower. It also helps to prevent those moist conditions in the turf that favour diseases such as Fusarium. Brushing will achieve the same results but has the added benefit of acting as a mild scarifier, lifting the procumbent growth ready for mowing. Brushing is also carried out as a method of incorporating or working in topdressing into the turf surface. On fine sports turf it is desirable to carry out one or other method every morning before play commences, primarily from the point of view of maintaining a clean playing surface and facilitating more rapid drying of the surface for play.

Switching and Brushing Tools

The switch, traditionally made of bamboo but now usually consisting of metal tubing with a 2m fibreglass extension piece, is simply a long flexible rod. It is used with a vigorous side-to-side motion, the fibreglass extension or tip held flat along the ground as the switch is progressively worked over the surface. The drag brush is a 1.25–1.5m-wide brush with whalebone, or now more

Tractor-mounted brush – a very useful tool for dew dispersal and presentation of sports turf areas. (Photo: GreenTek)

commonly synthetic, bristles, and is simply dragged behind the operative until, again, the whole surface has been covered. Larger tractor-mounted brushes are available for larger areas of grass such as golf-course fairways. A third variety of implement is sometimes used for the same purpose, this being a specialized type of roller with very light, narrow rolls 2.10m long and only 75mm in diameter. When dragged over the green, the rapidly spinning rolls disperse water back into the soil and so facilitate rapid surface drying. Dew rollers work best on flat areas with good surface levels, such as a flat bowling green.

CHAPTER 6

Diseases, Pests and Weeds

In the UK, the range of turf pests and diseases is limited when compared with those occurring in warmer climates. A few are very common and so occur frequently (such as *Fusarium* on fine turf), needing constant vigilance by the turf manager if surfaces are not to be irrevocably damaged. However, most of the problems described in this chapter are an issue only for intensively managed turf. It is a feature of turf culture that the more intensive the management the greater the prevalence of pests and diseases. This can be explained by the fact that the grasses of such surfaces are subject to great stress, such as close mowing, and usually extreme wear, and therefore are more susceptible to disease attack in particular.

The practice of any control for pests and diseases must be balanced against those of surface requirements, the needs of users and any benefits to be gained. This is especially the case where any form of chemical is to be used, as the welfare of people and the environment must be paramount. An integrated pest management approach and emphasis on sound agronomic principles to sustain vigorous grass growth is the best answer to such problems. When these methods are used and environmental conditions are maintained vigilantly, the occurrence of most of these problems is lessened. The growing awareness and concern of environmental issues in recent years has meant that the appearance of weeds such as daises in the lawn is now considered less of a problem; this philosophy of grassland maintenance should be positively encouraged.

Diseases of Turfgrass

Diseases are caused by pathogenic organisms, which disrupt the normal plant physiological and developmental processes. In horticulture generally, plant diseases may be caused by fungal, bacterial and viral agents, although in turf culture the vast majority of diseases are caused by fungi. In turfgrass, diseases have two important effects upon the sward:

1. The aesthetic value of turf (in other words, its visual appearance) may be reduced by disease attack. Many diseases discolour the grass or leave scars, which are unsightly. The quality of an area of sports turf as judged by the player is often based on visual appearance only.
2. In sports turf situations disease may often have detrimental effects on the playing qualities of the sward. In games such as golf and bowls, where the ball and turf surface closely interact, this can be critical.

It must be remembered that not all fungi associated with turf and soils are harmful. Many are extremely beneficial. as they aid the decomposition of plant materials (for example, thatch) and organic matter to release nutrients into the soil; some are also antagonistic to disease-causing organisms.

Most fungi grow as thread-like structures called hyphae. These can form larger aggregations known as mycelia, which are often visible on the grass plant or in the soil. Fungi are spread through the release of microscopic spores, which geminate into hyphae and continue their life cycle given appropriate environmental conditions. Spores are transmitted either through the air (usually released from fruiting bodies, like mushrooms and toadstools) or through water (such as the dew found on fine turf in the morning).

The factors affecting fungal growth, development and spread are varied as there are many different species, and in many instances they are still not fully understood or known. For most, the following factors will influence the processes to a greater or lesser degree:

• Temperature: fungi do not grow well below about 5°C; they flourish at around 20°C.
• Moisture. This is necessary for germination of fungal spores. Rainwater may spread the disease around by splashing and run-off. High humidity also encourages the spread of fungi. In addition, extreme wet or dry soil may weaken the grass plant, making it more prone to infection.
• Light: plants in the shade are more prone to disease because of weak growth.
• Air movement: moving air removes water from the grass, keeping turf dry and therefore less susceptible to disease. It also spreads or disperses fungal spores to new areas.
• Soil pH can affect fungal growth and development – many fungal diseases, such as Take-all Patch, prefer alkaline soils and become more troublesome as pH increases.

Diseases of grasses are far more prevalent in fine turf. This is often a result of the following conditions:

• Mowing – a cut leaf is an open wound. Close mowing continuously places great stress on the grass plant. Mowing also results in small plants that are crowded together, and this in turn restricts air movement and increases moisture retention. In addition, spores are spread by mowing.
• Fertilizer use – too much nitrogen applied late in the season can cause soft, lush growth, which is prone to disease attack. Many diseases are also encouraged by conditions of low fertility.
• Problems of soil compaction and lack of aeration.
• Thatch – some fungi can exist saprophytically on a thatch layer and then later cause disease.

The recognition and avoidance of these conditions are key factors in disease management.

Disease Identification
Identification of turf diseases is not always easy because the symptoms of one disease can vary dramatically depending on climatic conditions and the time of year. It is also common for more than one disease to be present and active within the turf. Correct identification is essential for control as not all diseases can be controlled by the same means, and conditions that may hinder some diseases can promote the activities of others.

If there is any doubt about a particular disease, a specialist with knowledge of the subject should be consulted. There are independent advisory organizations and consultants who can provide advice about turf diseases and their control, including identification services. The number of diseases that commonly affect turfgrass in the UK is relatively small, being confined in the main to approximately a dozen types and/or species. The major diseases, their symptoms, seasonality and controls are given in Table 21.

Note that not all the symptoms exhibited by an area of turf or grass may be caused by pathogenic organisms. Any harmful deviation arising from a cause other than a known pest or disease is termed a disorder – for example, fertilizer scorch or drought stress. Problems caused by incorrect nutrient availability and supply are known as deficiencies or toxicity. Identification is hindered when disease symptoms are similar to those caused by a disorder or nutrient availability problem.

Table 21: The main diseases of turf in the UK

Common name	Causative organism	Symptom	Species affected	Seasonality	Conditions favouring attack
Fusarium patch	*Microdochium nivale*	Orange/brown circular spots increasing in size	*Poa annua* and *Agrostis* spp.	Late autumn to spring (severe)	High N, high humidity, thatch
Pink snow mould	*Microdochium nivale*	Patches of bleached dead grass/pink mycelium	All, but especially *Poa annua*	Winter	Only under prolonged snow cover (10–14 days)
Damping off	Many, including *Pythium* spp. *Fusarium* spp.	Patches of dead grass, rotten seed, thin grass	All, but especially bents, fescues and Smooth-stalked Meadow Grass	Early spring or late autumn	Very wet or very dry conditions, uneven sowing
Dollar spot	*Sclerotinia homoecarpa*	Small white to yellow (dry) spots measuring 10–20mm	Slender Creeping Red Fescue and sometimes bent species	Summer and autumn (warm and moist)	Low fertility (particularly low N), warm humid conditions
Red thread	*Latisaria fuciformis*	Patches in turf measuring 50–200mm, 'red needles' on affected leaves	Red Fescue and Perennial Ryegrass	Mid- to late summer and autumn	Lower fertility (particularly N), warmth and moisture
Pink patch	*Limonomyces roseipellis*	White or pink mycelia on leaves	Red Fescue and Perennial Ryegrass	Mid- to late summer and autumn	As for Red Thread (it usually occurs with that disease)
Take-all patch	*Gaeumannomyces graminis*	Small patches of failing grass with rotted roots	Mainly *Agrostis* spp.	Mid-autumn	Rapid pH increase, excessive thatch, poor drainage
Anthrancnose	*Colletotrichum graminicola*	Yellow plants with rotten base	*Poa annua*	Late summer to winter	Compaction and prolonged surface wetness

(continued overleaf)

Table 21: The main diseases of turf in the UK (*continued*)

Common name	Causative organism	Symptom	Species affected	Seasonality	Conditions favouring attack
Type 1 fairy ring	*Marasmius oreades*	Ring of dead grass or bare soil between stimulated areas	May occur in any type of turf	Most obvious in dry summer weather – may persist for years	Not fully known, though moisture may be important
Type 2 fairy ring	Many, including *Agaricus campestris* and *Lycoperdon hiemile*	Rings of darker grass – stimulated growth	More noticeable on fine turf, although occurs on all areas	Active in summer and autumn	Not known, although symptoms most obvious when N is deficient
Type 3 fairy ring	Many, including *Hygrophorus* spp. and *Psilocybe* spp.	A ring of less distinct pattern or fruiting bodies	Autumn, sometimes in spring or early winter	All types of turf except heavily worn areas	Not known
Superficial fairy rings (or thatch fungus)	*Trechispora alnicola* and *Coprinus* spp.	Fungal activity in thatch layer, characteristic musty smell	Any, but particularly fine turf	Any time of year	Most troublesome in deep thatch areas

Control of Turfgrass Diseases

The decision to exercise disease control procedures will obviously be influenced by the area in question and the severity of the problem affecting it, as will the exact control measure implemented. As more and more chemicals are withdrawn and pesticide regulation in Europe and the UK is tightened up, the modern approach to the control of diseases (and indeed pests) is that of integrated pest management (IPM). Adopting such a strategy means that a number of control measures are utilized in a managed programme, the emphasis being that chemicals are used only as a last resort. The management practices adopted for the control of disease with an IPM programme will include cultural methods, biological control and use of pesticides.

Cultural Control
Good disease management commences with the adoption of sound turf culture practices that will reduce the incidence of disease. The following measures will assist in the control or eradication of turfgrass disease depending upon the particular disease organism present and its damaging effects:

- The maintenance of a vigorously growing sward.
- Moisture control to prevent the occurrence of humid surface conditions (for example, by switching or brushing).
- Free movement of air over the turf surface.
- Regular aeration treatment.
- Reduction of thatch through scarification/verti-cutting.
- Boxing off of clippings where possible, as they provide a substrate for disease development.
- Avoidance of excessive nitrogen application during cool conditions (autumn).
- Avoidance of lime application aside from exceptional circumstances, particularly on

fine turf. Water and topdressings should also be tested for lime content prior to application.

- Use of resistant grass cultivars when possible.
- Judicious use of fertilizers – a balanced fertilizer regime is essential.
- Sterilization of loams and topdressings.

Biological Control

This consists of deploying antagonistic fungi and bacteria to control (parasitize) the pathogenic fungi that cause disease (*see* Chapter 4 for more details). The pursuance of sound cultural practices will mean that soil microbial populations – including such antagonistic organisms – are maintained in the soil. However, in many sand-based sports turf areas such populations may be reduced, especially if management practices foster the overuse of fungicides, fertilizers or irrigation. The theory of biological control is sound, but in reality the application of such agents is far more complex when dealing with soil and living organisms in the field. The applied fungi or bacteria need particular conditions in order to thrive and have the desired effect; most likely, this will mean the correction of soil growing conditions. Bacterial inocula are now available in the USA, but as yet none has been released in the UK.

Chemical Control

The decision to use chemicals to control or eradicate a particular disease-causing organism should be made only when symptoms have been physically observed in the sward. Preventative sprays used as a matter of course are unnecessarily expensive in labour and material costs, are often damaging to both beneficial organisms and antagonistic fungi/bacteria, and increase the likelihood of disease resistance to that pesticide. Preventive sprays can, however, be useful when site experience dictates that a particular disease will occur. Fusarium, for example, occurs all too frequently every year on many areas of fine turf and preventative spraying in these instances is often justified.

Chemicals for the control of fungal disease organisms are termed fungicides. There are two main types of fungicide available for use on turf:

1. Systemic fungicides. These are mainly used during periods of active grass growth, are absorbed by the foliage, move throughout the plant, and give a longer period of protection than contact types. They are site-specific fungicides that affect cell division and so disrupt germination and growth of the pathogen. They are technically known as acropetal penetrants.
2. Contact fungicides. These chemicals act upon the disease on contact with it. They are frequently used during dormant growth periods but can be used at any time of year if desired. Technically referred to as localized penetrates, they act on more than one biochemical process within the pathogen and are less likely to create resistant disease strains.

In practice, fungicides should be used only as part of an integrated management programme for disease control. It is important to remember that repeated use of the same fungicide will often lead to problems of disease resistance. To minimize this likelihood, aim to:

- Employ a range of both cultural and chemical controls as appropriate.
- Exercise careful and judicious use of chemicals.
- Alternate between different chemicals and chemical groups.
- Treat the disease when first seen rather than using preventative sprays.
- Follow maximum recommended dosage rates and numbers of applications.

Turf Physiological Disorders

Dry Patch and Black Layer are often associated with extremes of weather condition pertaining to specific times of the year – summer and the autumn to spring period, respectively. The general occurrence of both phenomena is limited predominantly to fine rather than coarse turf areas, especially to bowling and golf greens.

Dry Patch

Dry Patch is a condition whereby the soil or growing medium becomes repellent to water, therefore resulting in dry patches of soil and turf within a given area. The soil in an affected area will be bone-dry and dust-like, resisting all attempts at re-wetting, whilst the adjoining area may be quite moist. Dry Patch is most severe on sandy soils, and so is most common on many constructed fine turf surfaces used for sport. Symptoms first appear during spells of dry weather as patches of thin, moisture-stressed turf. Where present, bent grasses will darken in colour whilst Annual Meadow Grass will die out completely.

The exact primary causes of this disorder are not fully known, although conditions such as compaction, slope, poor irrigation coverage and thatch are contributory factors affecting the severity. There is a potential link between its occurrence and soil fungal organisms – it has been found that soil fungi do have the ability to impart a degree of water repellence to soil particles, although these organisms have been found in soils that do not have dry patch. It is possible that the phenomenon occurs as fungal organisms move in the soil and that micro-organisms other than fungi are responsible for the condition.

Currently, the only treatment is to apply soil-wetting agents to the affected area. Greater efficacy will be achieved if preventative treatments can be made to those areas most susceptible to the condition. Wetting agents should be applied from the commencement of the growing season and should be continued at regular intervals throughout the summer period. Better results will also be achieved if the affected area is aerated by spiking or slitting prior to treatment, as this affords better soil penetration. There is a variety of suitable preventative products on the market in various formulations.

Black Layer

Black Layer arises when soil drainage is impeded and therefore soil oxygen is correspondingly depleted, leading to anaerobic conditions. The resulting action of anaerobic bacteria in the presence of sulphate ions leads to the production of sulphides such as hydrogen sulphide, along with other noxious compounds. Being toxic, these substances cause the death of roots and, ultimately, of the grass plant. Aside from a putrid smell, symptoms include the usual appearance of a black layer within the soil profile and an accumulating thatch problem. Control is best achieved by deep aeration, preferably hollow coring and topdressing with a more free-draining material. Charcoal may also be useful to reduce the effects.

Pests of Turf and Grassland

The few animal pests that cause damage to turf and grassland areas within the UK can be categorized according to the nature of the damage they create. They are either of the type that eat live plant tissue, or those that mix or disturb the soil and/or turf surface.

Tissue-eating Pests

In the main, these are species of insect, of which the two most common and damaging are the leatherjacket (*Tipula* spp.) and the chafer grub (*Phyllopertha horticola* and *Hoplia philanthus*); these are larval forms of the Daddy-long-legs, or Crane-fly, and the chafer beetle (actually several species, including the Garden and Welsh chafer), respectively.

Leatherjackets

The adult Daddy-long-legs emerges from its pupa in the soil during the cool evenings of late August and immediately lays its eggs, which hatch within two weeks. The leatherjacket larvae feed throughout the winter on grass roots, but damage is first apparent only in the spring when their activities intensify and grass growth increases. The grubs are 20–40mm long, brown or greyish in colour, and are found in the turf surface layers. The damage is usually first seen as patches of pale straw-brown grass, most obvious and severe in dry sunny weather. Leatherjackets are quite common on large, open areas of grassland that are relatively undisturbed, and they prefer sandier soils. Damage to turf is often exacerbated by the actions of birds such as crows and rooks, as these peck at the turf to retrieve grubs. The presence of such bird flocks is often a sure sign that a large population of leatherjackets or other pest is living in the soil.

Chemical control is usually necessary, especially on areas used for sport, and approved insecticides are currently available. Another method favoured by some is the use of a biological control agent carried the entomopathogenic nematode Steinernema feltiae. The nematode does not kill the insect grub but infects it with a lethal bacterium. The product is administered in liquid form with a watering can and must be applied under the correct environmental conditions to have any effect. The cost and application method limit its use to smaller areas of turf.

Chafer Grubs

In late May and June, adult chafer beetles emerge from pupae in the soil and lay eggs to begin another generation. The eggs hatch within a few weeks and the larvae begin feeding on grass roots. The grubs have fat, pale, waxy bodies with a characteristic brown head, they may be up to 40mm in length and they are always comma-shaped. The damage caused by chafer grubs is similar to that of leatherjackets and is most evident in the early autumn, by which time the grubs are almost fully grown. The grubs burrow deeper in the winter and hibernate before pupating in the spring. Secondary damage by mammals such as Badgers, which forage for the fat, juicy grubs, can be particularly severe.

The control of chafer grubs is more difficult than for leatherjackets as they burrow deeper into the soil, sometimes beyond the reach of pesticides. The same pesticides and biological controls used for leatherjackets can be used.

Soil- and Turf-disturbing Pests

The most serious pest of fine turf areas in this category is the earthworm. Occasionally, birds such as Rooks and Starlings may cause damage to the turf surface in their search for grubs and worms, but this is rarely a serious problem. The remaining pests within this category are mammals such as Moles and Rabbits.

Earthworms

More than 25 species of earthworm have been recorded in the British Isles. Only the three casting species of earthworm present a problem in fine turf. These are *Lumbricus terrestris*, *Allolobophora longa* and *Allolobophora noctuma*. Conditions favouring earthworm activity include:

- Damp soils with high organic matter content.
- Soil temperatures between 7°C and 13°C.
- Soils with a high pH (chalky/alkaline soils), although they occur in pH 5.1–8.0.

The benefits of earthworms in turf/soil systems are as follows:

- They break down organic matter in soil and thatch in turf.
- They reduce soil compaction.
- They improve surface drainage.
- They help to aerate the soil.
- They improve soil structure – organic matter and soil mineral particles are bound together in the worm's gut with lime.
- They may help to reduce disease (worms eat fungal hyphae).
- They reduce layering caused by topdressing by mixing materials within the soil.

The problems of earthworms on fine turf are in the main caused only by their casts, which are deposited upon the sward surface. The casts are detrimental in the following ways:

- They may smother fine turfgrasses.
- They are unsightly.

- They 'smear' on the playing surface.
- They may contain small stones that can damage a fine turf mower.
- They provide ideal seedbeds for germinating weeds (they may also contain weed seeds brought to the surface).
- They produce an uneven playing surface that affects ball roll, speed and direction.
- They may produce a squelchy, slow-drying sward.
- Their presence may encourage mole activity.

Earthworm activity can be significantly reduced, if not eliminated, by appropriate cultural methods. By reducing soil pH and organic matter content, earthworm populations can be controlled – worms do not like acidic conditions and they feed off soil organic matter. Soil pH can be reduced through the application of acidic fertilizers, and regular scarification and aeration will remove thatch and organic matter.

Chemicals for the control of earthworms in the UK are now very limited and currently only two fungicide products are approved for use. Both chemicals are short-lived in their effects and repeat treatments will often be necessary. It is only on fine turf surfaces used for sport that any worm killing is practised; for all other areas the benefits of earthworms generally far outweigh any detrimental effects populations may have. There have even been instances where earthworms have been reintroduced into soils, including football pitches, especially where these are suffering from the effects of compaction, poor aeration and low fertility.

Moles

Moles (*Talpa europaea*) are potentially a pest of any area of grassland where worms are present. Their soil heaps are obviously very damaging to surfaces used for sport or recreation, as is the disturbance to grass plants, but the unseen hazard is moles' tunnels, which can be very close to the surface. These readily collapse under the weight of a person or vehicle, possibly leading to personal injury. Moles can

be trapped, gassed or poisoned, all of which are effective between October to April, when the moles are most active. When using traps, it is important not to damage the run and to use fresh bait in the form of worms dipped in strychnine sulphate.

Rabbits

Rabbits (*Oryctolagus cunniculus*) have once again become a major pest on many areas of turf and grassland; this is often attributed to a reduction in the practice of control methods. Their burrowing activities are potentially very damaging, but on playing surfaces the scrapes they leave on the surface are of most concern. Scrapes are usually no more than 60–100mm in diameter and often not visible in the grass. These are potential accident blackspots for twisted ankles or even more serious injuries. Rabbits are best controlled by shooting at night or by gassing their burrows. For both these methods, there are strict regulations and requirements that must be followed.

Nematodes

Nematodes are microscopic roundworms, generally between 0.15mm and 2mm in length. There are many species of nematode and many are known as serious pests of horticultural and agricultural crops. Over 50 species are known to parasitize turfgrasses, although relatively few instances are reported in the UK. Very little research has been done in the UK regarding nematodes in turfgrasses and the full extent of this problem is still unknown. Nematode activity is favoured by warm soil temperatures and is more likely in sandy soils. They are positively discouraged by very dry or very wet soil and compacted root zones. They move in the soil in a similar manner to earthworms but are often spread over great distances in surface water or when soil is moved.

The symptoms caused by nematodes vary depending upon the nematode type. There are two basic types of nematode: ectoparasites, which attack and remain outside the plant; and endoparasites, which enter the plant tissues. Symptoms include swollen plant stem bases, roots and stunted growth. Nematode infection will affect a plant's ability to take up water and nutrients, and will be visible as a change in turf vigour and colour. If the turf is not responding to adequate water and nutrient input and is looking discoloured, nematodes may be the problem. Many nematode species are able to persist in the soil for many years, even remaining dormant as cysts until the right environmental conditions prevail for their activity. Currently there are no approved chemicals for controlling nematodes in turf.

Broadleaved Weeds in Turf

A weed has been defined as a plant growing in the wrong place. In sports turf, broadleaved weed species can be particularly troublesome and persistent, causing the following problems:

- They compete with desired grasses for water, nutrients and light.
- They create uneven playing surfaces.
- They spoil the aesthetic value of the turf.
- They can affect ball speed, roll, direction and bounce.
- They may harbour damaging pests and diseases.
- They can reduce the drought tolerance of the turf as a whole (larger leaf area leads to greater transpiration).
- They generally do not wear as well as grasses.
- They may affect player–surface traction.

Weeds can be propagated by seed or by vegetative means and can be spread or distributed in various ways, including:

- Windblown.
- Localized flooding.
- Birds and animals.
- On machinery brought from contaminated areas (especially mowers).
- On the shoes/boots of players and maintenance personnel.

- Use of poor-quality topdressing that is weed-infested.
- Via contaminated grass seed (especially *Poa annua*).
- Through the use of poor-quality, infested turf for repair work.

Weeds are able to survive, and even thrive, in mown turf areas because:

- Turf weeds are naturally low-growing – for example, daisies.
- They seed prolifically under varying conditions and even at low heights of cut.
- Some have taproots from which regrowth is possible – for example, dandelions.
- Many, such as speedwell, are vegetatively spread by severed fragments.
- Many have underground rhizomes or surface stolons from which regrowth occurs – for example, yarrow.
- Many have features or characteristics (such as waxy cuticles) that make them resistant to herbicides.
- Their habit of growth ensures that any chemical used for their control does not settle on their leaves.

Control of Weeds in Turf

The temptation is always to resort to chemical means to control weeds, but there are a number of cultural practices that should be implemented first to minimize the problem. That said, in many cases, especially on playing surfaces, a chemical will nearly always have to be used. Despite this, the best control for turf weeds is a healthy vigorous turfgrass sward!

Cultural Control
- Height and frequency of mowing will influence the botanical composition of the sward. Collect clippings where possible.
- Thatch weakens turf and may offer opportunities for weed invasion. Regular scarification is therefore good practice, with arisings collected.
- Aeration will improve surface drainage.
- Control of earthworms, whose casts are ideal seedbeds for germinating weeds.

Seeds are also brought to the surface by worms.

- Diseases will weaken and kill grasses, leaving bare patches for weed invasion. They should therefore be controlled.
- A balanced fertilizer regime to maintain soil fertility is essential.
- Irrigate when necessary to maintain healthy grass growth.

Chemical Control

There is a wide variety of approved chemicals available for use on established turf for broadleaved weed control. Herbicides used on established turf are known as translocated or growth-regulator herbicides. They are selective in that they target broadleaved weed species, leaving grass relatively unaffected. This occurs in part because grass has a vertical leaf orientation and narrow leaves, as opposed to the weed species, which have broad procumbent leaves and therefore receive a higher dose of the chemical. Translocated herbicides are absorbed by the leaf and move throughout the plant, killing all vegetative parts including roots, rhizomes and stolons. The effects of the chemical are seen as distorted growth, including twisted leaves and stems that quickly brown and die. Many products on the market contain a mix of two or more chemicals. These broader spectrum herbicides able to suppress or kill a greater range of weed species. There are a number of factors to consider when using such chemicals, including:

1. Timing of application. Translocated selective herbicides can be applied at any time of year when weeds and grass are in active growth; this usually means between the months of April and September, with best results from treatment given in April/May. The reason for this is that the chemical is carried much more quickly from one part of the plant to the other when the sap is flowing freely under active growth conditions. In addition, the grass plants are able to fill in the gaps more quickly at such times where weeds have been killed out. If bare patches have

to be sown shortly after spraying, a higher seeding rate than normal can often compensate for impaired germination caused by the herbicide.

2. Effect of weather. Fine, warm weather and moist soil give best results. Application during drought when the temperature is high may cause serious damage to the grass. Light showers of rain soon after application are not likely to cause appreciable loss in efficiency, but heavy rain may nullify the treatment and it is therefore inadvisable to spray in rainy weather.

3. Effect of fertilizer. As stated above, the best results are obtained when both grass and weeds are growing vigorously. An application of nitrogen should therefore be given one or two weeks before spraying.

4. Effect of mowing. It is best if two to three days have elapsed between the last mowing and application of the herbicide so that the weeds present a large leaf surface area to the spray. Turf should not be mown for at least two days after treatment to allow time for the herbicide to be translocated. It is not safe practice to use grass clippings for compost or mulching for at least one month or the first four mowings after spraying, whichever is the longer (refer to the manufacturer's instructions for details).

5. Effect of application rate. Overdosing must always be avoided or the weeds and grass will be scorched, and weed control will be impaired since the herbicide cannot be translocated from the scorched foliage.

Broadleaved Weeds in Amenity Grassland

The perception of weeds in amenity grassland has changed in recent years especially on those areas of requiring less intensive maintenance. The practice of differential mowing where some areas of grass are mown less frequently and at different heights to others has become more common in recent years. This can be used to both dramatic visual effect. Pathways can be mown through long grass areas for added effect, and the

---

Table 22: Common weeds of turf and amenity grassland

Species	Common name	Species	Common name
Ranunculus repens	Creeping Buttercup	*Veronica serpyllifolia*	Thyme-leaved Speedwell
Ranunculus bulbosus	Bulbous Buttercup		
Ranunculus ficaria	Lesser Celandine	*Veronica filiformis*	Slender Speedwell
Cerastium holosteoides	Mouse-ear Chickweed	*Prunella vulgaris*	Self-heal
		Plantago major	Broadleaved Plantain
Stellaria media	Common Chickweed	*Plantago media*	Hoary Plantain
Sagina procumbens	Pearlwort	*Plantago lanceolata*	Ribwort Plantain
Geranium molle	Dove's-foot Crane's-bill	*Plantago maritima*	Sea Plantain
Erodium cicutarium	Common Stork's-bill	*Galium verum*	Lady's Bedstraw
Medicago lupulina	Black Medick	*Galium saxatile*	Heath Bedstraw
Trifolium dubium	Suckling Clover	*Bellis perennis*	Daisy
Trifolium repens	White Clover	*Achillea millefolium*	Yarrow
Lotus corniculatus	Bird's-foot Trefoil	*Cotula coronopifolia*	Cotula
Potentilla anserina	Silverweed	*Cirsium acaule*	Dwarf Thistle
Potentilla reptans	Cinquefoil	*Hypochaeris radicata*	Cat's-ear
Aphanes arvensis	Parsley Piert	*Leontodon autumnalis*	Autumn Hawkbit
Hydrocotyle vulgaris	Marsh Pennywort	*Leontodon hispidus*	Rough Hawkbit
Polygonum aviculare	Knotgrass	*Hieracium pilosella*	Mouse-ear Hawkweed
Rumex acetosella	Sheep's Sorrel	*Taraxacum officinale*	Dandelion
Rumex acetosa	Common Sorrel	*Juncus bufonius*	Toadrush
Veronica chamaedrys	Germander Speedwell	*Luzula campestris*	Field Woodrush

---

longer grass areas will be richer in plant diversity. Mowing once or twice a year after flowering will lead to a wide range of broad-leaved species establishing themselves, especially if both soil and fertility are low and vigorous invasive species are controlled by appropriate means. Management, which approximates to mowing for hay followed by autumn grazing, fosters the widest species diversity of grasses and herbs.

Annual Meadow Grass and Fine Turf

There is no doubt that Annual Meadow Grass (*Poa annua*) is a dominant grass within many of our fine turf surfaces in the British Isles. Such is its significance in the fine turf industry that it is often the subject of lively debate and discussion amongst those charged with managing fine turf playing surfaces. Its presence and control have, over the years, stimulated great interest amongst greenkeepers and other turf professionals, and the very mention of this grass will invariably promote a strong response or reaction. The debate has led to many myths and half-truths becoming established, which sometimes serve only to complicate understanding of the real reasons for the species' success, the actual problems associated with it in fine turf and the best approaches for its control.

Annual Meadow Grass (AMG) is a cool-season turfgrass and is widely distributed throughout the temperate and sub-tropical regions of the world, including most of Europe and North America. One characteristic of AMG that is certain is that it is a highly variable grass. It is thought to have originated from a cross between two other closely related meadow grass species, these being *Poa infirma* and *Poa supina*. It is found mainly in locations of human habitat or influence, and within turf culture two common subspecies have been described. One form has a tufted, upright growth habit and is very prolific in its capacity to produce seed. This type is an annual plant that continually regenerates itself from its almost permanent flowers and seed-heads, and has been given the subspecies designation *Poa annua* var. *annua*. A second form displays more procumbent growth and is actually a short-lived perennial that roots freely at the nodes of its prostrate stolons and tillers. This form is also recognized as a subspecies, *Poa annua* var. *reptans*. The latter form is actually the one most frequently occurring in fine turf surfaces. While these two subspecies commonly occur in turfgrass situations, there are also many intermediate types.

The inherent ability of AMG to adapt to widely differing environmental conditions and its ability to flower and set seed almost all year round are significant reasons for its success in fine turf surfaces in the UK. It has been estimated that British soils may contain as many as 70,000 AMG seeds per sq m. These seeds are ready to germinate when conditions permit, such as when the sward is damaged by wear from play or pest and disease attack. In conditions of heavy wear, soil compaction, shade or excessive moisture, AMG will persist and even thrive at the expense of the desired fine turf species. Once this aggressive plant species is established, it becomes difficult for the finer species to compete with it.

Given that AMG is such a successful grass and occurs so frequently in our fine turf surfaces, what are our concerns relating to its presence? AMG is a very successful colonizer species and is quick to exploit bare or weakened growth areas within fine turfgrass swards of bent and fescue grasses, but it is itself prone to certain environmental stresses. For instance, we know that it is particularly prone to some common turfgrass diseases,

including Anthracnose and Fusarium. AMG also suffers at extremes of temperature. As temperatures increase above 21°C or fall below 10°C, it is prone to injury or complete kill, with often dramatic effects for the affected turfgrass sward. In addition, it is very susceptible to injury and death when temperature increases are allied with drought conditions. Fine turf swards containing AMG often have bumpy surfaces in the spring, which can be attributed to the initial slow growth of this grass. The coarser leaf texture and ever-present seed-heads also affect playing surface quality, and together with its distinctive blue-green coloration create a negative impact on visual or aesthetic quality. This markedly different appearance often leads to a patchy surface as AMG grows between the more desirable bent and fescue grasses. Being fast to establish itself and because of its almost continual renewal in the sward, AMG is also a thatch-productive grass. This contributes to the soft, spongy swards and subsequent slow playing speeds often encountered on fine turf surfaces.

Although AMG is a highly variable grass and has many characteristics that contribute to its success in fine turf, it is also important to recognize that this can often be directly attributed to incorrect or misinformed fine turf management practices. Fine turf professionals in the UK have often been put under pressure by players and sport officials to provide the verdant greens of turf in such countries as the USA as seen in the media. This is despite the fact that we have different turfgrass species and climatic conditions. The consequent misuse of automatic irrigation systems and applications of high levels of nitrogenous fertilizer by some fine turfgrass managers in an effort to achieve this goal have certainly contributed to the success of AMG in fine turf swards used for sport.

AMG can, however, be controlled and eradicated by sound agronomic practices based on an understanding of the factors responsible for its ingress into our fine turf surfaces. It must be understood that there is no quick fix solution, but that a long-term strategy of thatch control, soil aeration and topdressing, together with responsible nutrient and irrigation inputs, will produce the firm, dry surfaces required for play. Only when this has been achieved can one begin to reintroduce the desired bent and fescue species. Again, this will need to be a long-term managed programme if the botanical composition of the sward is to be changed successfully. Such sound greenkeeping practices will often need to be allied with education of players and sport officials about what is effectively sustainable in British conditions with regards fine turf surfaces and maintenance of the best surfaces for play.

Moss

Mosses are primitive plants that belong to a division of the plant kingdom known as the Bryophytes. These non-flowering plants can be found growing in a wide and diverse range of habitats, including mown turf. The moss plant consists of slender stems that are soft and fleshy, green or brown leaves and slender roots known as rhizoids, which absorb water and anchor the plant. Moss will readily establish on any areas of thin turf where there is a lack of competition from grass growth. Factors favouring the growth of mosses include:

- A moist surface/poor drainage, which encourages fern-like and tufted mosses.
- Very dry soil (for example, on mounds or over drains), which encourages upright types.
- Mowing too close (scalping), which weakens grass growth.
- A soft, spongy sward with excessive fibres.
- Surface compaction.
- Shade.
- Low soil fertility.
- Low pH (4).

Types of Moss
Around 600 species of moss have been recorded in the UK, although the number found in mown turf is limited. These are generally grouped into three main types:

1. Upright mosses (*Polytrichum* spp.), comprising of upright tufts, usually found in dry, acid conditions such as dry mounds adjacent to golf bunkers. They are seldom a serious problem.
2. Trailing or fern-like mosses (*Hypnum* and *Eurhynchium* spp.), which are normally associated with symptoms of bad drainage, shade and areas of thick fibre.
3. Tufted or mat-forming mosses (*Ceratodon purpureus* and *Bryum* spp.), which are found on acid soils areas that are continually scalped by the mower. Growth of these tends to become progressively worse unless checked.

Control of Moss
The best solution is to find the cause and remedy it. Most moss killers are palliative and moss will soon returns unless the factors responsible for a thin sward and moss ingress are removed. 'Lawn sand' can be used for moss control, made up of the following ingredients:

1 part ferrous suphate
3 parts sulphate of ammonia
10–20 parts medium/find dry sand corner

This mixture is applied at a rate of 140g/sq m. It is also useful for controlling some broad-leaved weeds in turf. In addition, approved chemicals are available for moss control.

Algae

Green or black slime can occur during wet weather on the turf surface, causing problems of slipperiness, especially on sloping ground. This slime is made up of tiny-celled algae (for example, *Nostoc* spp.), which are able to colonize bare areas in turf that may have been created by excessive wear or compaction, such as on approaches to green. Under wet conditions these algae can multiply rapidly, resulting in a dense algal slime that when walked upon will rise to the surface and become exceedingly squelchy, hence its nickname 'squidge'.

The conditions under which squidge develops are shade, damp and poorly drained turf. These problems can be rectified only by paying attention to drainage, or through the removal of waterholding thatch by scarification, spiking and top-dressing with sand. When infestation is heavy, the slime can be brushed or raked into heaps and removed. Affected areas can then be treated with iron sulphate mixed with sand or cresylic acid. Approved moss killers are often also effective.

Lichens

Lichens are a combination of fungi and algae, and although they are not as troublesome as moss they can cause some problems in turf, particularly in damp or dry acid conditions when grass growth is weak. A very common lichen found mainly in neglected lawns is *Peltigera canina*. This appears as overlapping, leafy plates, the upper surfaces of which are brown or black. When the lichen is dry the surface fades to grey and curls upwards to reveal a white underside. Control is best effected by general improvement of soil fertility. Chemical control is through the application of calcined sulphate of iron, cresylic acid or approved moss-killer.

The Application of Pesticides

The chemical control of fungus-causing diseases through the use of fungicides, pests with pesticides, and weeds with herbicides, needs careful preparation and regulation. The chemicals come in many forms and can be applied in several ways, but they are also dangerous to health, and so should be treated with caution. Most chemicals used on areas of turf and amenity grassland are applied as liquid sprays. The most commonly used forms of chemical available for use in sprayers are:

- Concentrates. These contain the active ingredient plus other materials such as wetting and spreading agents. They are usually very easy to dilute evenly when mixed with water.
- Emulsions. When added to water and mixed thoroughly, the ingredients form a suspension.
- Wettable powders. As the name suggests, these are powders that can be wetted easily. The resulting solution must be stirred or agitated to maintain an even distribution.
- Water-soluble powders. These are finely ground powders that form a homogeneous solution when added to water.

Chemicals not used in sprayers include the following types:

- Granules. These consist of active ingredient incorporated in an inert carrier material. They are ideal for applying to areas where drift may be a problem.
- Dusts. These also consist of a mix of inert and active ingredients, both of them finely ground.
- Fumigants. These are liquids or crystalline solids that can easily be converted into fine fogs or vapours.

Spraying Equipment

The main function of a sprayer is to convert the liquid chemical into droplets of an effective size and to distribute them uniformly over the surfaces to be treated. The main type of sprayer used for turf and grassland areas is the hydraulic nozzle type, which operates by forcing liquid through small nozzle holes attached to a lance or boom. Such sprayers come in a wide range of sizes, from the pedestrian knapsack to larger tractor-mounted or towed machines. Most commercial sprayers consist of several basic parts that differ only in their configuration, design and size depending upon the size of sprayer. These are:

1. The tank. This is the main body of the sprayer and contains the chemical for spraying. Tanks should be constructed of non-corrosive materials such as polythene

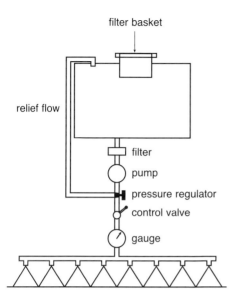

filter basket

relief flow

filter

pump

pressure regulator

control valve

gauge

Basic sprayer layout – typical components.

or reinforced fibreglass. They should also have a large filler opening with a filter basket to prevent coarse particles entering the sprayer.

2. The pump. This may be powered by hand, by the sprayer's own engine or, as in larger tractor-mounted machines, by the PTO. Again, it is important that the pump is constructed with non-corrosive materials and that there is a means of controlling the output pressure, such as a relief valve.

3. Control unit. This will vary depending upon the size and sophistication of the sprayer. It may be as simple as an on/off tap or as complex as an onboard electronic system in a vehicle cab.

4. Filters. These are a vital part of any sprayer. They are designed to prevent any solid particulates from blocking nozzles or the associated distribution system, including the pump. They will normally be present at the filling point, pump circuit and the individual nozzles.

5. Nozzles. The nozzles atomize the diluted chemical before it is applied to the tar-

get. There are three different nozzle types commonly used, the fan, cone and anvil.

Fan-type nozzles are ideal for spraying relatively flat surfaces such as areas of turf or grass, but they can also be used effectively with plants where penetration of the canopy is required. They come in a range of designs and pressure ratings to cope with different situations. Fan nozzles used on boom sprayers have a triangular spray pattern – in other words, they are spaced out on the boom so that the sheets of spray will overlap to produce a reasonably even distribution. In contrast, a knapsack sprayer (fitted with a single hand lance) will have a fan nozzle that produces a more rectangular spray pattern – a nearly even distribution will be produced across the full width of spray (hence the term 'even-spray' nozzle)

Cone-type nozzles are usually designed to produce a fine swirling spray that gives a good overall coverage of the plant's leaf surface. They are ideally suited to the application of insecticides and fungicides. The most common type is the hollow cone, which has a small swirl chamber built into the nozzle head to create the swirling spray. They produce a rectangular distribution spray pattern.

Anvil-type nozzles are designed to produce coarse droplets in a fan-shaped sheet and are normally operated at low pressures. They are most often used for herbicides, especially when applies with knapsack sprayers.

The droplet spectrum of hydraulic nozzles depends on the nozzle spray angle and its operating pressure, and these factors in turn determine the spray quality. Product labels now specify the application spray quality in terms of very fine, fine, medium and coarse categories, with the medium category being the most common. Choosing the wrong nozzle and/or operating pressure can lead to serious environmental problems through spray drift (as well as being grossly inefficient and uneconomic). Manufacturers are now producing a range of reduced drift nozzles (mainly based on fan nozzle design) that can help to minimize spray drift. These nozzles are suitable for spraying near watercourses or other sensitive landscape areas or habitats.

Most nozzles today are made of a special hard plastic, although stainless-steel and ceramic types are also used. There is now a standardized reference system for nozzle types produced by the British Crop Protection Council, which uses four parameters to describe a particular nozzle: nozzle type, spray angle, flow rate (litres per minute) and the rated pressure (normally in bar). For example, a nozzle with the reference F110/0.8/3 is a fan type with a spray angle of 110 degrees, a flow rate of 0.8 litres per minute and a pressure rating of 3 bar. There is also an international colour code (ISO 10625) for flat fan nozzles, though not all manufacturers use this yet.

Hand-operated Sprayers
Most of these are air-pressurized – in other words, they contain a volume of compressed air that forces the spray out of the nozzle when the trigger valve is opened. The two common systems used are:

1. Compression sprayers, in which there is compressed air above the level of the liquid. The air space in this unit occupies about a quarter of the total tank volume.

The air is compressed by pumping more in from outside by means of a built-in hand piston pump. One drawback of this design is that the nozzle output will fall as spraying continues and the air pressure falls. This can be partially overcome by installing a pressure-control valve on the output side (normally on the hand lance), which will maintain a constant output pressure and hence a constant nozzle output. This will only work if the pressure in the tank is kept above the pressure-control valve setting. As a safety measure, a pressure gauge and a pressure-relief valve should be fitted. The sprayer is usually carried on the shoulder, although larger units are carried on the back or mounted on a pedestrian trolley.

2. Lever-operated knapsack sprayers, in which there is a pressure chamber within the tank. This sprayer is carried on the back of the operator. A side lever operates either a diaphragm or piston pump, which forces the liquid chemical from the tank (via a one-way valve) into the pressure chamber thus compressing the trapped air inside. When the trigger valve is opened, this compressed air will force some of the liquid in the chamber out to the lance and nozzle (via another one-way valve). Pressure is maintained by a continuous pumping action of the lever. As a safety measure, a pressure-relief valve is commonly fitted on the pressure chamber or pumping

Selection of small sprayers and knapsacks for different applications.
(Photo: Hardi)

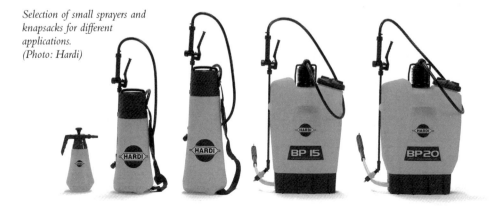

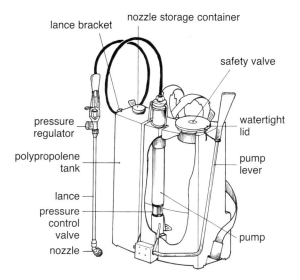

lance bracket — nozzle storage container

safety valve

pressure regulator

watertight lid

polypropelene tank

pump lever

lance —

pressure control valve

pump

nozzle —

Features of a knapsack sprayer.

Pedestrian barrow-type sprayer – a very useful sprayer for treating small lawns and turf areas. (Photo: Allen Power Equipment)

mechanism. In addition, it is advisable to have either a pressure gauge or a pressure-control valve fitted onto the lance to ensure that the spray quality is maintained. Even better is to fit a special flow-control valve that will operate only within a defined narrow pressure range (in other words, it has a minimum as well as a maximum pressure requirement before it will allow liquid through).

There have been a number of design improvements to knapsack sprayers in recent years, particularly to tanks and pumps. Even so, many models still suffer from poor ergonomics, are difficult to clean out thoroughly and leak after a relatively short period of use. To remove the drudgery of manual pumping, some manufacturers now use electrically operated pumps powered by rechargeable batteries.

Power-operated Boom Sprayers
These are designed for larger areas and can vary in size from the pedestrian controlled barrow sprayers, through small ride-on ATVs (all-terrain vehicles), compact tractors or utility vehicles, tractors and purpose-built self-propelled spraying vehicles. Up until the 1980s and the introduction of stricter chemical regulations, most boom sprayers were relatively simple in design, consisting of the basic components of a tank, pump, agitation system, control regulating equipment and boom assembly. Today, however, they tend to be much more sophisticated in design, with the overall emphasis being on minimizing the risk to the operator and the environment. Major developments have taken place in the following areas of sprayer design:

• Chemical transference. One of the greatest contamination risks to the sprayer operator occurs when concentrated liquid chemical is poured into the tank. This can be avoided by using a suction probe in the chemical container or by using a low-level induction hopper. An improvement on this is to use a closed transfer system, whereby the chemical container is opened up, emptied and washed thoroughly within a closed environment and with no risk of contamination to the operator. Recent sprayer designs that use direct injection systems eliminate the need for pre-mixing by metering the chemical supply directly into the water flow to the nozzles. This has the additional benefit that the main tank is not contaminated and the final number of washings is very much reduced.

- Control systems. To achieve uniform spray application on a basic sprayer, the operator has to ensure that both the vehicle forward speed and the nozzle set pressure are kept constant. On more sophisticated sprayers, it is possible to install control systems that will allow some variation in speed without seriously affecting the application rate. An accurate forward speed detector (such as a trailed, wheel or radar system) is linked to a microprocessor, flow-controlled valves

and metering pumps to match flow to speed. On direct injection-type sprayers the separate flows of water and pesticide can be regulated.

With the advent of geographical positioning systems (GPS), it is now possible to record the localized areas that require spraying. The onboard computer of the sprayer can then be programmed so that only those areas are sprayed. On a smaller scale where total weed control is required – for example, on paths and hard surfaces – it is possible to have ride-on sprayer units whose nozzles are individually activated by optic sensors that can detect the presence of plant chlorophyll.

- Boom systems. On large boom sprayers it is important that the boom system is as stable as possible to prevent over- or underdosing of spray. Modern sprayers can be fitted with independent boom suspension systems to reduce the yawing (back and fore) and bounce (up and down) effects. Some booms are now fitted with shields or shrouds to contain the spray drift. By carefully setting up air vortices under the shroud, the possibility of pesticide gathering on the shroud itself is much reduced. Another innovation is the use of air-assisted boom sprayers to give better crop penetration and reduce drift. Some designs use air-sleeves or air-bags along the boom to blow air into the nozzle spray. Alternatively, pressurized air can be

ABOVE: *Trailed sprayer for large turf and amenity areas. This model has its own power source in the engine, mounted on its chassis. It requires only a vehicle to tow it along. (Photo: Hardi)*

RIGHT: *Large pesticide sprayer with shrouds on the booms to prevent spray drift. (Photo: Hardi)*

Ground-crop sprayer specifically designed for turf application. The sprayer is mounted onto a basic turf utility vehicle. (Photo: John Deere)

supplied to special twin fluid nozzles to produce aerated droplets.

Sprayer Calibration

It is critical that all sprayers are correctly calibrated to ensure that the correct amount of material is applied. Calibrate the sprayer using clean water on a hard surface, and using the recommended nozzles and pressure ratings for the particular product application rate.

Knapsack Sprayers It is first necessary to find the value for operator walking speed. This can be determined by recording the time (in seconds) it takes the operator to walk at a steady pace over 100m whilst operating the sprayer. Divide this figure by 360 to arrive at the speed in kph.

Next, the effective spray width needs to be determined. To do this, the nozzle is held at the correct height for spraying above a dry surface and the width of the spray output is measured.

Finally, the nozzle output needs to be ascertained. To do this, spray water into a measuring cylinder or jug, marked in millilitres, and record the volume of water delivered in one minute. The sprayer output can then be calculated using the formula given below:

Volume (litres/ha) = [600 × nozzle output (litres/minute)] ÷ [spray width (m) × speed (kph)]

For example, a sprayer with a nozzle output of 3 litres per minute, a spray width of 1.7m and an operator walking speed of 3.75kph will have an output of:

(600 × 3) ÷ (1.7 × 3.75) =282 litres/ha

If the area to b covered measures 1,000sq m, one-tenth of this volume should be applied.

Mounted Boom Sprayers The sprayer application rate for a mounted boom sprayer can be calculated whilst the machine is stationary by running the sprayer for a time period equivalent to that required to spray 1ha and then applying the following formula:

Time (minutes) =
600 ÷ [spraying width (m) × speed (kph)]

For example, the time taken to spray 1ha using a sprayer with a spray width of 6m and a speed of 5kph will be:

600 ÷ (6 × 5) = 20 minutes

Next, with the PTO set at 540rpm and the engine on, run the sprayer for 20 minutes and record how much water has been emptied from the tank. This volume will be the application rate per hectare at these settings.

Sprayer Maintenance

It is absolutely essential that sprayers are cleaned thoroughly after use. This must include all spray lines, nozzles, pumps, filters and the tank, as well as any induction devices or low-level filler hoppers. Any trace of chemical remaining will contaminate future tank fills and, on the next occasion of use, possibly lead to serious damage to turf or grass. Most sprayers, especially larger machines, are used to spray a range of chemicals including both herbicides and fungicides. The worst damage will occur when traces of herbicides are inadvertently applied to a turf surface with another chemical. When using knapsacks, it is good policy where possible to have one for each chemical type and to label them clearly so that they are used only with that type.

Washing of sprayers should preferably be done in a specially constructed wash-down area where the residues are prevented from contaminating watercourses or other sensitive areas. In addition, the operator must wear the appropriate protective clothing required for the particular product. Finally, the machine should be checked over for any signs of damage or leakage. For winter storage, remove all nozzles and store them separately, and make sure that pumps are drained.

Chemical Regulations

Anyone who advertises, sells, supplies, stores or uses a fungicide, pesticide or herbicide in the UK is bound by legislation. There are numerous UK statutory controls regarding these chemicals, but the major legal instruments and their requirements of the user are detailed below.

• The Food and Environment Protection Act 1985 (FEPA) and Control of Pesticide Regulations 1986 (COPR). FEPA introduced statutory powers to control pesticides, with the aims of protecting human beings, creatures and plants, safeguarding the environment, ensuring safe, effective and humane methods of controlling pests, and making pesticide information available to the public. Control of pesticides is achieved by COPR. The main restrictions under COPR for the user of pesticides are:

1. Only approved products may be used.
2. Users must be competent to apply pesticides – appropriate training followed by examination leading to a certificate of competence is necessary.
3. Users of pesticides must comply with the conditions of approval relating to use.

• The Control of Substances Hazardous to Health Regulations 1988 (COSHH). These regulations, which came into force on 1 October 1989 and made under the Health and Safety at Work Act 1974, cover virtually all substances hazardous to health, including those pesticides classed as very toxic, toxic, harmful, irritant or corrosive, as well as other chemicals used in industry or the workplace. The basic principle underlying the COSHH regulations is that the risks associated with the use of any substance hazardous to health must be assessed before it is used, and the appropriate measures taken to control the risk. In order of preference, the measures should be:

1. Substitution with a less hazardous chemical or product.
2. Technical or engineering controls (for example, the use of closed handling systems).
3. Operational controls (for example, operators in cabs fitted with air-filtration systems).
4. Use of personal protective equipment, including clothing.

Consideration must be given to whether it is necessary to use a chemical control at all in a given situation, and, if so, the product posing the least risk to humans, animals and the environment must be selected. Adequate records of all operations involving chemical application must be made and retained for at least three years.

If there is any doubt about an aspect of pesticide application, the advice and guidance of a qualified person should be sought or, better still, the Health and Safety Executive contacted.

CHAPTER 7

Turf Establishment and Renovation

The two main methods for establishing a turfgrass sward in the UK are turfing and seeding. The choice made and its implementation depend on many variables. In addition to these two methods there are more specialist techniques, such as the use of seeded mats. These methods are usually employed on sites where it is difficult to establish grass by turfing or seeding, or, more likely, where there is a need for erosion control.

For successful turf establishment it is necessary to have a sound knowledge of the reasons for the operation and of the variables that affect it. This will enable selection of the most appropriate option for a particular site after the local conditions have been evaluated so that turf establishment is successful and a satisfactory sward is produced. Economic criteria must also be considered, but it must be remembered that the cheapest option will not always be the best and that a little more expense at the beginning may pay dividends later.

The success of the operation will also be affected by the quality of both the materials used and the workmanship. All stages of the operation must be carefully monitored and regulated in order to ensure that success is achieved, and no quarter should be given for substandard materials or workmanship. When ordering materials, specify in detail the precisely what it is you want so that there can be no confusion or misunderstanding. Ensure that the supplier adheres to these requirements, checking purchases when they are delivered to the site.

Selection of Grass Species for Use in Turf

Turfgrasses have many characteristics that make them suitable for a range of turf surfaces and amenity landscape situations. Having established the criteria for the particular surface, the next stage is to select appropriate species and cultivars for that surface or area. In amenity turfgrasses, the following characteristics are important and are used in the selection of particular species for particular situations and uses. They are often also used by seed companies in breeding programmes for new grass cultivars:

- Sward density. A dense sward (one with a high number of tillers per unit area) gives good cover and keeps out weeds and undesirable grasses because of its competitive ability. High tiller density results in speedier recovery of the sward after damage.
- Leaf texture. This is a measure of the width of the leaf blades and largely determines the quality of the turf. The leaf texture influences the compatibility of different species in mixtures.
- Speed of establishment. A fast establishment is required, to ensure a speedy ground cover, to suppress weeds and prevent soil erosion. Large differences occur between species in this characteristic.
- Cleanness of cut. Tough vascular bundles in the leaf blades will resist cutting, adversely affecting mowing quality. This is an important characteristic for fine

sports turf where there is intimate contact between the ball and sward surface.

- Greenness under low temperatures. Cultivars should maintain an attractive green colour under low temperatures. This characteristic is partly influenced by the occurrence of turfgrass diseases and is partly an inherent characteristic of the plant gene type.
- Tolerance of low fertility. Grasses grown on sandy soils that have a low inherent fertility level, such as those found on links golf courses and constructed sand-carpet systems, should be able to withstand these conditions. There are large differences between species and cultivars.
- Colour. Distinct differences in colour exist between species and between cultivars within species. The preference for a certain colour is largely subjective. In light-green turf the presence of Annual Meadow Grass, also light green, is not so striking. Colour can be influenced to some extent by the application of fertilizers.
- Tolerance of close mowing. This is another important characteristic for fine sports turf, where the grass may be mown down to 3mm on occasions. Large differences occur between species and between cultivars within species.
- Presence of stolons/rhizomes, which contribute greatly to turf strength. This is often an important characteristic for those grasses that will receive heavy wear, such as those used for winter sports. Large differences occur between species.
- Resistance to wear and tear. The sward should maintain its density under treading. Testing can be done either under natural playing conditions or with a treading machine.
- Winter hardiness. This is a complex subject covering the ability to survive all the factors of a winter environment, including temperature, snow or ice cover, rainfall, light intensity, management practices and diseases.
- Resistance to disease. Amenity grasses can be affected by various diseases, which may cause anything from negligible to

severe damage to the sward. Newer cultivars of certain species are resistant to some grass diseases, such as red thread.

- Slowness of vertical growth. Fast growth necessitates frequent mowing, which is undesirable. Slow growth makes the species more vulnerable to diseases, especially in ryegrasses.
- Greenness under drought. A cultivar should maintain its attractive appearance under dry conditions. Differences between species exist, and large variety differences occur within the species.
- Tolerance of salt. This can be an important characteristic where the grass variety is to be grown in coastal areas or on roadside verges in urban areas. Large differences occur between species and cultivars.
- Shade tolerance. This is dependent on the height and frequency of cut, the available moisture and the microclimate of the shaded area. Disease resistance is an important factor for plants grown in shade, as they tend to be weaker and hence more prone to infection.
- Seed productivity. Even when a cultivar scores highly for all the above characteristics, its seed production capability will ultimately determine its commercial success.

For independent information comparing new turfgrass cultivars, consult the Sports Turf Research Institute's annual publication *Turfgrass Seed*. This contains tables that compare the relative merits of new grass cultivars for a range of important characteristics following trials for many of the above traits at Bingley.

Choosing Between Seeding and Turfing

In the UK, the choice of materials for creating a grassed area is one between seed or the use of turves. There are several factors that may have a bearing on this decision and that need to be considered. There is no difference in the work required to prepare the soil for either seed or turf.

- Cost. The costs of purchasing either seed or turf are very variable and depend largely upon the particular grass species involved, the quantities required and the transportation costs. In general terms, turf is more expensive than seed and as it is a bulky product is certainly more costly to transport.
- Speed of visible establishment. For most applications, turf produces a sward in a shorter time than one from seed. Seed may take up to 18 months to produce an area that is playable although the final quality is often better. It may be that a surface created from turf will take a similar length of time before it is playable depending upon the levels required and the initial standard of workmanship.
- Tolerance to wear during the establishment phase (at 100 days). Areas that have been seeded are generally better than those produced from turf in tolerating wear at 100 days. This is in part due to the better initial rooting from germinating seeds as opposed to transported turves, which take more time to re-establish themselves once moved.
- Weed invasion. This is much more likely to be a problem in those areas that have been seeded, although it is dependent upon the initial quality of soil preparation. Turf is very likely to contain weeds or weed seeds, and even possibly pests or diseases unless it is of a very good quality. Turf is a very variable commodity whose quality is often dependent upon its source. Weed invasion in seeded areas tends to increase as the proportion of natural topsoil increases in the root zone.
- Size. The area that is being prepared may simply be too large to make turfing a sensible proposition – as with a 5ha sports field used for soccer. Smaller areas such as an ornamental lawn or a bowling green leave the choice open.
- Turfgrass species/cultivars. The option to select specific turfgrass species and cultivars and to ensure a uniform root zone are the major reasons why establishment from seed is preferred in the UK for virtually all high-specification sports turf areas. It is generally accepted that these benefits outweigh the advantage of immediate establishment from turf. With many types of bought-in turf there is not the opportunity to select the species of grass to suit the area, although, depending upon its particular use, this may not always be deemed necessary. When buying grass seed if it is not possible to select species of seed mix; if this is important for the particular area, buy the species separately and sow at the desired ratio.
- Turf root-zone composition. For turf intended for use as sports turf, it is often desirable that the root zone consists of a soil with a high or even pure sand content to facilitate good drainage. The nature of the soil is critical in determining the quality of the finished surface. Some sports in which ball bounce is a critical factor (such as cricket and tennis) rely on a soil with a high clay content. A problem arises with purchased turf in that it is not always possible to procure the required root-zone composition or specific soil type that is required. For general landscape operations, this will probably not be a factor, but for sports turf it can be critical.
- Existing site topsoil/root-zone mix. It is more difficult to establish a turfgrass sward from seed on sand-dominant topsoil and proprietary root-zone mixes, because of their potentially poor water retention ability. In contrast, a 'natural' soil will generally be better in this respect. Young seedlings are susceptible to drought and this problem can be exacerbated by light, sandy mediums. Irrigation will be required for spring sowings and may even be needed for autumn sowings on some soils.
- Time of year. There are two suitable times of the year to sow grass seed: April and late August/early September. Seed can, of course, be sown at other times but there may be more risk of failure due to drought, frost, heavy rain or weed invasion. Sowing is preferable at the end of August because the land is warm and

moist at this time and so germination should be rapid. The young germinating seedlings will have time to form a reasonable root system before the onset of the worst winter weather. Seedlings arising from spring sowings will not have formed such an extensive root system before the dry summer weather arrives. Sowing in the autumn will also mean that the ground will have had more time to fallow, and weed germination/activity will be reduced.

Turfing can be carried out at any time of year providing the ground is not frozen or waterlogged and irrigation can be provided if necessary. The effective period for turfing operations is thus much greater than for seed sowing operations.

Preparation of Land Prior to Seeding or Turfing

A number of steps need to be completed before seeding or turfing commences:

1. Ploughing. On larger areas of land, ploughing will probably be necessary as the initial soil preparation method unless an imported root zone is to be used.

Smaller areas may be manually dug if this is appropriate. On virgin ground, a more satisfactory result will be obtained if it is ploughed in the autumn prior to the year of establishment so that any existing vegetation has time to rot down and decay in the soil. On grassland, any fibrous material together with the actual grass cover should be well buried.

2. Cultivation. On a field scale, fine cultivators and disc harrows will be used to break down the soil clods remaining after ploughing and winter frost action. Rakes and lutes can be used on smaller sites. Cultivation should be carried out after any drainage installation works have been completed and up until the actual seed sowing or turfing operation. The aim is to produce a suitable tilth for reception of the seed or turves.

3. Fallowing. This is a process whereby the weed seeds within the soil profile are allowed to germinate and are then eliminated by either mechanical or chemical means. For thorough weed eradication, the fallowing process should be continued over a period of months prior to sowing or turfing.

Herbicides may be used to eliminate germinating weeds – the choice is large-

Tractor-mounted stone burier and cultivator unit leaves a surface ready for seeding. This particular model also has a seeder attachment and can therefore seed as well as bury stones in one pass of the machine. (Photo: BLEC)

ly dependent upon actual weed species present. For specialist areas, soil sterilization may be carried out. Extreme caution should be exercised with these materials and relevant recommendations concerning their use must be followed implicitly (many materials can now be applied only by licensed contractors).

4. Rolling. In order to form a consolidated surface, rolling may be necessary. Initially, a Cambridge roller may be employed to break down larger soil clods, and later a flat roller can be used to aid the formation of a smooth surface. Care should be taken not to roll when the soil is too wet, otherwise it will compact and create problems of water and air infiltration into the soil.

5. Surface grading. Where a rough tilth has been prepared by cultivation, surface grading with a blade grader or tru-lute will be required to smooth out the immediate soil surface and to correct minor surface levels. Major grading operations involving topsoil stripping and subsequent replacement should have been carried out well before any initial cultivation if necessary.

6. Stone removal. Stones within the soil tend to rise to the surface with time and subsequently may be injurious to players or damaging to maintenance machinery. For fine turf areas, stones exceeding 25mm in any one dimension, or on other turf surfaces those greater than 40mm, should as far as is practicable be removed before sowing or turfing. Rolling will bury some stones, whilst hand picking on smaller areas may be necessary. Specialist stone-burying machines are now available and can be utilized during the preparation works.

7. Soil improvement. If finance permits and if it is deemed necessary, the physical nature of heavy soils should be improved during the cultivation stages. Addition of sand and/or organic matter (for example, well-rotted compost) can improve soil structure. Light soils may also need the addition of an organic material in order to improve their water-retention characteristics. Such materials should be carefully evaluated for any potential peat, disease or weed content and should ideally be obtained from a known source.

For specialist areas such as golf and bowling greens, an imported root-zone mix is often used. These are often based on specifications recommended by organizations such as the STRI (Sports Turf Research Institute) or the USGA (United States Golf Association). Where imported root-zone mixes are not used, the existing topsoil can still be improved by the addition of sand and organic matter. Off-site mixing is usually done, whereby the existing soil is removed, sterilized and mixed with suitable quantities of materials such as sand and peat. The specific proportions of the materials used should be determined by laboratory tests aimed at producing mixes of good hydraulic conductivity.

8. Lime application. Acidic soils should be corrected by the application of a lime dressing. Lime should be applied only when it has been proved necessary by soil analysis for pH. Application rates can also be calculated following soil analysis. For most situations, a soil pH of around 5.5–6.0 is preferable for turfgrass swards.

9. Fertilizer treatment. To ensure that there are adequate quantities of phosphate and potassium in the soil for newly laid turves or seedling grasses, it is recommended that an appropriate compound fertilizer (determined through soil analysis – *see* Chapter 4) is raked or harrowed into the soil a short time before seeding or turfing.

10. Pest control. The more damaging pests such as leatherjackets or moles will need to be controlled or eradicated. For many turf areas, it is often advantageous – or indeed easier – to control such pests prior to actual turf establishment by the use of an approved pesticide (*see* Chapter 6).

REAL SEED VALUE

When analytical purity and germination results have been obtained, two or more seed lots can be compared using the following equation:

Real seed value =
(% purity × % germination) ÷ 100

For example, sample A has 98 per cent purity and 80 per cent germination, so its real seed value is:

(98 × 80) ÷ 100 = 78

Sample B has 94 per cent purity and 85 per cent germination, so its real seed value is:

(94 × 85) ÷ 100 = 80

Therefore, if seed samples A and B cost the same, B would be the best buy.

Establishing a Grass Sward from Seed

As already stated, the option of establishing a sward from seed is generally preferred in the UK when dealing with high-quality specification surfaces (for example, fine sports turf); or with large or extensive areas, which by their very size make turfing an unviable option, especially in economic terms. The advantages of seeding have already been discussed. The following section will discuss the selection of seed, seed quality and the seed-sowing operations.

Seed Quality

There are three main factors to evaluate when judging the quality of a particular seed lot or sample:

1. Analytical (or species) purity. A small sample of seed is examined and split up into pure seeds, which are the actual seed being purchased (in other words, the desired species); other species, which are seeds of other crop species, including

weeds; and inert matter, including husks, damaged seed, dirt and other materials.
2. Germination. A sample of seed is grown under ideal conditions to determine the germination percentage. Seed lots may vary enormously in this area, and as a rule, most seed lots deteriorate with age. Both analytical purity and germination can be tested in a laboratory at an official testing station.
3. Purity of seed cultivar. This is very difficult to test for – the seed has to be sown and then inspected when it has become established. It is preferable to rely upon certified seed to ensure purity of seed cultivar. For many of the main turfgrass species, it is no longer possible to purchase uncertified seed.

Seed Certification

The purchaser of certified seed knows that the seed has reached a minimum legal requirement for varietal purity, analytical purity, germination and other seed content. A certified seed is one that is officially placed on the UK national list or EU common catalogue for marketing. Before a variety can be listed it has to have undergone several years of trials to satisfy the authorities that it is distinct from other known varieties, that all the plants are the same (uniform), and that when reproduced subsequent generations are identical to the original (stable).

Seed ready for certification is broken down into lots of 10 tonnes, and each lot is then tested separately. Each bag of seed contains an official label that details the species, the variety/cultivar, the date of sealing, the weight of bag, and the seed lot reference number. The latter contains the following information: the last digit of the harvest year (this is the first figure in the reference number); the category code (the second figure in the reference number); the registered processor number; and the seed lot number.

Seed may be sold as an individual variety or mixed with others. Official certification labels are used for mixtures. The older seed becomes, the lesser its viability, so do not purchase too much. Buy fresh seed when you need it.

Seed Mixtures

From knowledge of turfgrass species – and in particular of their growth habits and tolerances – it can be determined that each is infinitely more suitable to a particular set of conditions than another. The more certain the end use and maintenance regime, the easier it is to select specific turfgrass species and cultivars to match. Competition between turfgrass species is continuous within a sward, and altering the management regime can favour one species or cultivar over another. It is often necessary to formulate a mixture of species to achieve good cover of the ground so that it will not only withstand wear (even if only light) but will also allow the species to complement each other instead of competing adversely. For intensive use (such as close mowing, hard wear or both), turf requires:

- Suitable grass species.
- Good cultivars.
- Adequate water and nutrient supplies.
- Satisfactory drainage.
- Freedom from weeds, pests and diseases.

The two most important turfgrasses sown for such use in the UK are Browntop Bent and Perennial Ryegrass. These two species are the foundation for fine sports turf and heavy-duty turf respectively, and in certain cases they may be used alone. They are, however, more frequently used with other grasses in mixtures to ensure turf adaptability and freedom from disease damage.

For non-intensive use, the choice of grasses is generally greater as there are no restrictions. However, consideration should be given to:

1. Potential special soil conditions (for example, fertility, pH and moisture).
2. The envisaged height and frequency of cut.
3. Whether the area will receive much or any wear/traffic.

4. Whether the schedule for completion will allow sufficient time to enable slow-establishing species to be used.

There is a wide range of pre-set mixtures available from seed houses designed for all sports turf and landscape situations. In practical terms and in most casea, a pre-set mixture will be purchased and used. When ordering, the following terms need to be understood: mixture (a mix of two or more different species); and blend (a mix of two or more cultivars of the same species).

Seed houses are always happy to impart advice concerning seed mixtures for specific situations, although for independent advice you should always consult a qualified reputable agronomist or seek the guidance of an independent advisory organization.

Seeding or Sowing Rates

The factors that will influence the successful establishment of a sward from seed, and thus the seed rate, are:

- The species used. Speed of establishment varies enormously with different grass species. The longer it takes for a plant to establish itself, the greater the chance of failure. Browntop Bent contains a very large number of seeds per kilogram, but it is weak in its early growth. Some species are erect-growing or tufted and so require more plants per unit area to cover the ground effectively. Because of these factors, some species will require a heavier seed rate than others.
- Sowing method. Seeds need to be placed at the correct depth in order to germinate – a depth of about 12–15mm is considered correct for most species as an average. The sowing method used will obviously influence depth and thus potential success or failure, thereby affecting the seed rate chosen.
- Time of year. Higher seed rates are sometimes used when ground conditions are less than favourable, such as in early spring when ground temperatures may be low and a higher rate is used.

149

Table 23: Seeds of the main turfgrasses

Species	Perennial Ryegrass	Red Fescue	Smooth-stalked Meadow Grass	Timothy	Browntop Bent
Weight in grams of 100 seeds	1.7	1.0	0.330	0.250	0.067
Number of seeds in 1g	600	1,000	3,000	4,000	15,000
Days to emerge (at 10–13°C)	9	9	12	8	9
Days to reach 50mm height	18	27	33	26	32

- Weather conditions. Drought, rain or waterlogging will all affect seed establishment and thus influence the seed rate.
- Seedbed conditions. Poor seedbeds may prohibit even depth of planting or may be affected by disease and/or weed invasion. Poorer ground conditions may often necessitate higher seed rates.

Traditionally, seed rates have always been relatively high, no doubt because of the dubious nature of the seed being supplied in the past. However, since the introduction of certified seed and the general higher standards of production, many of the older seed rates are no longer justified.

The seedbed preparation is probably the most important single factor in affecting the actual sowing rate. The better the seedbed preparation, the lower the sowing rate will need to be. The use of a high sowing rate may help to overcome ingress of weeds, but the additional cost that this entails is rarely justified. Sowing rates will also be dependent to a certain extent upon seed quality and, in particular, the percentage germination rate – a higher value attributed to this characteristic will allow lower sowing rates to be employed.

Finally, the sowing rate will most obviously be affected by the particular method adopted for sowing. It is worth remembering that too high a rate will often lead to failure caused by damping-off disease. The cost of the seeds and the sowing rate used will determine the actual grass seed cost per unit.

Sowing Operations

Prior to sowing it is critical that a clean, firm seedbed of a suitable tilth has been prepared. It should be well consolidated and have received a base dressing of a suitable fertilizer. It may also be necessary to irrigate the area beforehand to ensure sufficient moisture status for seed germination. The stages of actual seed sowing will be as follows if sowing seed by hand:

1. Mark out the area into multiples of 1sq m.
2. Divide the seed into the correct quantities to cover each of the marked areas.
3. Sow the seed in two halves per marked area. Two lots are sown in opposing directions to give even coverage of the area.
4. Lightly rake in the seed and irrigate if necessary.

Under ideal conditions, grass seed will take approximately 10–14 days to germinate depending upon the temperature and moisture content of the soil. For successful germination, there needs to be adequate soil moisture, soil oxygen and soil temperatures.

There are two main methods for sowing grass seed:

1. Broadcasting. This is the method whereby the seed is scattered across the area by

Table 24: Suggested sowing rates			
(per sq m for a range of situations using three application methods)			
Area	Seed drill	Spreader	Hand
Bowling greens	20g	35g	45g
Golf greens	20g	35g	45g
Golf fairways	15g	25g	30g
Golf tees	20g	30g	35g
Golf roughs	15g	30g	35g
Tennis courts (with ryegrass)	15g	25g	30g
Tennis courts (without ryegrass)	20g	30g	35g
Playing fields	15g	25g	30g
Playing field renovations	20g	25g	30g
Cricket tables/outfields	15g	25g	30g
Croquet lawns	20g	35g	45g
Parkland (with ryegrass)	10g	20g	30g
Parkland (without ryegrass)	15g	25g	35g
General landscape areas	20g	35g	45g

NOTE: the above rates are intended as guidelines only and should be adapted depending on prevailing site conditions. The rates for the machine seeder are low owing to the accurate placement achieved by these machines; in some instances, even lower rates may be used successfully.

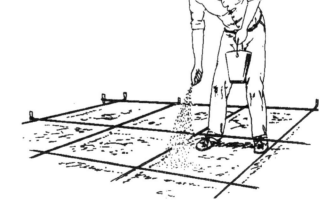

Sowing grass seed by hand on a small area. The site has been divided up into 1m squares.

either hand or the use of a spinning disc-type fertilizer distributor. The seed needs to be raked into the surface and sometimes light rolled to ensure that it is in intimate contact with the soil.

2. Drilling. There are machines available that have been designed specifically for sowing amenity grass seeds. Some drills work on the principle of discs cutting a channel into firm ground or a spiked

Tractor-mounted disc seeder for seeding of large areas of new turf or grassland. (Photo: BLEC)

roller that makes holes into the surface. The seed then falls from a hopper into these channels or holes. Seed drilling ensures accurate seed placement, usually to a pre-set depth. It will be necessary to cross-drill in two or three opposing directions to ensure good ground coverage, and so seed rates may have to be adjusted accordingly.

For either of the above methods, the soil preparation is still the same and still needs to be executed efficiently.

Seed Establishment Failure
The success or otherwise of an area to establish satisfactorily from seed is predominantly dependent upon prevailing weather conditions, although there are several other factors that may also have an effect:

• Moisture. There must be an adequate supply of moisture in the soil to allow germination and growth. The underlying soil may be moist but the surface can be dry, thus allowing the seeds or seedlings to dry out and die. A firm seedbed and correct sowing will greatly reduce this risk.
• Temperature. In general terms, most grasses do not grow actively at temperatures below 4–5°C. The slower the

growth during the establishment phase, the greater the risk that the seedlings may be placed under stress from other factors.
• Frost. Air and ground frosts will severely check the growth of grass seedlings. Frost heave of the soil will sever young roots, while aerial temperatures can destroy plant cells in the leaf and stem. Due consideration should therefore be made to the possible risk of frost when sowing grass seed.
• Waterlogging. Oxygen is a vital constituent for seed germination and healthy root growth. In waterlogged conditions, oxygen is not available to the seed/plant and thus germination and/or growth will suffer accordingly.
• Depth of planting. Seeds that have been drilled or raked into the soil too deeply, will fail because their food reserves will expire before the young seedling shoots reach the soil surface. Conversely, seeds placed at too shallow a depth are prone to moisture stress.
• Consolidation. Insufficient soil consolidation will lead to pockets of air in the soil, which are void of moisture. Young roots growing in such regions will be unable to access sufficient moisture. Rolling the soil with a Cambridge roller can consolidate the soil surface to eliminate such air pockets.

- Soil fertility. The soil must be adequately fertile to promote rapid growth and establishment. Phosphorous and potassium are particularly important. A base dressing of fertilizer should have been incorporated prior to seeding after soil analysis results. Soil pH should also be corrected as appropriate.
- Weed competition. Weeds will compete with young seedlings for water, nutrients and light. A clean seedbed is essential and should have been obtained prior to sowing using chemical or mechanical fallowing techniques. It is critical that perennial weeds are eliminated prior to sowing, while annual weeds will usually be mown out later.
- Soil contamination. Previous chemicals applied to the area may persist and affect seedling germination. Young plants are extremely susceptible to chemical damage. Follow the manufacturer's instructions and allow the appropriate period to lapse before sowing any grass seed onto the area.
- Pests. The two major pests of seeds and seedlings in turf are leatherjackets and wireworms (*see* Chapter 6). Wireworms can be particularly troublesome in older areas of grassland that are cultivated and re-sown. Both pests eat the roots of plants and thus cause their rapid death – large areas of the sward can be affected. For both these pests, chemical control with the appropriate pesticide may be necessary.
- Disease. A range of fungal organisms may cause damping off in the sward, including *Fusarium culmorum*, *Microdochium nivale*, *Rhizoctonia* spp. and *Pythium* spp. Symptoms include rotten seed; thin, patchy germination; decayed/rotten bases of young seedlings; and leaves of affected seedlings turning red, purple or yellow in colour. Very wet or very dry conditions, uneven sowing and inadequate or excessive seedbed fertilizer use favour the disease. The best control is good seedbed preparation, good soil drainage and correct seed sowing rates.

There are no UK-approved fungicides available for spraying, although fungicide seed dressings are available.

Establishing a Grass Sward with Turves

Turfing is probably more common in general landscaping practice and in repair work than for specialist surfaces, which are almost invariably grown from seed. Turfing does, however, have its place and is particularly favoured where an instant effect is desired. When electing to establish a surface from turf, the type of turf first needs to be considered. There are several types available, each containing different grasses and suited to different uses:

- Meadow turf/pasture turf. This is turf lifted from agricultural grassland. It consists predominantly of coarse agricultural cultivars of ryegrass and often has a high incidence of broadleaved weed species present within it. It is only of use for large areas that will not require a high standard of maintenance.
- Parkland turf. This is turf from older established grassland, and is invariably of better quality than meadow turf. Good samples will contain finer grass species, such as bents and fescues, which may make it suitable for reasonably good-quality lawns and amenity areas.
- Sea-washed/Cumberland turf. This is natural turf that is harvested from sea-washed marshland and river estuaries, predominantly along coastal areas of Lancashire. It consists in the main of fine-leaved grass species, such as bents and fescues, and has been used extensively in the past for fine turf surfaces, especially golf and bowling greens. Its relatively high cost, short supply and, more importantly, its high soil silt content now restrict its commercial use in all but very limited circumstances.
- Cultivated/purpose-grown turf. This turf has usually been specially sown using

Turf harvesting in operation at a large turf producer. (Photo: Sovereign Turf)

selected grass species and cultivars. It is often grown on sandy soils for ease of harvesting and for reasons of more rapid growth and crop rotation. The best-quality purpose-grown turf would be suitable for specialist sports turf use and all forms are usually suitable for general landscaping and amenity use. Some turf producers offer washed turf where the soil has been removed from the turf-root mat. This is often used in situations where the preservation of the existing soil type is critical, as is often the case on high-quality golf green constructions. Washed turf is more expensive and so its use is generally limited to smaller areas.

• Seedling turf. There are several turf production systems that have been developed and patented by a variety of suppliers in recent years. In the main, such systems employ a material such as plastic form or netting to provide reinforcement for the young turfgrass plants. Such turf is quickly produced and can be grown to order depending upon the customer's exact requirements. Slow-release nitrogen fertilizers are often incorporated into the soil-less growing medium to ensure sustained growth and development. Those systems that do not employ netting or other reinforcement material are often grown on polythene, rely upon a restricted depth of root zone, and depend on root growth to hold the turf together. All such materials will require regular watering after lying and particular attention to nutrient inputs. Depending upon the firmness and thickness of the turf, it will also require probably more topdressing and other operations than traditional turves to create a level surface should this be required.

Sizes of Turf

The size of turf used depends on the specific purpose for which it is intended and, to some extent, on supplier availability. Smaller sized turves are desired to facilitate the accurate levels needed on fine turf swards, while sites that are more extensive will require larger turves to save on laying times and costs. Soil type will also influence turf size – those in a sandy substrate, for example, may need to be smaller to ensure that they hold together. Sizes most often encountered for purchased turf are 1sq yd (16 × 81in) and 1sq m (16 × 97in).

One of the most recent innovations in turf production has been the release of larger sizes and rolls of turf, such as the 'big roll' system. This turf measures 75cm in width, and a single roll provides 20sq m of turf. Some companies even supply turf larger than this. Such large rolls necessitate the use of specialized lifting and laying equipment.

They are of particular use for large sites, and turf areas laid with these rolls can have up to 90 fewer joints than conventional-sized turves. Suppliers of big roll turf often stipulate a minimum requirement in terms of quantity ordered (for example, 1,000sq yd) before providing their large tractor-mounted laying equipment for installing the turf. Specialized DIY machines are, however, also available for hire if necessary. Obviously, the use of these large turves will be economically viable only on large sites where the cost of the work justifies their use.

The standard thickness of turf varies enormously with the supplier and the size of turf required or supplied. Most frequently, turf thickness will range from 25mm to 40mm.

There are now available turfs grown in special trays (turf tiles) that can be laid in situ upon delivery. The turf is grown in plastic or galvanized steel trays, usually 100 × 75cm, and has a depth of 50mm plus. Turf tiles need motorized handling equipment as they can weigh 100kg or more. They are promoted for, and used in, stadiums that are given over for other purposes such as music concerts, during which the turf trays can be easily removed. The size and weight of the turf tiles are aimed at giving greater surface stability under playing conditions.

Assessment of Purchased Turf

One of the most important tasks for the person supervising the turfing operation is that of inspecting and assessing the turf upon delivery to the site. Turf can be very variable in its quality, even between turves of the same batch received from the same supplier. The on-site supervisor should ensure that the turf fulfils the requirements of the initial order placed, both in terms of quality and quantity. Such a procedure should be followed before accepting any delivery of turf. Depending upon the exact nature of the work being carried out, the following items are likely to be important:

- Grasses present. The turf should contain the desired grasses for the purpose for which it is to be used – for example, fescue and bent species for fine turf. It should ideally be free of weed grasses such as *Poa annua* (Annual Meadow Grass). As well as containing the correct species, these should also be within the desired proportions, again in relation to

The big roll system – laying the turf with a tractor-mounted frame. (Photo: Sovereign Turf)

the intended purpose. Verification should be sought from the supplier concerning the actual grass species, cultivars and their proportions in the turf.

- Soil. The type of soil on which turf is grown is frequently ignored when ordering and receiving turf. For most situations, a light sandy soil will probably be best, although this would be disastrous for specialized areas such as cricket squares and tennis courts where a clay loam is needed. The turf must be grown on a medium that is suitable for its final usage. Failure to do this could result in a 'capping off' situation, whereby the turf is totally incompatible with the underlying soil surface and fails to root satisfactorily.
- Stone content. Any stones or other solid materials in the turf could be injurious to potential players and/or hazardous to maintenance machinery, especially mowers. Naturally, such matter is undesirable and should be limited within the turf substrate.
- Turf thickness. It is a common fallacy that thick turf is better than thin. In fact, the opposite is true, particularly with modern turf production techniques that can produce turf 6–12mm thick. When transplanted within a period of four to eight hours, such turf has a speedy rate of re-establishment – often twice as fast as more conventionally cut turf.
- Turf dimensions. The turf should be of the desired size – in other words, the size ordered. All turves should be of the same size or as specifically stated, if different. Most turf suppliers offer a range of sizes that will be suitable for varying conditions. With respect to both turf thickness and dimension, the most important factor is uniformity. Turves that are all the same size and thickness will be easier to lay and, generally, a higher quality finish will result.
- Age of turf. For conventionally produced turf, that which is less than 12 months old is more likely to be immature and not sufficiently strong to be handled and moved. Turf that is more than three years old is likely to contain thatch, fibre, pos-

sible weed species and turfgrass disease organisms. Specialist turves are available for purchase and laying that are less than one year old (seedling turf).

- Depth of organic material. Excessive amounts of thatch and/or fibre are to be avoided. This is especially the case for sports turf, where (in most cases) it would prove to be too problematic later. However, for general landscape and amenity situations, this factor is less important.
- Weeds, pests and diseases. All of these are undesirable, especially for turf supplied for the highest quality work. The extent to which any can be tolerated will depend upon the exact agent present and its stage of establishment. Weeds that are particularly difficult to eradicate and diseases that are most damaging should be absent.

For further guidance, reference can be made to the British standard BS3969 (1990) 'Recommendations for Turf for General Purposes', which outlines the criteria for turf used for landscape and amenity situations.

Turf Lifting

Small quantities of turf are usually lifted manually with turfing irons or floats. It will be necessary to mark out the area accurately to the desired turf sizes using tapes and lines. A plank will often prove invaluable in providing a solid straight edge against which a half-moon can be used to cut the turf to the required size. The turves may also need to be boxed off to ensure conformity (see box). When the turf has been cut to size, the turfing iron is used to lift the turf in parallel strips over the area.

For larger scale areas, lifting turf-cutting machines can be used. These vary in size from pedestrian machines to tractor-mounted units. They can usually be adjusted to cut the turf to a pre-set depth and, on some larger machines, to cut turves to a pre-set length. As a result, they produce turves of uniform thickness and can lift relatively large areas very quickly. Such machines can be hired when necessary, although contractors engaged in regular turf lifting and laying will

Pedestrian turf lifter – a very useful machine for those with large areas of turf to repair or with their own turf nursery area. (Photo: RansomesJacobsen)

BOXING OFF TURF

For turf that has been lifted by hand, it may be necessary to 'box off' the turves to achieve a uniform thickness. To do this, the turf is placed upside-down into a wooden box with sides of the desired depth or thickness, and the excess soil is then shaved off using a knife or scythe blade. It is important that the box contains no debris and that the turf is inserted properly to ensure that all turves are of the same finished thickness.

---

usually find it more practical to purchase a turf-lifting machine.

Turf Laying

Good soil preparation is vital to the success of turf laying, and final soil levels need to be established well before turfing operations commence. The turves are laid in rows adjacent to each other, close-butted, with individual turves laid in a brick-like fashion (in other words, staggered) to ensure the production of a close-knit sward. When laying turf, one should, if possible, refrain from walking over the prepared soil surface but should instead work from boards or planks laid onto turf that has already been laid and thus progress forwards over the area.

It is more effective to lay turves around the perimeter in the first instance and then to fill in the main area. This perimeter edge should be two turves wide. In certain circumstances, a single row of turves laid upside-down with their tops flush with the soil surface is placed around the perimeter. Turves are then laid the correct way up on top of this row – this aids the formation of a firm, strong edge and is often practised on areas such as bowling greens.

The pattern of laying will depend upon the nature of the site, the size of turf being used and the desired levels of the finished work. On areas such as flat bowling greens, the turf is laid in a diagonal pattern to avoid surface 'furrows' that would affect the bowl's passage over the surface. Full turves should always be used for the edging and smaller pieces used for infill, only where this proves necessary. Turves should be close-butted only and not laid so that they overlap or that they create tension so that the joints pull apart.

157

*The turfing operation –
working forwards from planks
on top of the turves just laid.*

On completion of turfing, the area should be topdressed with an appropriate material to fill in the joints between the turves. Irrigation should be provided as and when necessary until the turf is sufficiently well established. Protection in the form of temporary fencing or rope may be necessary to keep people and animal pests off the turf; this must also remain in place until the turf is sufficiently well established that it can withstand normal wear and tear.

Turf Storage

Turf should be laid in its new position as soon as possible after harvesting. Turves must not be allowed to dry out, as this will cause them to shrink and then die back, eventually irretrievably. Turf can be stored temporarily by one of three methods:

- Stacked turf to turf and soil to soil in a pile.
- Rolled and stacked.
- Laid out face upwards in a single layer.

The first two methods are possible only for short-term storage as if the turves are left for a longer period they will turn yellow and die. The third method may be used for longer periods, especially if the turves are kept watered. Turf can survive for up to two days from harvesting in summertime and up to five days in wintertime. Turf must be laid within this timescale or unrolled onto a 'holding bed' for up to ten days only. After laying any turf that has been stored, even temporarily, water it well.

Turfing Slopes

On slopes exceeding 30 degrees, turves should be laid diagonally or horizontally on the banking in a stretcher bond pattern. They will need to be close-butted, firmed and secured by the use of stout wooden pegs 100mm in length, or by 4mm galvanized wire pins, bent or hairpin pattern, at least 200mm long. On such slopes, it is desirable to ensure that there is a minimum depth of topsoil of at least 75–100mm. Where the gradient encountered creates difficulties in topsoil retention, the soil should be spread in narrow strips across the bank, starting at the bottom. Proceed by laying two or three rows or turves before placing the next topsoil strip. To aid retention and establishment on very steep banks, netting can be placed over the turf and this subsequently pegged down. The netting can be reinforced if necessary to rope off the area to prevent damage from people and/or animals.

Specialist Methods of Sward Establishment

A range of geotextile materials and alternative methods are available for establishing

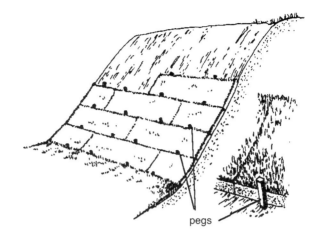

*Turfing to banks exceeding
30 degrees.*

pegs

grass swards on difficult landscape areas such as embankments, riverbanks, floodplains and reclamation sites where conventional seeding and turfing techniques would be impractical or simply not possible. Some of these methods (such as hydroseeding) are suitable for other landscape areas and can provide a more rapid means of turf establishment where this is required.

Seeded Mats
A couple of types are available:

1. Biodegradable jute matting. This material consists of layers of recycled jute fibres and has seed (and sometimes fertilizer) embedded into it during the manufacturing process. The seed is held in a middle layer to provide the best conditions for germination and seedling development. The matting retains moisture and provides a warm environment for grass germination and growth, and it also provides protection from competition as it suppresses weed growth from the underlying substrate. Mats generally come as rolls up to 25m in length.
2. Mats of straw and/or coir fibres. These materials are sewn between two light polypropylene woven meshes. They are essentially straw mulches with a small degree of reinforcement and are very effec-

tive for short-term erosion control. They are most often supplied and installed with a seed mixture already embedded into them.

For both of the above materials it is critical to facilitate good contact between the material and the soil surface. This will require the preparation of a loose, stone-free surface with no major undulations. The mats will need to be pegged down firmly to the soil with 300mm steel pins or staples, usually placed 0.5m apart. Edges are overlapped as appropriate, and most mat manufacturers provide installation details and specifications.

When assessing the stabilization of a slope with the use of either turf, seeded mat, netting or other techniques, it is always advisable to seek the advice of an engineer or other suitably qualified person. This will often be necessary when the particular slope is extremely severe and/or unstable. The work involved in such laying procedures can be inherently dangerous and needs a thorough risk assessment and attention to health and safety.

Hydraulic Seeding (Hydroseeding)
Hydroseeding involves applying grass seed in a liquid medium to the required surface or area where grass establishment is needed.

159

Hydroseeding tank unit. This model has a capacity of 2,500 litres and is suitable for mounting onto a trailer or pick-up truck. (Photo: BLEC)

The mixture, which is sprayed under pressure with specialized equipment, consists of water, grass seed, fertilizer and a mulch material. Water is the carrier for the mixture and provides moisture for seed germination. Seed content can be varied according to the site requirements and the method can be used for non-grass species such as wildflowers and even trees. The mulch material is normally either wood or paper-based and is incorporated to enhance plant germination and establishment. It retains moisture, nutrients and provides a seedbed for germination and initial growth. Other products such as soil amendment materials can also be added. To aid adhesion of the slurry mix to the surface of slopes, materials known as tackifiers are usually added. This technique has been applied on conventional turf areas, including those used for sport, and is promoted as being considerably cheaper than turfing, faster in its execution and having the advantage of easily covering inaccessible areas.

Hydroseeding is usually carried out by specialist contractors.

Vegetative Methods
Certain grasses such as Creeping Bent can be propagated by planting stolons that will thicken up to form a grass sward. Stolons of Creeping Bent are commercially available in the USA and in some European countries. This method of establishing turf is rarely attempted in the UK. When grassing sand dunes, some form of vegetative establishment (for example, with rooted plants of Marram Grass) is usually necessary.

Initial Maintenance of New Turf Areas

In order for any new area of turf to establish itself and form a thick, vigorous sward, it is necessary to implement a few basic maintenance practices within the initial months, immediately after sowing or turfing. The exact nature of these initial maintenance practices will vary in detail according to the specific turf sward being created. The following are guidelines only and will need to be adapted to the particular site and usage of the area. Many new areas of turf have been spoilt or ruined by neglect in the immediate few months following turfing or seeding. The effectiveness and extent of all initial maintenance practices form the key to creating a vigorous turfgrass sward to any given standard. The initial maintenance requirements for seed differ from those required of a turfed area.

Seeded Areas

On any seeded areas, the following operations may be necessary during sward establishment:

- Disease control. Various damping off diseases can affect newly sown grass, causing either the seed to rot and so prevent its germination, or else the young seedling to rot and collapse at its base. Both lead to bare patches arising within the sward. Newly sown grass can be particularly prone to damping off in the autumn period, when mild, damp conditions, suitable for the disease, are likely to prevail. The key factor in avoiding these diseases is to ensure rapid germination, for which three vital conditions are required: warm soil; moisture without waterlogging; and correct sowing depth. Fungicide treatment of seed can improve establishment under inadequate conditions but should not be necessary.
- Stone removal. Stones need to be removed to prevent possible future injury to players and/or damage to maintenance machinery, especially mowing equipment. Obviously, it is desirable to remove as much of the soil stone content as possible prior to seeding, although a quantity will always remain. After the grass has attained a height of 25mm for fine turf, stones having a dimension of 13mm or more in any one dimension should be

removed. For other areas of turf, again allow the grass to achieve 25mm in height, but remove only those stones exceeding 40mm in any one dimension.
- Rolling. The removal of stones should be followed by rolling. Hand rollers of 250kg are most suitable for fine turf areas whilst tractor-drawn agricultural flat rollers can be used on coarser and larger areas of turf. Rolling helps to re-true surface areas after the soil heave caused by germinating grass seeds. Rolling should be carried out only when the soil is dry to avoid both surface soil compaction and possible damage to the developing sward. Rolling will probably be necessary on two or more directions across the surface.
- Mowing. During the establishment period, it is vital that the young grass is cut regularly with a well-sharpened mower. For the initial cuts it is often better to employ a rotary-type mower as cylinder mowers may pull at the weak-rooted grass seedlings and thus possibly damage the sward. On all mowers, the blades must be sharp to ensure clean cutting of the grass without tearing. The grass should never be allowed to grow away as this will encourage the coarser grass species to invade at the expense of the desired finer species and will inhibit the development of a dense turfgrass cover. Many broad-leaved weeds will be suppressed by an early first cut, especially annual species.

Particular attention needs to be paid to the surface conditions for the first cut. Young swards are often soft and are easily rutted, and these disturbed levels are always difficult to correct satisfactorily later. The surface therefore needs to be dry enough and adequately firm to support the particular mowing equipment that is being used. For these reasons, on fine turf area a hover-type mower such as a Flymo is often used for the first cut as this type of machine exerts very little downward pressure on the surface, causing no rutting or damage to levels.

As regards to mowing height, this will vary enormously depending upon the intended use of the area. For fine turf, the young grass is often left to grow to 40mm before initial cutting as this helps to promote the formation of a deeper root system that is vital for subsequent turf recovery from wear and tear. Never remove more than one-third of the height of the grass at any one mowing. After topdressing to improve surface levels, this may be reduced still further; subsequently, the cutting height can be gradually lowered until the standard height of cut for the particular turf area is attained (fine turf areas are gradually reduced to 12mm in height over a period). For areas of fine or ornamental turf or other high-quality sports turf, it is always desirable to remove arisings. Removal of the grass clippings will help to reduce the spread of weed species and inhibit the formation of thatch.

- Topdressing. In order to achieve the required finished levels on areas of fine turf such as golf greens and bowling greens, topdressing with an appropriate soil or compost should be carried out approximately eight to ten weeks after sowing. The rate of application will need to be in the region of 1.5–2.0kg/sq m on each occasion. More than one application will be necessary during the first year following sowing. It is important not to smother the young grass and to work the soil into the sward thoroughly. Specialized areas such as cricket squares will need topdressing with the appropriate clay loam. All areas of turf, including those for general use, will benefit from topdressing, but on larger amenity areas costs may be prohibitive and unwarranted.
- Fertilizer treatment. During the initial growth phase, the young grasses will have a greater fertilizer requirement than subsequently when they have become established. For those swards sown in the autumn, it will often be necessary to apply a complete dressing of nitrogen, potassium and phosphorous nutrients in the following spring, followed by four or five summer dressings of a nitrogen fertilizer (for example, 1.5kg of sulphate of ammonia

per 100sq m). For those swards sown in the spring, the application of a pre-sowing fertilizer eliminates the need for such a spring application of nitrogen, potassium and phosphorous, although subsequent summer dressings will be required.

- Weed control. Commencement of mowing operations will eliminate any annual weeds that have grown in the sward. Perennial species are more problematic and should be eradicated prior to seed sowing by leaving the land fallow and applying a contact or translocated herbicide. There are no herbicides available for use on seedling turf, so a clean seedbed is essential.
- Irrigation. Young grasses are very prone to damage from drought during the initial stages before they have established an adequate root system. It will therefore probably be necessary to irrigate at some stage and this will almost certainly be necessary for those swards sown in the spring. Frequency and exact timing of irrigation will depend on local weather conditions and soil moisture status.
- Protection. The use of temporary fencing/netting to deter pests, especially rodents such as rabbits, may be necessary and is always advisable as a precaution. The extent of any such measures will be dictated by the value of the work and its intended use. Protective fencing should be removed as soon as is practical in order to ensure that other initial maintenance operations can be carried out effectively.

Turfed Areas

The initial maintenance for areas that have been turfed is essentially the same as for those created by sowing seed, especially in respect of rolling, mowing and fertilizer treatment. Topdressing will be required to fill the joints between the turves to ensure binding of the sward and trueness of surface levels. The exact quantity and application rates of topdressing will be dependent upon the level of skill with which the turf has been laid, the intended purpose of the sward and the material used. An application of about 2.5 kg/sq m will usually be required immediately after turfing. Subsequent applications may be necessary, dependent upon the actual levels and those levels that are required for the final surface. In most cases, sandy loam or sand alone is used for topdressing, except for specialized areas such as tennis courts and cricket squares where a clay loam will be required.

Irrigation is also essential to ensure adequate root growth and turf establishment, especially in periods of dry weather. Swards that have been created from turves should not be treated with selective weedkillers during their first summer. Instead, such weed-control measures are best left until the following season.

Repair and Renovation of Turf and Grass Areas

The repair and renovation of grassland is an essential part of their maintenance. This remedial work can have a significant effect upon the quality of the surface that is produced. Running repairs to sports surfaces can be particularly testing, as they usually have to be done during the playing season and restricting players is always difficult.

Resourcefulness is often the greatest asset for the turf maintenance professional. In most cases, time is limited and there is a demand for the areas to be back in use as soon as possible. This and the fact that repairs will often have to be carried out at the wrong times of year for grass establishment causes obvious problems. End-of-season renovation allows a little more time so that more extensive work can be carried out, but it must still be completed before the onset of late autumn/winter, when grass growth declines.

Causes of Damage to Turf and Their Prevention

A turf sward or surface may be damaged through a variety of causes and by a diverse range of agents. Following are some of the more common damaging agents with suggestions for their prevention.

Play Wear and Tear

On sports surfaces, the players using the green, pitch or court cause most damage. The amount of damage caused will be dependent upon the nature of the game being played, the frequency with which it is played and the ground conditions pertaining at the time of play. Damage may be very severe and localized (for example, divots on a golf tee), severe and widespread (for example, the centre circle and goal mouths on a football pitch), or less severe and damaging only in small areas. Damage will be greater when an area is subjected to too much use (in other words, it is overused), or it is used during poor conditions, particularly in wet weather, when the surface will be more prone to damage. The damage resulting from play can be prevented or reduced to a minimum by employing a range of management techniques:

- Move the actual playing areas regularly – for example, move pins on golf greens and rinks on bowls greens.
- Reduce the amount of play (the number of games per period), particularly when there is only a short interval between games.
- Restrict play or stop games completely during periods of inclement weather, especially when ground conditions are poor.
- Where there is more than one area for play, rotate the use of these – for example, at multiple tennis courts those courts that have been played upon can be taken out of use and allowed to recover whilst other courts are brought into play.
- Where possible, use artificial (non-turf) surfaces in wet or winter weather. These can be used as a back-up for natural turf areas when these are not suitable for play.
- Where possible, have back-up natural turf areas too. Many golf courses, for example, have greens and tees for winter use. These winter greens are often nothing more than areas of close-mown fairway that have been created for temporary use only.
- If possible, move the court or pitch. On larger areas where there is sufficient space,

a 'new' court or pitch can be marked out by mowing the old one sideways or up/down a little. This will help to spread wear and tear and allow worn base lines and goal areas more chance to recover.

Pests and Diseases

Damage caused by pests and diseases is very variable depending upon the actual causative organism, but in extreme cases large areas can be affected. Many insect pests such as leatherjackets and chafer grub will kill grass plants by eating their root systems, earthworm casts can smother fine turf surfaces if left unchecked, and larger animals such as moles cause devastation by their burrowing and by their molehills on the surface. Fungal organisms tend to cause the decay and death of affected plants also. The only preventative measures that are practical are the prompt treatment/eradication of such pests and diseases when first noticed. Vigilance is essential to ensure they are treated as soon as possible. In most instances, some repair work will still be necessary.

Chemical Damage

This includes a wide variety of substances that will invariably kill the grass and may contaminate the soil, thereby preventing any successful re-establishment. Damage may result from fuel and oil spillage from maintenance machinery or, more commonly, through incorrect fertilizer/pesticide application. To avoid such damage, any materials that are applied to turf should be done so only as per the manufacturer's guidelines and in accordance with the relevant legislation, and any application machinery should be correctly calibrated before use and cleaned out afterwards. Fertilizers will often have to be watered in afterwards to prevent scorch of the grass. All maintenance machinery should be regularly serviced and particular checks made for oil and fuel leaks, with particular attention paid to hydraulic pipes, motors and fuel lines.

Poor Maintenance

Workmanship and materials can have a detrimental effect on the sward if they are not up to standard. Problems may arise because of operator incompetence and in particular through the use of badly adjusted machinery. A common fault is scalping of grass caused by too low a mowing height or the incorrect machine being used for the situation. Poor topdressing material may be contaminated with disease and this may lead to disease outbreak occurring later. Again, prevention is better than cure. Turf maintenance staff need to set and maintain their machines correctly and be trained in their use. Only good-quality materials from known reputable suppliers should ever be used.

Neglect

All turf areas need a minimum amount of maintenance, and mowing alone will often lead to an eventual deterioration in sward quality (especially if clippings are also removed) whereby invasive weed species dominate. Obviously, the more intensive and demanding the use on the area the more maintenance will be required.

Vehicle/Traffic Damage

Vehicles on turf can cause considerable damage, especially when ground conditions are the wet. Turf maintenance vehicles should ideally be fitted with turf-type low-ground-pressure tyres and even then driven onto the turf only if ground conditions permit. Rutting caused by vehicles on verges and lawns adjacent to paths and roads can be severe and difficult to repair. It is not only the larger vehicles that are damaging – on the golf course, trolleys and golf carts will wear away paths in the grass if left to travel over the same area constantly. The same is also true for pedestrian traffic. People will often take the shortest route to their destination, and this may mean that they walk along the same line continually until a path is worn into the grass.

To prevent such damage, ensure that only turf maintenance vehicles drive on the grass or that other vehicles are restricted to certain areas for only limited periods. Bollards or other solid barriers can be placed along the edges of grass areas adjacent to hard surfaces to prevent traffic overrunning the edges. Change the routes taken by trolleys and carts by roping off damaged areas to allow for sward recovery. Consider laying permanent hard paths or using materials such as grass-crete to take vehicle/pedestrian traffic over grass areas.

Weather

Weather on its own or as a partner with other agents can cause damage to turf. Young seedling turf is particularly prone. The two most damaging factors are drought and frost. Drought will obviously induce stress and ultimately death, while frost can kill young seedlings; severe ground frosts can cause heaving of the surface. Water can also be a problem, especially on bankings where erosion may occur, and if turf cover is thin or the medium is particularly loose (for example, sandy soils). Finally, prolonged snow cover (10–14 days) may promote the rapid spread of fusarium and pink snow mould in which whole areas of turf can be destroyed.

Little can be done to prevent damage caused by some weather conditions. Prestige or high-value areas should be irrigated when necessary, and slopes should be stabilized if appropriate. Sow seed only at times of year when germination and establishment are favourable or utilize netting materials for protection. Snow should not be allowed to remain for extensive periods, especially on high-value fine turf. Finally, vehicles and people should be kept off frozen turf if possible as they will bruise the grass and possibly kill it.

Vandalism

It is an unfortunate fact that occasionally vandals may damage areas for no reason at all. Damage can be extreme and widespread, from that caused by motorbikes scrambling over park areas to the actual lifting and theft of turf. Areas that are isolated and left unattended for long periods are most prone to this type of damage. It may be possible to increase security and start regular patrols, although most instances of vandalism are isolated cases that are unpreventable.

The above factors are the main causes of damage to turf, but this list is by no means exclusive. However, in most situations good maintenance and control in terms of the area's usage will go a long way to restricting and/or preventing damage to the sward. With many of these causes, prompt attention will need to be limited and repair costs restricted.

Factors Affecting the Type and Extent of Repair Work

The specific method adopted and the extent of works required in the repair of a turf sward will often depend upon the following factors:

- Extent and type of damage. The type of damage will often be closely related to the use of the particular area, ranging from wheel ruts caused by vehicles to spike wear from golfers' shoes on a green. Severity is variable and is affected by many other factors such as the prevailing weather conditions. The extent may also vary considerably and is largely determined by the particular damaging agent. The problem can range from small patches on a discrete area of a lawn or a whole football pitch in need of repair or renovation.
- Time of year. This will affect both the nature and extent of the damage and the success of any repair works that are implemented. Grass recovery and establishment will be successful only if the weather conditions allow, the critical factors being soil moisture status and temperature. Damage can be exacerbated by weather conditions, particularly if these are extreme.
- Standard of facility. To a large degree, the standard of the facility will dictate to the extent of repair work – the requirements for a Premier Division football ground, for example, will obviously be greater than for a local community football pitch for general use. Similarly, an ornamental lawn of high quality in a prestigious location will require more input than areas of rough in parkland. Usually, the higher the standard of provision, the more sophisticated the construction required, which

in turn will need greater maintenance and attention to reparative works.

- Available time for repairs. This is a critical factor for many areas and especially so for those used for sports. Time may be limited between that available from one game to the next or that between playing seasons. In many situations, the time during the close season is becoming increasingly shorter, and for some sports there may be no actual close season as play continues year-round. Ideally, an area that has been repaired should be left as long as possible until it is brought back into use. Most repairs are conducted using seed or turves, materials that in the initial construction process would have been left for a full year to establish themselves. With repair work, however, this is usually not possible. For areas that can be taken out of use altogether, time is a less restricting factor.
- Standard of maintenance. This will have a great influence upon a sward's vigour and its ability to withstand wear and tear, and is closely linked to the standard of a facility (see above). A high standard of maintenance does not always mean that more expensive operations are appropriate; the competence of turf maintenance personnel is equally important.
- Availability of materials, machinery and labour. All of these can be limiting to the actual repair works conducted. It is more important, however, to make sure that the right materials and machinery are available for the task. The availability of some materials, such as grass seed, can be dependent upon the grower or producer and are not always readily available. In most situations, requirements are known in advance and materials should therefore be obtained before they are actually needed. For some operations, specialized machinery, such as an overseeder, may be necessary, and again it is best to order such items in advance to make certain of fulfilling requirements. Labour will obviously be dependent upon staff availability and the overall workload. On large sports complexes, the autumn is a busy time for renovation and labour

requirement can increase accordingly. There are specialist contractors who can complete all the necessary works and/or provide machinery and operators for hire.

- Available finance. Finance is always a limiting factor and will directly influence both the extent and quality of the renovation work to be executed. Money will obviously be needed to pay for labour and materials, and possibly also the hire of machinery or contractors. It must be remembered that money can be lost through cancelled matches, gate receipts and penalty fines if sports areas are not ready for play when needed. Ground staff therefore face a constant battle to maintain playing areas suitable for use. Running repairs to sports areas are always ongoing.

Factors Affecting the Timing of Repair Work

Depending upon the nature of the particular area and the extent of the repair work, the following factors will influence the exact timing of the work:

- Playing season. Because of the demand for games on many surfaces, full-scale repair work is left until the end of the season, when complete renovation is often necessary. For those areas that are played upon all year round, running repairs have to be made or areas taken out of use and play moved to other areas. The problem with some sports facilities, such as football pitches, is that the playing season ends when turf re-establishment is difficult because of environmental conditions at that time of year.
- Time of year. Turf repairs are carried out by seeding or turfing, and these will be successful only if environmental conditions allow for germination and/or root growth. Spring and autumn best for successful turf repairs and seed germination. Repair at other times of year will often need additional care for their success, such as irrigation in dry spells.
- Material availability. Materials are needed for repair work and availability is not

always guaranteed. Turf may be available only during the autumn–spring period, although many producers now have year-round harvesting and distribution. Seed also may be in short supply because of harvesting quantities. On-site turf nurseries will overcome the former problem, whilst seed can be stored for longer periods if bought in advance. Naturally, a situation whereby repair work is held up because of material unavailability is undesirable.

- Labour availability. For many grassed areas, up to 75 per cent of the time (and money!) is spent on mowing. This may mean in some instances that repair work has to be left until a quieter time of year, perhaps when grass growth is reduced.
- Finance. Most organizations work to budgets according to pre-set financial years. Costs for repairs should be allowed for in maintenance budgets, although when damage is particularly severe there may not be sufficient funds available in that financial year. In most situations, depending on circumstances, it may be possible to defer payments for materials and so on until the following year.

Methods of Repair Work

There are only two methods used to any extent for repairing turf areas, namely seeding and turfing. The basic operations are essentially the same as for establishing any new areas from turf or seed, the only differences being that small, finite areas are generally involved and the time of year may not always be appropriate for turf sward establishment.

Repairs with Turves

The method for repairing a worn or damaged area using turves is as follows:

1. Mark out the affected area.
2. Use a half-moon and turfing iron to remove the damaged/worn area of turf.
3. Fork over the soil to prepare a tilth and relieve surface compaction.
4. Incorporate suitable pre-seeding fertilizer.
5. Firm the areas by treading.
6. Rake to obtain a suitable tilth.

7. Carry out further raking and firming as necessary.
8. Lay new turves on prepared soil, ensuring all joints are staggered and leaving the turves about 6mm proud of the surrounding area to allow for future soil settlement.
9. Firm turf.
10. For larger areas, work from planks or boards to minimize possible damage to turves previously laid.
11. Topdress with the appropriate material.
12. Work the topdressing into the joints with a tru-lute or levelling bar.
13. Ensure the area is irrigated as and when necessary.
14. On larger areas, carry out a light rolling as the turves begin to 'knit' together.
15. On specialized areas such as cricket and tennis courts, omit the light forking but simply puncture the ground with the fork to allow for turf rooting.

Choice of Turf Choose turf that will blend in with the area being repaired. It should contain the appropriate grasses for the area and have the correct soil type, especially if it is sports turf. Order only the quantity required and lay it promptly or as soon as conditions permit.

Turf Nurseries Many golf courses and sports grounds have an area of land set aside for the production of their own turf for use in repair and renovation work. It is best to establish such a nursery by preparing the ground and sowing the appropriate seed mixture. The area is then managed and maintained in the same way as the areas for which it is produced. It is also possible to create a turf nursery by working down an existing area of ground, but invariably the final quality will not be as good as that from a purpose-sown area. Whichever method is adopted, maintenance must be both thorough and exactly as that carried out on the final area where it will be used. The advantages of a turf nursery are that turf is always available whenever it is needed and it is cheaper than buying it in; in addition, you are not reliant upon a supplier who may deliver your turf when ground conditions restrict laying.

Obviously, areas that have been lifted will need to be topped up with soil and re-sown. Normally, it will take up to two years for turf produced in this way to be strong enough for lifting and handling. For specialist areas such as bowling greens, it is better to use turf already on the green for repairs to control areas and to use the nursery turf for edges only. Again, ensure that the soil type is appropriate for the area being repaired.

Repairs by Seeding
Repairing an area with seed is essentially the same as for establishing a new area from seed. It may mean adopting the following procedure or similar:

1. Establish and mark out the area to be repaired.
2. Break up the soil by forking or use of a mechanical cultivator.
3. Rake to produce a suitable tilth.
4. Top up soil levels if appropriate with a suitable soil/root-zone material.
5. Consolidate the surface by treading or using a Cambridge-type roller.
6. Apply a suitable pre-seeding fertilizer.
7. Lute or rake to produce final tilth.
8. Sow the grass seeds, broadcasting in two or more opposing directions.
9. Rake the seed into the soil surface.
10. Ensure the area is level with surrounds.
11. Firm by rolling if required.

Overseeding Overseeding is a method used to thicken an existing sward by inserting or placing grass seeds that will then germinate, grow and fill in the turfgrass surface. Overseeding can be done by hand broadcasting and rubbing in the seed, but better results are probably obtained by the use of specialized machines. Various types of machine are available, or attachments are available for others (for example, scarifiers) to convert them into overseeders for one-off use. These machines employ spiked rollers or coulter discs to cut or insert holes into the turf, into which grass seed from a hopper is allowed to fall. The

best results are obtained when the operation is carried out in two or more directions at slight angles to each other, as this will achieve a better coverage of the area.

The machines, in most cases, are also suitable for seeding other worn areas on which little or no grass cover is present. When overseeding grass areas, lower seed rates are used, and because of the accurate placement achieved by some machines, lower rates can also be used for worn/bare areas. Machines are normally calibrated to a pre-set sowing rate and this can usually be adjusted to pre-set depths for different grass species.

Seed Choice The species sown will depend upon the area being repaired and should be appropriate to that area's usage. Purchase certified seed from a reputable supplier that has met quality standards for analytical purity and germination percentage. When sowing more than one species, it is often better to sow the seeds separately as they will often require varied sowing rates and depths of sowing.

Sowing Rate This will be dictated by the species sown and the particular area concerned. It may also be governed by the amount of existing grass cover, if any, and the condition of this. Lower rates are possible with seeding machines compared with traditional broadcasting methods.

Depth of Sowing Larger grass seeds from vigorous species will tolerate deeper sowing than smaller seeds of less vigorous species. For most mixtures, aim for a sowing depth of 10–15mm. The shallower figure (10mm) would be most suitable for fine turf mixes (bent/fescue) on moist soils and the deeper figure (15mm) for the same mixtures in dry conditions. Seed of bent grass should be raked only very lightly into the surface, whilst Perennial Ryegrass seed can emerge from a depth of 25mm or more in good conditions. As already mentioned, seeding machines can achieve very accurate placement of seed and shallower sowing (5–10mm) is possible.

Tractor-mounted overseeding unit suitable for most areas of turf renovation and repair. (Photo: BLEC)

When soil conditions are dry, ensure that the seed is covered and in contact with the firmer soils underneath. Rolling may be needed to ensure that the seed is in intimate contact with the soil so that it can imbibe water for germination. The soil will need to be kept sufficiently moist at all times in order that growth continues unimpeded once it has started.

Pre-chitted Seed Some groundspersons and greenkeepers pre-chit their seed before using it for repair work, whereby the seed is encouraged to sprout before sowing and thus establishment is speeded up. The faster the grass can establish itself, the less likely are the chances of failure through pest, disease or environmental damage.

Pre-chitting consists of mixing the required amount of grass seed with moist soil or compost (the material used should be appropriate for the area it will eventually be used on) and leaving it for a few days in a warm, sheltered environment. It is advisable to turn the mixture periodically to ensure thorough germination throughout. After germination, the seed can be used on the damaged area, being carefully worked into the soil surface. The mixture must not be left too long after germination, as any delay will result in long, drawn, etiolated seedlings that will be useless. Nor should the young seedlings be allowed to dry out, otherwise their growth will be checked and the result will probably be failure.

The Effect of Soil on Repair Works

The soil type (texture) will determine its moisture-holding capacity, nutrient retention, aeration and temperature. Clay soils are heavier and hold more water, and so they are also colder and have less air content. The

169

THE CHOICE – SEED OR TURF?

Choosing between seed or turf for repair work will largely be determined by available time and finance. The reasons for either would be the same as if establishing any new area from seed or turf. Some people advocate the use of turf for its instant effect, although it will still need time to establish, particularly if it is to be played upon. Seeding is more economically viable for larger areas and, of course, is the only method that can be used in overseeding existing turf. Turf is often be used for small repairs on even large surfaces (for example, turfing goal mouths on a football pitch), whilst seed is used for the maintenance of the area. In most situations, a sward established from seed will be more tolerant of tearing-type wear at 100 days than an equivalent turfed area.

---

opposite is true for sandy soils, which are usually freer draining, nutrient-poor, well aerated and generally warmer. For successful seed germination the soil must have some moisture whilst not being waterlogged, be well aerated and be of sufficient temperature. In such conditions, Perennial Ryegrass (the fastest grass to emerge after sowing) will show in four to nine days, but in poor conditions it will take 15 days or more to germinate. Generally, bents and meadow grasses prefer higher soil temperatures and establish best during the period June–August in the UK.

The speed at which different species emerge and their initial growth rate will strongly influence the species balance within the new sward. For turfing soil, conditions are not as critical. although there must still be adequate moisture and a high enough temperatures to promote root growth. Root growth for most cool-season grasses is strongest or most active with soil temperatures of 10–18°C, although cell division at the root tips can occur at temperatures just above 0°C. Drainage is critical for both seed and turf – roots will decay, as will seeds, in waterlogged soils. Seed estab-

lishment can be difficult on sandy soils or sand root-zone constructions because of the low water availability and the inherent likelihood of seed desiccation.

For both seeding and turfing operations, the best time of year overall is undoubtedly the autumn. At this time the soil is still warm after the summer and contains sufficient moisture for germination and root growth. The grass also has time to establish a root system before the worst of the winter weather and the onset of the following year's dry season. As with other seedling or turfing, ensure that the soil is free of weeds, pests and diseases as far as possible. When initial growth has commenced, soil nutrient status will significantly affect subsequent growth. Pre-seeding fertilizers based upon soil analysis should therefore be broadcast prior to seeding and turfing to ensure an adequate nutrient supply.

Turf Renovation Using the Koro Field Topmaker

This is a machine and renovation method developed in the Netherlands that has recently been used increasingly for the renovation of turf areas, particularly those used for sport, in the UK. The basic machine, which is mounted onto a tractor, consists of a rotating shaft attached to which are blades like those found on a rotavator or flail mower. These rotate at speed, being powered by the tractor PTO, and remove surface vegetation and soil. The blades can be set to different depths up to 50mm, where the turf surface is removed completely in order to leave it ready for re-turfing.

Fraise mowing is the term used to describe the operation whereby surface vegetation only is removed. The intention here is to remove weed species, notably Annual Meadow Grass, which dominates many turfgrass swards, and to leave the basal crown tissues of grasses such as Perennial Ryegrass, which will regrow and with overseeding lead to a renewed sward of desirable turfgrasses. In addition to controlling weed grasses and other undesirable species, the machine will also remove thatch and soil to alleviate surface irregularities, resulting in a smoother

The KORO field topmaker – an innovative machine used in turf renovation and surface restoration. (Photo: Campey Turfcare)

surface with reduced organic content. The removed material is collected onto a conveyor that will feed the material to a trailer being drawn alongside the machine, thus allowing rapid and efficient removal of the spoil from the surface and site.

A sister machine, the Koro recycling dresser, is often used with the field topmaker. This machine, which again is tractor-mounted and -powered, removes soil by means of coulters, decompacting the surface and leaving removed material for its integration into the surface by drag-mats or other means. This is the same concept as hollow coring followed by the reintegration of the removed cores, and is essentially aeration and topdressing in one operation. In recent years, both of these machines have been used on a variety of winter sports pitches, cricket squares, golf greens and other surfaces as an intensive renovation method where severe wear or other factors have led to a decline in surface quality.

Repairs and Renovation
Related to Function
In all aspects of turf maintenance, good-quality workmanship and use of materials is critical, probably no more so than in the case of renovation of playing surfaces. Some operations will need to be carried out dur-

ing the playing season and at a time of year not ideal for grass recovery and establishment. The following guidelines are intended only to illustrate the work that is likely on specific sports areas; they will need to be adapted to specific situations depending upon local circumstances and conditions.

Fine Turf Areas – General Operations
In spring, spike thin areas, remove moss, lightly scarify and topdress to maintain the surface. Overseed to thicken the sward. Shallow pricking is useful prior to seeding. At the end of summer, overseed as soon as possible. Spike and rake to a depth of at least 13mm to obtain a good tilth, topdress to maintain levels and then sow seed. Alternatively, use a mechanical seeder. Do not mow until the seedlings are at least 25mm long. Turfing can be done for smaller areas. It is better that the turf is not laid proud but that topdressing is used to correct levels later as required.

Bowling Greens
At the end of the playing season, scarify the area thoroughly after close mowing to remove thatch. Overseed with appropriate seed mix - for example, 80 per cent Chewing's Fescue/20 per cent Browntop Bent. Aerate, to depth if necessary, normally using hollow coring or solid tines. Finally, topdress with

171

appropriate sandy loam compost (for example, 70/30 or 60/40 sand/soil mix); 4–6 tonnes will be required. Ensure that low spots receive adequate amounts and that it is worked well into the surface.

Cricket Squares

As wickets come out of play and are not required again for at least three to four weeks, they can be lightly scarified, watered and spiked. Small depressions such as bowlers' footmarks should be gently eased up with a fork and levelled by topdressing if required. Bare areas should be re-seeded and deep depressions plugged with turf if necessary. Seeded areas should be well watered. Chitted seed is often used on wicket ends to promote rapid recovery of the sward. The end-of-season treatment will also consist of overall deep aeration, scarification, overseeding/seeding, turfing repairs and topdressing. Apply overall topdressing of a suitable clay loam and work into the surface (this will be significantly easier to achieve if both the surface and topdressing material are dry).

Tennis Courts

Wherever possible, courts should be grouped in such a manner that they can be shifted from year to year so that the same area will not be used for serving. In early spring, the levels of base lines should be checked and if necessary topdressed with a suitable heavy loam topsoil. End-of-season renovation is similar to that for cricket squares. Particular attention may be needed on baselines and turfing is often carried out to repair these.

Golf Tees

The permit markers of large tees should be moved over a greater area so that they are more effectively spread. Ensure that the markers are moved frequently. Separate tees for winter play are desirable. Divot marks should be filled with a soil/seed mix throughout the growing season as necessary.

Large Playing Areas

These areas in the main are used for winter sports and as cricket outfields. Most of the actual wear caused in winter is due primarily to play in wet conditions; to this end, site drainage is essential. Regular spiking and sanding of worn/wet areas is essential to keep the surface draining effectively. Individual areas that become wet merit extra attention, such as careful prising with hand forks and dressing of sand. Rolling must be kept to a minimum. The surface can be restored after a match by manually replacing divots and brush harrowing. These operations need to be carried out as soon as possible after the match so that frost does not harden to form an uneven surface.

The end-of-season renovation needs to be conducted both efficiently and quickly.

The Quadraplay is a multi-tool, tractor-mounted implement often used in the renovation and preparation of play areas, especially winter-games pitches. (Photo: SISIS)

Bare areas should be broken up by disc harrowing, raking and so on to form a seedbed, and rolling and further harrowing carried out until a suitable tilth is obtained. Pedestrian machines or hand tools can be used on small areas. During this process, the soil may be ameliorated with sand to improve surface drainage. Prior to sowing, broadcast a pre-seeding fertilizer based on soil analysis. Sow grass seed at around 35g/sq m (depending on the chosen method and grass species). For professional use, it is probably best to use Perennial Ryegrass alone because of its fast establishment and hard-wearing capacity. Allow the grass to attain a height of 75mm before topping to 50mm and then lowering further as appropriate.

Protection and Aftercare

In order that the repaired area can establish itself before it is subjected to use, it must be allowed sufficient undisturbed time to do so. Protection is vital if the repair work is not to be damaged and need further repair work itself at a later stage. Protection may be needed from players, the public, vehicle traffic, animal pests, the weather and weed invasion. All of these will limit the success of the repair work and need to be controlled if they are not to destroy the repaired areas. Depending upon the exact nature of the problem, this can be achieved in a number of ways:

- Roping or fencing off the area.
- Erecting warning signs.
- Netting or laying string (to deter birds in particular).
- Using treated seed (as a bird repellent).
- Using pesticides and animal-repellent sprays.
- Fallowing (if possible).
- Irrigating (when necessary).

The particular area and its use will in the main dictate the necessary aftercare. The aftercare of repair surfaces will, however, be the same or largely similar to that for any newly seeded or turfed area. A major difference is that repair works are often conducted at times of year that are not suitable

to good root growth and grass establishment, and so extra attention may be needed. Aftercare will consist of:

- Disease control (particularly damping off).
- Rolling.
- Initial mowing.
- Topdressing (for turfed areas and all areas used for sport where levels are important).
- Fertilizer application (light nitrogen following initial growth).
- Weed control.
- Irrigation (vital for the success of all repair work, whether by seed or turf).

Turf Reinforcement Systems

The use and variety of materials for turf reinforcement has grown in recent years for both sports turf and general landscape application. Many amenity grass areas receive intense wear, often very localized when they are overused or subjected to inappropriate use, such as for temporary car parking or any other practice that normal turf and soil cannot withstand without some form of protection or reinforcement. Sports turf surfaces on sand-dominant root zones often benefit from the stabilization properties that turf reinforcement systems can afford. The materials can improve turf wear tolerance and quality in several ways:

1. By spreading the load of compacting forces, which will reduce soil compaction and hence lead to better surface drainage and aeration.
2. By protecting the crown tissue of grass plants, allowing for the rapid regeneration of cover.
3. By increasing the mechanical strength of the root zone.

Reinforcement materials can be categorized into two groups:

1. Those in which the reinforcements form part of the surface layer. This group of materials includes a variety of products,

including mesh structures, concrete grids, plastic tiles and needle-punched geotextiles. The materials spread the weight of players, users and vehicles, thus reducing the effects of compacting forces (compression) and in some cases protecting plants from shearing wear.

2. Those in which the reinforcements are mixed into the root zone. These materials are incorporated into the root zone primarily to increase the mechanical stability of the surface. The most common materials in this category are Fibresand, Rufford's Fibremaster, Netlon Mesh elements and Desso DD GrassMaster. Fibresand consists of single-thread polypropylene fibres, typically around 0.1mm in diameter and 35mm in length. These are blended in a mixing plant into either pure sand or a sand-dominated root-zone mix with a fibre rate of 0.25–0.35 per cent by weight for most turf applications. Fibremaster uses polypropylene fibrillated fibres with an average length of 40mm, which again are incorporated into the root zone. Unlike Fibresand, the individual strands of Fibremaster are cross-connected to form bunches of five or six interconnected fibres. Netlon mesh elements are discrete pieces of oriented polypropylene mesh measuring 100 × 50mm, with apertures of 10 × 10mm, that can be mixed into the root zone material. The DD GrassMaster system utilizes nylon fibres or threads, injected into the surface to a depth of 200mm so that 15–20mm is left above the surface to form part of the sward. The roots of grasses grow and intertwine with these fibres, thereby strengthening the surface.

Using Turf Reinforcement Systems

There is no doubt that many of the materials available do indeed improve the quality and wearing ability of turf and grass surfaces, but there are a number of important factors to consider in determining both their implementation and the selection of an individual material. Consider whether using such a material or system will indeed solve the identified problem or if reconstruction or improvements to turf management are a better option.

The key factors to look at here are likely to include surface levels, surface sealing and ease of aeration work, topdressing and user/player safety. Problems can arise in the installation of materials and in retaining surface levels, and can be particularly acute with materials that are mixed into the root zone. The effectiveness of these materials can be lost by accumulation of fine soil or sand particles near the surface, and by the build-up of organic matter. Such problems are most likely to occur with the denser mat-like products installed near the soil surface. Topdressing will often bury the reinforced layer without good management, thereby negating the purpose of the reinforcement material at the surface.

CHAPTER 8

Species-rich Swards

Flower-studded meadows and pastures were once commonplace features of the British landscape and culture. Such traditional grasslands have suffered more than any other habitat from the changes of recent decades. Since 1947, 97 per cent have been destroyed. Other habitats have experienced similar, if less drastic, decline. Many people are now concerned to halt such losses and if possible alleviating the situation. Attitudes to the green landscape in general are also changing, with greater value put on the 'natural' and less on the formal. Most amenity grass areas are dominated by fast-growing rye-grasses on fertile soils that are species poor and intensively managed. This short-turf grassland maybe satisfactory for intensive use but has very little benefit for wildlife and is often expensive to maintain. Most managers of turf and amenity grassland areas have been faced with financial cuts, and those seeking alternative, cheaper ways of managing land may be interested in 'naturalistic' habitats: the creation of landscapes similar in appearance to natural ones. Many areas of amenity grass, especially those, which not trampled make ideal sites for species rich swards, these can, include roadside verges, railway embankments, river and canal bankings and golf course roughs. Set-aside agricultural land allows new amenity grasslands to be created on the urban fringe. Many golf courses and other areas of amenity grassland have been designated as Sites of Special Scientific Interest (SSSI) because of their wild flora and fauna. Because working with natural processes is easier- than changing them, lower man-agement costs could result in the long term. Short-term costs however, including re-training and new machinery, may be higher.

The creation of flowery grasslands, attractive to people and animals, can bring variety to landscaped areas, varying subtly from year to year with age and weather. Their different management requirements shift work away from the mowing peaks. The new grasslands are not faithful mimics of truly natural plant communities (which show great variation), but they can provide new homes for some of the plants and animals characteristic of such areas. Grasslands can be one of the most difficult naturalistic habitats to create and maintain successfully. They can require innovative, ecological and practical skills that are in short supply. All too often, the story of wildflower grassland is one of a showy second year, but diminishing interest thereafter as coarse grasses, docks and thistles replace the finer wild flowers. Unmanaged areas are seen as signs of neglect and may even be prone to fire and vandalism.

Ecological and Management Principles

In order to understand grassland and its requirements for effective management, one must firstly understand the ecological processes that govern these plant and animal habitats. On most soils in Britain, grassland would soon turn into woodland without the action of man or other animals. To keep an area as grassland, it must be managed.

Most areas of lowland grassland in the British Isles are referred to as plagioclimax vegetation as they exist in this state through the intervention of management practices and sometimes because of prevailing environmental conditions, which may include fire, drought, shade, waterlogging, disturbance, nutrient levels, and soil pH. If these influences are removed, the vegetation structure and composition will change and, for most of Britain, the climax vegetation would be that of deciduous woodland. This is known in ecological terms as succession. When grassland is not mown or grazed, woody plant species will start to colonize the area and grow through stages of scrub to full tree cover. In many situations, a small number of competitive species or even a single plant species dominates plant communities. Where such dominant plants grow then, obviously, species diversity will be limited and there will be little botanical or con-

Table 25: Grasses for different conditions

Species	Common name	Dry acid	Dry alkaline	Good loam	Wet	Shade
Agrostis stolonifera	Creeping Bent	•	•		•	
Agrostis capillaris	Browntop Bent	•	•	•		
Alopecurus pratensis	Meadow Foxtail	•	•	•	•	
Anthoxanthum odoratum	Sweet Vernal Grass	•				
Agrostis capillaris	Browntop Bent	•	•	•		
Alopecurus pratensis	Meadow Foxtail	•	•	•		•
Anthoxanthum odoratum	Sweet Vernal Grass	•				
Cynosurus cristatus	Crested Dog's-tail		•			
Deschampsia flexuosa	Wavy Hair Grass	•			•	
Festuca arundinacea	Tall Fescue			•	•	
Festuca longifolia	Hard Fescue	•	•			
Festuca ovina	Sheep's Fescue	•	•			
Festuca pratensis	Meadow Fescue			•		
Festuca rubra commutata	Chewing's Fescue	•	•			
Festuca rubra rubra	Creeping Red Fescue	•	•			
Festuca tenuifolia	Fine-leaved Fescue	•	•			
Holcus lanatus	Yorkshire Fog			•		
Lolium perenne	Perennial Ryegrass			•		
Phleum pratense	Timothy			•		
Poa annua	Annual Meadow Grass			•	•	•
Poa nemoralis	Wood Meadow Grass	•	•			
Poa pratensis	Smooth-stalked Meadow Grass			•		
Poa trivialis	Rough-stalked Meadow Grass	•	•	•		

servation interest. This situation often occurs where soils are nutrient rich and aggressive plant species oust botanically more desirable but weaker species.

Grassland ecosystems contain many plant species, all of which have different growth forms and strategies for survival. Most species are perennial, living for several years and flowering many times during their lifetime. Some species are annual, persisting for one season or less and usually senescing and dying after flowering. Annual species usually occur in grassland where disturbance has led to bare areas for their seeds to alight and to germinate. Where there is a thick sward of grasses or other plant species there are few opportunities for such plants to gain a foothold. These opportunists rely on the wind for seed dispersal from parent plants, seed persisting for long periods in the soil until it is disturbed, and environmental conditions favouring their rapid growth, development and setting of seed for the next generation. Perennial species established within the sward often rely on vegetative spreading mechanisms such as stolons or rhizomes rather than seed alone. The important point for grassland management is that once a plant species has been lost from a sward it is often difficult to reintroduce it without using plants or propagules. In Britain, areas of semi-natural and natural grassland are often classified in three groups:

1. Calcareous grassland (found on alkaline soils that have high calcium carbonate content, usually overlying limestone or chalk).
2. Acidic grassland (occurring on soils of low pH such as over granite, millstone grit or acid greensand).
3. Neutral grassland (often found on clays and loams) that are neither acid nor alkaline.

Such grasslands will obviously vary in the specific species found, and this will affect management strategies deployed. The less fertile the soil, the easier it will be to create and sustain a flower-rich community It may not always be worth attempting such a habitat on fertile soils without taking action to reduce fertility. There are plenty of examples, dominated by docks, thistles and coarse grasses, to show that it is very difficult to sustain grassland rich in wild flowers on fertile soil. The easiest way to determine soil fertility is by assessing what is growing on it. Soil pH, water regime and fertility can be changed, at a cost.

Any habitat needs to be part of a well co-ordinated landscape. Small areas of flowery grassland seem to work best when co-oriented with hedges, shrubs or trees. Larger areas can stand alone, but both need clear edges and paths. Meadows are not necessarily spectacular from a distance and need close inspection to appreciate the detailed tapestry of colour and form. Safety also has to be considered. All long grass poses some fire risk, and should therefore not be too close to buildings or areas of high public use or access.

Flower-rich grasslands must be managed, usually by mowing. The only exceptions are communities on some extremely infertile sites. One of the commonest reasons for the failure of wildflower schemes is lack of proper management, not just in the early stages but every year. Management of grasslands with wild flowers is more complex than standard amenity programmes, requiring different machinery and skills and a more flexible approach. If such management is not feasible, it is better to opt for some form of enriched rough grassland or some other appropriate habitat, such as shrubs, coppice or woodland.

Grassland Management

In the European agricultural system, grasslands have been traditionally managed either as pastures or as meadows. Pastures were grazed for most of the growing season. Meadows were closed in spring to allow the grass to grow long, harvested for hay after midsummer, and the aftermath grazed through late summer and autumn (sometimes also in early spring). These two types of management favoured different species. Meadows often had greater numbers of species, and, because many plants flowered while the meadows were closed up, were more attractive to people than pastures. Agricultural grassland management has changed greatly in recent decades. Modern grasslands contain few plant species and support little wildlife, while traditional grasslands have all but disappeared. One aim of management must therefore be to retain and maintain any surviving examples of species-rich or unusual grasslands, whether relics of former agriculture or those that occasionally develop naturally on golf courses. However, courses have few such sites, so attention must centre on newly created habitats. Management should aim to encourage the wildlife value of grasslands, and to increase their attractiveness to people. These can run concurrently, as grasslands good for wildlife (plant and animal) usually appeal to the human animal also. Management also needs to keep the grassland habitat intact by controlling unwanted species, preventing ecological succession to scrub and woodland, and minimizing damage by people.

Many wildflower mixtures have been sown only to degenerate within a few years into unattractive rough grassland with few species. For a flower-rich habitat to survive long-term, it is best to create stressed conditions before sowing. This will deter problem weeds such as docks, thistles, nettles and charlock. Such small invasions, which survive stress and mowing, can be hand-weeded or spot-treated with approved herbicides. Grasses are essential to a meadow, to form a matrix and to provide winter cover but vigorous grasses will suppress wild flowers. If stressed conditions have been created, mowing can control these grasses. Stress will also reduce the quantity of herbage produced, lessening the amount of cuttings to be composted. In some new wild flower grasslands, large amounts of clover have invaded. Legumes are attractive species and essential to some insects (for example, common blue butterflies depend on bird's-foot-trefoil).

However, they have the ability to fix atmospheric nitrogen, so that a large invasion of vigorous agricultural species such as white clover is likely to raise the fertility of the soil, which in the long term could reduce the sustainability of the flowery grassland habitat. Legumes need moderate levels of phosphate to thrive, and should not be a problem if phosphate levels are sufficiently low. On areas where clover has been abundant soon after sowing, there is some evidence that amounts decline naturally after 5–7 years: long-term monitoring is needed to confirm this. It is difficult, but not impossible, to control clovers by herbicides, therefore the best control is to choose sites or substrates with low levels of phosphate. To avoid problems of rising soil fertility, native legumes should be sown, not agricultural cultivars bred for high growth rates.

Grazing, regular burning or mowing can theoretically prevent succession to woodland. Only the latter is practical in most urban areas, and is essential to maintain diverse grassland. Controlled burning, if feasible, can sometimes be useful, for example in reducing accumulated leaf litter to allow new seed to germinate. Damage from people takes two main forms. Firstly, inappropriate maintenance: a well-trained, sympathetic workforce is necessary, with suitable machinery and flexible work-programmes to cope with seasonal variation. Where contract maintenance is envisaged, contract documents should set out the requirements very clearly. Secondly, damage, whether intentional or not, caused by sports players. The more they can be involved in their landscape, and the more they understand it, the less damage there is likely to be. Communicating with users, and enlisting their help from the design stage onwards, is therefore vital. Good design will obviously help: careful path layout to allow access without trampling and avoidance of areas where long grass could be a nuisance. You cannot please all of the people all of the time, and there are bound to be some who would prefer a formal course. Ideally, both formal and naturalistic should be available to everyone, but at present, the formal predominates.

Managing Existing Areas

On any grassland, it is possible to mow different areas in different ways to get a pattern of varying grass lengths. This 'differential mowing' can be quite attractive, but in the vast majority of cases do not expect a diverse show of wild flowers – the attraction will be mainly sculptural. However, carefully timed mowing can make the most of whatever flowers are there. A simple botanical survey will show if any wild flower species are present in quantity in the sward. An eye-catching effect can be achieved with just one species. On many grasslands, stopping mowing for a few weeks in June will produce a 'flowery hiccup' of buttercups and daises, without making it difficult to resume mowing using existing machinery. The 'hiccup' needs to be timed to match whichever flowery species are already abundant – May for dandelions, July or August for cat's-ear and hawkbits. Such management would reduce a typical amenity-mowing regime of 12 cuts a year to about 5–7 cuts, spread unevenly through the season.

A related concept, of particular value when wildlife is a prime consideration, is 'rotational mowing': using a different pattern of mowing in successive years so that some part of the site is left long each year. The long area provides a refuge for invertebrates and small mammals, while the shifting pattern prevents anyone part of the site developing into coarse grassland or scrub. Existing efforts at differential mowing often experience problems of public acceptability, and long grass in flower seems to be a problem to hay fever sufferers. This approach therefore has to be used carefully, with management chosen to make the best of the sward, and good publicity and interpretation. It needs to be clearly distinguished, both on the ground and in the minds of the community, from wild flower meadows, traditional or newly created.

Even in amenity or unmanaged grasslands, it is quite common to find small areas of grassland different from the typical ryegrass or false-oat swards. Such areas may not be species-rich, but this is not necessary to give an attractive effect; they do relieve the monotony and may contain some unusual species. Such patches could be enriched by more species, or just managed to make the best of what is there. On such areas, the mowing can be relaxed to allow flowering,

but otherwise cut as usual – the species present have survived mowing for some years, so it is likely they will continue to do so. On most soils, the vegetation will have grown reasonably long during flowering and will need to be cut and removed. If the cut can be delayed until after seeding of the attractive species, this will help to ensure their survival. If the interesting areas are on rough grassland, mowing paths and neatening edges will show them off and help lessen abuse.

Managing New and Old Grasslands

Many amenity and park areas have so much close-mown grassland because it is easy to maintain. Grasslands rich in wild flowers require less mowing, but in consequence, the foliage is longer, which makes problems for current machinery and makes it impossible to leave cuttings on site. Timing and frequency of cuts cannot be so closely fixed, and are best determined by someone with ecological knowledge, as the weather and the age of the habitat influence the mowing needed. However, some guidelines can be given to help landscape managers. This needs to be related to soil fertility and the water supply, as this control the vigour of grass growth. More nutrients and more water entail more cuts to prevent the grasses smothering the herbs. In the first year after sowing, the herbage needs to be kept low to allow smaller and slower-growing species to establish. This may need up to 4 cuts between April and October on moderately fertile sites in the west, but drought stresses grasses more than broad-leaved species. Less mowing is therefore needed in the drier east of Britain. In dry years, especially after spring sowing, only one or two cuts may be needed on any site.

Thereafter, mowing regimes have to be devised to fit the flowering period desired and the amount of grass growth. In the wetter west, two to three cuts each year may be needed, in the drier east, only one to two. Only dry, very infertile or grazed sites will thrive on just one (September) mowing each year. Mowing needs to match the flowering period of the species chosen. Most wild flowers have only one main flowering season, the timing of which varies by two to three weeks from year to year. Artificial meadows are usually classed as 'spring' (cut after June) or 'summer' (cut in April/May and September). However, with a well-chosen seed mix, flowers can be available from May to September, and a long-lasting meadow is better for invertebrates. (Any mowing between April and September will do some damage to invertebrate populations). If the grassland is cut in April/early May (exact timing depending on whether the spring is early or late and when ground conditions are suitable for machinery), this will depress grass growth for the next two to three months.

All sites need an end-of-season cut in September/October, before soils get too wet for machinery (especially on sticky clays). These cuttings can be reused as a seed source if sites are available. If a real spring meadow is required then this cannot be mown in spring, but should be first cut in July after the desired species have seeded. Precisely when the mowing is best done will vary with the season. Cuts may be delayed in a late year, or brought forward to prevent weeds seeding. During dry summers, it may be possible to miss a cut, but a wet spring may entail an extra one.

Varying the mowing regime within a site will produce somewhat different displays.

HEIGHT OF CUT

This must stress the grasses but minimize damage to wild flowers. A guide would be 30–70 mm during establishment, falling to 20–70 mm after 2–3 years. On rough ground, the cut has to be set high enough to avoid scalping. Areas to be mown need to be clearly marked out, especially before the first cut of the year. It will help the man on the mower to do the correct areas if the specified height for wild flower areas is different from that for amenity grassland.

Cutting a summer meadow species mix in April will probably produce peak floral interest in early July. A slightly later cut in May will delay the peak of flowering by a few weeks. A portion of a site left completely uncut will protect overwintering insects, but the portion left must be rotated each year to preserve the habitat.

Machinery

There is a range of mowing machinery available, mostly of the reciprocating knife type mower and mainly from Europe. Some flail type mowers with grass collection facility may also be appropriate for use on many areas. The requirement is for machines capable of cutting long grass, on somewhat rough sites; and manoeuvrable for small sites and on slopes. Remember that picking up the cuttings removes the insects as well, especially if the job is done in one operation with no gap between cutting and lifting.

Cuttings

Cuttings should be removed on all except the most infertile sites to avoid a gradual increase in fertility and to prevent long cuttings smothering the sward. Ideally, the cuttings should be left on the ground for three to five days to allow insects to move back into the sward. However, this may not be practical, and does increase costs by splitting the work into two operations. This can be up to two to three times more expensive than collecting the cuttings immediately in a forage harvester.

Weed Control

As mentioned above, the best weed control is stressed growing conditions. However, some undesirable species may occur, particularly in the early stages, such as creeping thistle or ragwort (both of which are notifiable weeds and must be controlled in farming areas). These can be removed by hand or by spot weeding with approved herbicides, but a reasonably skilled person is needed to identify the plants correctly; for example, some thistles are desirable to encourage butterflies, but creeping thistle is very invasive. If major infestations should occur, it is possible to allow the weeds to grow taller than the general sward, and then apply herbicide with a tractor-mounted weed-wiper.

Fertilizers

Fertilizers should not be applied! On very infertile sites, negligible growth and yellow leaves may indicate that a small application of nitrogen is needed. If in doubt, do not apply fertilizer.

Harrowing

In traditional meadows animals created gaps in the sward by trampling. Meadow species are mostly perennials, but some replacement from seed is needed. Usually, cutting a tall sward in autumn will leave plenty of gaps. However, if a sward becomes too thick (perhaps because of rabbit grazing), it may be opened by harrowing. This could be necessary at three- to five-year intervals, and is best done in October/November, when the ground is dry.

Turning Existing Grassland into Flowery Swards

Any project to create flower-rich grasslands has to start with the soil. Mown grasslands may all look similar, but on closer examination, the plants growing there can give an adequate guide to soil. The treatment needed is determined by the soil fertility.

Fertile Soils

This is a difficult problem, so first be sure a naturalistic habitat is really the best option? Would a productive habitat such as coppice be better? If you do want wild flowers, it is best to reduce the soil fertility. There are several possible approaches: all need some information on the depth of topsoil and type of subsoil on the site. Most of the options involve removing the turf and some or all of the topsoil. Such drastic measures remove nutrients and the perennial weed seed bank: invasion by docks, nettles or creeping thistle is a major cause of failure.

The options are:

1. Strip and sell the turf and all the topsoil to leave infertile subsoil. This removes most of the soil nutrients and the seed bank, which is likely to contain mainly undesirable species. On flat sites, this may take the land level below winter water table, in which case you will get a marsh instead of a meadow. This technique is simple and relatively cheap (especially if the topsoil can be sold). However it is restricted to sites with an infertile and cultivatable subsoil, for example sand, at an accessible depth <30cm), and where stripping will not cause problems to adjacent land by disturbing drainage patterns. It is likely to produce a damp site in most situations, which will influence the species suitable for planting After stripping, the subsoil can be cultivated and a wild flower mixture sown. Fertilizer should not be applied.
2. A related idea sometimes advocated is 'reversing the profile' – stripping top and subsoil separately and replacing in reverse order. Apart from wasting a valuable resource (topsoil), there is a danger that deep-rooting species will eventually penetrate to the fertile topsoil layer and grow to dominate the habitat.
3. In many amenity situations, such drastic changes in land level is problematical, especially where topsoil is deep or only small areas of wild flowers required. The alternative is to strip (and sell) the turf and the top 10cm or so of topsoil. This removes much of the nutrient supply. Then apply 10cm of a suitable waste material and rotavate to 20cm depth, to give a 50:50 mixture (the precise depth can be adjusted to suit the rotavators available, but at least 20cm is advisable). After rotavation, the new soil can be harrowed, sown and rolled. No fertilizer is to be applied!

Making a Small Site

To create small areas of wild flowers a good approach may be to make a mound. To do this, the topsoil (with or without turf) is sealed off by a layer of material hostile to plant roots, such as rubble. On top of this can be built a mound (at least 1m high) of some infertile substrate. Good successes have been achieved with chalk, but a sandy subsoil should be suitable, or a soil/waste mixture as suggested in the soil mixing technique. Make sure the shape can be mown. The mound can then be sown or planted with suitable species, whose attractiveness will be well displayed by the slopes. There is a slight risk that deep-rooted plants will eventually penetrate to the underlying topsoil, but on this small scale, any over-vigorous individuals can be weeded out.

Natural Colonization

In the past, many attractive and species-rich habitats have developed because places have been left alone. Unfortunately, such a strategy is rarely applicable. Three things appear to have been necessary for interesting communities to develop; low fertility in the substrate, a supply of suitable species, and time. Owing to the decline in many native species, an area of infertile habitat exposed today is less likely develops into an attractive wildlife habitat. The plant colonists will probably be such few plants common in the surrounding landscape as can survive the conditions, and a small selection of wind-dispersed species tolerant of low fertility, such as the marsh orchids (*Dactylorhiza* spp.).

Most native species will simply be too far away for their seeds to reach the site. Plant cover on an infertile site may take some decades to develop to an attractive condition. Allowing natural colonization to proceed is therefore most likely to be useful as a means of extending an existing rich habitat, at the expense of adjacent less interesting ones, and ecological advice will be needed.

Wildflower Seed

Seed mixtures are marketed for various soil types, for example moist loamy soils or calcareous soils. To give the species mixture a good chance of succeeding, it is essential to match the soil conditions on site as closely as possible to those for which a mixture is designed, considering pH, soil texture, water regime and aspect. The geographical location of the site to be treated is also important: some species used in mixtures are naturally confined to certain parts of the British Isles, for example, meadow barley occurs mostly in south and east England. Such species will be less successful outside their natural areas and are best omitted.

Consider your needs and the factors below before approaching a supplier when selecting suitable material. Factors affecting the choice of wild flowers are:

- County.
- Substrate soil fertility.
- Soil moisture regime.
- Aspect.
- Shade.
- Previous land use.
- Height above sea level.
- Is the site coastal?

A simple mix of species well adapted to the conditions available will be equally, if not more, successful than a complicated one, some of whose species are not suitable, or present as only a few seeds. Scientific names should be quoted, as vernacular ones vary. If you feel capable, there is much to be said for choosing your own mixture to fit each particular site perhaps using a simple standard mix and adding appropriate species. This is especially useful on unusual soils such as industrial wastes, but on any site allows the inclusion of particular, local or well-adapted species, and may increase the variety of grasslands developing in different places. Whether evaluating standard mixtures or designing ones own, a few guiding principles apply:

- Avoid rare species such as fritillary; they are likely to be particular in their habitat requirements.
- Do not use species outside their natural range. For example, clustered bellflower is restricted to calcareous habitats in southern England. Consult county floras or local experts such as the Wildlife Trusts as necessary. This can be extended to different ecotypes: northern forms of

knapweed *Centaurea nigra* lack ray–florets and look quite different to southern types.

- Do not use species known to fail in seed mixtures, no matter how nice this may make the mixture look on paper! Such species are best added as transplants once the sward is established.
- A long species list is unnecessary and expensive; a handsome grassland can be had with a relatively few, attractive species, chosen to suit the site conditions available. Given time and low fertility so that gaps remain in the sward, most species in a well-chosen mixture should appear.
- If a wide choice of species is available, try to choose a range of colours and flowering times, but remember the latter have to be compatible with the management regime.
- Consider attractiveness to insects, birds, and so on, and cost.
- If wild-collected seed is a possibility, remember to use only plants, which regularly grow in grasslands, are perennials, able to spread vegetatively, and not invasive species which form single-species stands in the wild.

Turf

Some purpose-grown, wildflower turf can now be obtained commercially, but is expensive. Very occasionally, it may be necessary to move an area of traditional species-rich turf. This should only be done if all attempts to conserve the site in situ have failed. The techniques are still experimental; some examples have achieved reasonable, though never complete, success, others utter failure. The key points appear to be:

- That the soil conditions (fertility, drainage, pH, topography) are matched closely between the donor and receptor sites and similar management can be applied.
- Before any work is carried out, several soil profiles should be dug on the donor site to see how deep the bulk of the roots go: this is the depth to which turf will need to be stripped. It is likely to be at least 20 cm, and could be up to 40 cm if it is necessary to move some subsoil as well.

- Turf is stripped from the receptor site and any necessary preparation done. Turf is then taken from the donor site, in as large pieces and with as little damage as the available machinery can achieve. It should be relaid as soon as possible.
- Usually the turves are re-laid as a carpet in their original positions with regard to one another, but they can be spread out and a simple seed mix sown in between.
- It is unlikely that all plant species will survive the move, but a reasonable proportion should do if the conditions above are met, and some animals will also have been transferred.

Making Unmanaged Grassland More Attractive

Some rough grasslands exist because money is not available to manage them. In the case of a golf course, it provides an important element of the course design. If finance allows, rough grasslands can obviously be stripped, the soil treated if necessary, and flowery grasslands established and managed. Careful biological survey work is doubly important before such drastic measures are applied, as even low levels of management will have an effect. Annual mowing each autumn (with cuttings removed) will allow a greater range of species to flourish. Alternatively, a hay-cut (and removal) in July may give a better floral display in late summer than no management, and should remove the worst of the summer fire danger. As with mown grasslands, what can be achieved and the appropriate techniques depend on the soil fertility.

Fertile Soils

If no management can be applied, it is very difficult to diversify rough grasslands on fertile soils. The tussocks of the dominant grasses and the sheer mass of vegetation swamp less competitive species, and only a small range of species will survive. An annual cut and removal of material in autumn will increase the floral display, but in the absence of management, limited results will have to

Table 26: Flowers for different grassland conditions

Species	Common name	Acid	Alkaline	Neutral	Wet	Shade
Agrimonia eupatoria	Agrimony		•		•	
Stachys officialis	Betony	•	•	•		•
Lotus corniculatus	Bird's-foot Trefoil	•	•	•		
Centaurea nigra	Black Knapweed		•	•	•	
Silene vulgaris	Bladder Campion	•		•		
Hypochoeris radicata	Cat's-ear	•	•	•		
Cichorium intybus	Chicory		•	•		
Campanula glomerata	Clustered Bellflower		•			
Vicia sativa	Common Vetch	•	•	•		
Dactylorhiza fuchsii	Common Spotted Orchid		•	•		
Potentilla erecta	Common Tormentil	•		•		•
Viola riviniana	Common Dog Violet	•	•	•		•
Primula veris	Cowslip		•	•		
Succisa pratensis	Devil's-bit Scabious	•	•	•	•	
Orchis mascula	Early Purple Orchid		•			•
Knautia arvensis	Field Scabious		•	•		
Veronica chamaedrvs	Germander Speedwell	•	•	•		•
Centaurea scabiosa	Greater Knapweed		•	•		
Orchis morio	Green Winged Orchid			•		
Campanula rotundifolia	Harebell	•	•	•		
Dactylorhiza maculata	Heath Spotted Orchid	•			•	
Galium saxatile	Heath Bedstraw	•			•	•
Anthvllis vulneraria	Kidney Vetch		•			
Galium verum	Lady's Bedstraw	•	•	•		
Ranunculus acris	Meadow Buttercup	•	•	•	•	
Geranium pratense	Meadow Crane's-bill		•	•		
Malva moschata	Musk Mallow	•	•	•		
Leucanthenum vulgare	Ox-eye Daisy	•	•	•		
Leontondon hispidus	Rough Hawkbit	•	•	•		
Prunella vulgaris	Selfheal	•	•	•	•	
Onobrychis viciifolia	Sainfoin		•			
Scabiosa columbaria	Small Scabious		•	•		
Vicia cracca	Tufted Vetch		•		•	
Echium vulgare	Viper's Bugloss		•			
Silene alba	White Campion		•	•		
Origanum vulgare	Wild Marjoram		•	•		
Thvmus drucei	Wild Thyme	•	•			
Achillea milliefolium	Yarrow	•		•		•
Linaria vulgaris	Yellow Toadflax		•	•		

be accepted, or other habitats such as woodland attempted.

The best method of introduction is by transplants, grown in soil-based media, not peat. Apart from conservation of peat lands, plant roots spread more easily from soil-based media into the surrounding soil, especially in dry spells. A single grass cut (and removal) makes planting easier and may aid establishment. However, do not be tempted to rotavate the area as this merely allows undesirable species such as docks and thistles to take hold. Planting can be done in autumn or spring. Unfortunately, the plants are unlikely to be able to increase themselves in the sward, and the method is expensive. Plants and labour costs will be considerable unless voluntary groups are able to help. Ecologically, two approaches are possible. These are to plant natives, or to use some of the species from other countries that have become naturalized in many areas. Natives are more appropriate in locations such as country courses and those sited in urban fringes. However, in enclosed urban situations the naturalized species may be more successful and appropriate. This has been dubbed the 'prairie' approach, since many of the typical species (Michaelmas daisy, goldenrod, lupin, and so on) come from the North American prairies. However, each urban area has its characteristic species that can be exploited. Prairie species often prove more successful than others at surviving on coarse grassland on fertile soils. A number of nurseries now supply native species, or seed from appropriate seed suppliers can be grown up by normal horticultural methods.

It may be difficult to obtain suitable plants for the prairie approach. The latest garden varieties are often less suitable than strains closer to wild types. Collecting seed from existing populations (if they produce seed in this country) or even dividing mature plants could occasionally be possible.

Infertile soils

Most species growing on infertile soils are poor competitors, which makes introduction of wild flowers much easier. However, red fescue can sometimes form dense mats that deter establishment by other species. Never apply any fertilizer as a small amount of cock's-foot in the sward can rapidly become dominant if given nutrients. Transplants or rotavation are the best methods to enhance these areas. Infertile grasslands are more likely than fertile ones to allow introduced species to spread by seed, so that the impact of a relatively small number of transplants may gradually increase. Prairie species mostly thrive on fertile soils and are therefore, not recommended for infertile habitats.

Damp soils

Very wet areas are better treated as marshes. Damp grasslands vary in soil fertility, but water logging does restrict the growth of coarse grasses such as false-oat. Transplants are probably the best option. If machinery can be used, clearing and re-sowing would be feasible. However, on all but the most infertile soils, this could lead to invasion by Yorkshire-fog, which is one of the few grasses to have a seed bank in most soils, and is difficult to control once established.

Glossary

acid soil A soil with a pH of less than 7.0. For practical purposes, this typically relates to a soil with a pH of less than 6.5.

adventitious Applied to roots arising from stem nodes to distinguish them from those originating at or from the primary root emerging from the germinating seed.

aeration The penetration of the soil profile, resulting in soil air being replaced by air from the atmosphere. This helps to improve drainage and encourages deeper rooting of grasses.

air-filled porosity The amount of pore spaces within a soil that are filled with air.

algae Dark green slime (also called squidge) that can be present on poorly drained turf areas.

alkaline soil A soil with a pH of greater than 7.0. For practical purposes, this typically relates to a soil with a pH greater than 7.5

anaerobic soil Soil that contains an inadequate amount of oxygen for healthy aerobic bacterial activity.

annual A plant that completes its life cycle within one year.

auricle A small claw-like feature that is present where the leaf blade joins the sheath in some grasses, for example, Perennial Ryegrass.

available water capacity The water that is retained in a soil between its field capacity and permanent wilting point, and that is freely available to the plant.

biennial A plant that completes its life cycle in two years. Vegetative growth is achieved in the first year, flowering and seeding in the second year.

black layer This is the name given to a layer formed in the soil profile under wet and anaerobic conditions. The black colour comes from the production of iron sulphide.

blade The main part of a grass leaf, also called lamina.

brushing This is mainly used to remove dew from the grass or to help work topdressing into the sward.

bulk density The dry mass of soil per unit volume, or how much a certain volume of soil weighs, including the pore spaces within the soil. The standard measurement is g/cu cm.

calcareous soil Alkaline soil usually overlying chalk or limestone.

calcium An element whose chemical symbol is ca. Soils usually contain adequate amounts of calcium. It can also form part of other fertilizer components – for example, superphosphate supplies phosphorus, but also includes calcium.

capillary porosity The amount of water-filled pores within the soil, where the water is available for use by the plant.

caryoposis The grass fruit, normally dry at maturity, and consisting of a single seed within and including the ovary.

cation exchange capacity (CEC) The ability of negatively charged clay and organic matter particles in the soil to attract and retain positively charged ions (cations), usually plant nutrients.

chisel tine A thin tine, with a narrow blade that is broader at the end that penetrates the turf.

chitted seed Seed that has been allowed to germinate before it is sown. Used where quick establishment is needed, often in turf repair situations.

clay Particles with a diameter of less than 0.002mm. They are plate-like in shape.

culm Aerial stems of grasses. They are normally vertical but can be prostrate or spreading.

cultivar A cultivated variety with a characteristic that is slightly different from other cultivars of the same species. When cultivars reproduce, they retain their particular characteristic.

denitrification Loss of nitrate from soil through the action of various denitrifying bacteria.

dew Surface moisture on grass leaves. This is usually caused when atmospheric moisture condenses onto leaves and/or by guttation.

drag drush A bristle drag (which is about 2m wide and has bristles typically 75–100mm long), used for removing dew and worm casts, and also for brushing grass upright prior to mowing.

dry patch A physiological disorder of the soil where it is dry and repellent to water. Often a problem on fine turf surfaces with sand-based root zones.

endomycorrhiza A form of soil-borne fungus. The fungal hyphae infiltrate the grass root tissues and coexist with the grass plant in a mutually beneficial relationship. The fungus receives plant foods from the grass plant in return for water and soil nutrients. A very common relationship found in many plant species.

ephemeral A plant with a short life cycle that may be completed many times in one growing season.

family In plant taxonomy, a group of similar genera.

fertilizer This provides one or more essential plant nutrients to aid growth and health, and can be applied to the turf surface or root zone. The main fertilizer nutrients applied to turf are nitrogen, phosphorus and potassium, followed by iron and occasionally magnesium.

field capacity Following drainage in a soil, this is the amount of water that remains in the soil profile. It is the maximum amount of water that a soil can retain against the force of gravity.

fungicide A chemical used to control diseases caused by fungi.

genus A group of species with similar characteristics. Similar genera are grouped into a family.

green A very fine area of mown grass, such as a golf or bowling green, or a croquet lawn.

grooming This is the light combing of the surface of a fine turf area and is usually done to lift prostrate stems prior to or with mowing.

herbicide A chemical used to control or kill weeds; also called weedkiller.

hollow tine A hollow cylindrical spike with one part of the spike cut away to allow for the removal of soil cores from the tine during the hollow-tining operation.

hydraulic conductivity The rate of water flow through the soil.

hydraulic seeding, or hydroseeding The practice of establishing grass swards with a special slurry mix. Often used for difficult and inaccessible landscape situations.

infiltration rate The rate at which water enters the turf surface/soil. This is important in irrigation and drainage design.

inflorescence A collection of spikelets arranged on a common branching system

integrated pest management (IPM) A managed programme of pest control using a combination of cultural, biological and chemical methods.

irrigation The application of water to a grassed area. Small areas can be irrigated using a hose pipe and attachment. Larger areas, especially those with high-quality sports turf, will have fixed automatic pop-up sprinklers.

leaching The process whereby rainfall and irrigation water washes out soluble elements from the soil solution. Leached elements end up in streams, rivers and aquifers.

leaf The generic term for the sum of the grass blade, ligule and auricle (where present).

ligule Small, usually whitish, growth at the junction of the leaf and sheath. Some grasses have a small fringe of hairs instead of the whitish feature.

macronutrients Essential elements required by the grass plant in relatively large amounts. Macronutrients include carbon, oxygen and hydrogen (obtained from the air and water); and nitrogen, phosphorus, potassium, calcium, magnesium and sulphur (obtained from the soil solution).

macropore These are pores within the soil that are typically greater than 50–75µ (0.05–0.075mm) in diameter.

marcelling A wavy or washboard pattern on the surface cutting plane of mown grass. This usually occurs where the clip of the cutting cylinder exceeds mowing height.

meristem A cluster of dividing cells comprising the root and stem apices. An intercalary meristem occurs at the base of grass leaves, rendering them less damaged by mowing or grazing. Hence meristematic.

micronutrients (Also called trace elements.) The essential elements that are required only in relatively small amounts by the grass plant. They include iron, boron, chlorine, copper, manganese, molybdenum and zinc.

mycorrhiza A symbiotic association between a fungus and the roots of a plant.

neutral soil A soil with a pH of 7.0. For practical purposes, this typically relates to a soil with a pH range of 6.5–7.5.

nitrification The process whereby nitrites are converted to nitrates in the soil by nitrifying bacteria. It is an essential part of the nitrogen cycle as it releases plant-available nitrogen from organic material in the soil.

nitrogen cycle The circulation of nitrogen between living organisms and the environment.

node A point on a stem (which can be a grass shoot, rhizome or stolon) from which arises a leaf, shoot or root, depending upon the type of stem.

organic matter Material within the soil that consists of decaying and decayed organic remains of plants and soil animals.

panicle A branching inflorescence that in many grass genera is lax.

particle density The dry, solid mass of particles per unit volume of soil. It is how much a certain volume of soil weighs when it is squashed together, without the pore spaces within the soil. The standard measurement is g/cu cm.

perennial A plant that takes more than two years to complete its life cycle.

permanent wilting point Water held very tightly by soil particles and hence unavailable to the plant. To prevent wilting, water must be added to raise the water content above this point.

pesticide A chemical used to kill insects, mites and other pests that cause harm.

pH A measure of soil acidity or alkalinity – actually a measurement of the hydrogen ion concentration (activity) in the soil solution. Measured using a negatively logarithmic scale from 0 to 14, 0 being strongly acidic and 14 highly alkaline.

phloem Plant vascular tissue (in other words, an internal network of vessels) that carries nutrients in solution throughout the plant.

photosynthesis The process whereby light is captured by chlorophyll within a plant and is then used to make carbohydrates.

pollination The transfer of pollen from the male reproductive organs to the female in seed plants. It is normally effected by wind in grass plants.

PTO Power take-off. A mechanical means of deriving power from a power unit (tractor) to attached or trailed machines such as gang mowers.

rhizome An underground stem that gives rise to roots and shoots at the nodes.

ribbing A pattern of low ridges or ribs that appears during mowing. It can occur when a cylinder mower has been set incorrectly, with either the cutting height too short for the grass or the bottom blade too tight against the cylinder.

rolling factor A figure used to determine the effect of different rollers on a surface, calculated using the following formula: gross weight (kg) ÷ [width (cm) diameter (cm)].

root zone The term normally used to describe a proprietary material used as a growing medium for turf. Often root zones are sand-based and used for quality greens and other sports turf surfaces.

sand Particles with a diameter of 0.05–2mm. For turf culture purposes, sand is divided into several groups: very coarse (1–2mm); coarse (0.5–1mm); medium (0.25–0.5mm); fine (0.125–0.25mm); and very fine (0.05–0.125mm).

scarification 'Scratching' of the turf surface, to raise up flat vegetation or to penetrate the surface rooting area of turf in order to remove thatch.

sheath This is found at the base of a grass leaf or stem.

silt Particles that range in size between sand and clay, and with a diameter of 0.05–0.002mm.

slit tine A thin tine, either diamond shaped or narrowly rectangular, with a curved end.

soil aeration The exchange of atmospheric air and soil air.

soil air This is the composition of the air within the soil. The concentrations of the main gases are very similar to those found in the atmosphere.

soil moisture deficit (SMD) The amount of water required to restore a soil to field capacity.

soil porosity The amount of pore spaces within a soil, which is primarily influenced by the structure of the soil. Soil porosity is usually divided into air-filled and water-filled porosity.

soil structure The arrangement of the soil particles and aggregates within the soil.

soil texture The relationship between the sand, silt and clay particles that make up the soil. The different proportions will determine whether the soil is, for example, a sandy loam, a silty loam or any of the other textural classes that describe a soil. Technically, soil texture is referred to as the particle size distribution.

solid tine A narrow spike, similar to that of a garden fork, but usually chunkier.

species A group of individuals that interbreed with one another, but generally not with other species. Abbreviated to spp. (singular = sp.).

spikelet The key reproductive structure in grasses.

stolon A stem that grows above ground in a prostrate manner. It gives rise to roots and shoots at its nodes.

sward The total surface content of a grassed area, including grasses, bare areas, weeds, pests and disease content. Often synonymously referred to as turf or turf sward.

switching Sometimes called swishing. A long cane is attached to a handle and held by both hands, and is used to remove dew and earthworm casts on fine turf areas.

thatch General term used to describe the layers of organic fibrous material found in turf. Thatch accumulation is a natural phenomenon of turf development and can never be entirely prevented.

tine A spike or prong such as that on a garden fork.

topdressing The application of bulky material to the sward. The material can include soil, sand,

clay loam, or a mixture of sandy loam and organic matter. The exact composition will depend on the purpose the topdressing and on what sort of facility it is to be used.

total porosity The total amount of pores within the soil.

trace elements *See* micronutrients.

turf An area of grass that includes the leaves and roots as well as the root zone, or at least part of it.

verti-cutting The use of vertically orientated blades to sever lateral stems and growth on fine turf surfaces such as greens.

vertidrain A tractor-mounted implement for aeration. It typically has 12–18 solid or hollow tines 18–25mm in diameter and 300–400mm in length. These are punched into the ground and on their extraction can cause shattering of the soil profile to aid drainage and root growth.

water-filled porosity The amount of pore spaces within a soil that are filled with water.

wilting point (WP) As a soil dries out the plants will wilt if no further water is added to the system. This is commonly referred to as the wilting point.

xylem Plant vascular tissue (in other words, an internal network of vessels) that carries water and dissolved nutrients from the roots up to the other parts of the plant.

Metric/Imperial conversion factors

Metric	Imperial	Metric	Imperial
1 millimetre (mm)	= 0.0394 inches	1 millilitre (ml)	= 0.035 fluid ounces
1 centimetre (cm)	= 0.394 inches	1 litre (l)	= 1.76 pints
1 metre (m)	= 3.281 feet		= 35.211 fluid
1 kilometre (km)	= 0.621 miles		ounces
1 square centimetre (sq cm)	= 0.155 sq inches	1 kilowatt (kW)	= 1.341 horsepower (hp)
1 square metre (sq m)	= 10.760 sq feet		
1 hectare (ha)	= 2.471 acres	1 kilopascal (kPa)	= 0.15 pounds/sq inch (psi)
1 cubic centimetre (cu cm)	= 0.061 cu inches		
1 cubic metre (cu m)	= 35.310 cu feet	*Celsius to Fahrenheit:*	
1 gram (g)	= 0.035 ounces	Celsius (°C) × 1.8 + 32 = Fahrenheit (°F)	
1 kilogram (kg)	= 2.205 pounds		
1 tonne	= 0.984 tons		

Useful Addresses

British and International Golf
Greenkeepers Association
BIGGA House
Aldwark
Alne
Yorkshire
YO61 1UF
Tel: 01347 833800
www.bigga.org.uk

British Turf and Landscape
Irrigation Association
The Secretary
41 Pennine Way
Great Eccleston
Preston
Lancashire
PR3 0YS
Tel: 01995 670675
www.btlia.org.uk

Committed to Green Foundation
Jonathan Smith
Chief Executive
Fenton Barns
North Berwick
East Lothian
EH39 5BW
Tel: 01620 850 659
www.committedtogreen.org

English Nature
Northminster House
Peterborough
PE1 1UA
Tel: 01733 455000
www.english-nature.org.uk

European Turfgrass Laboratories
Unit 58
Stirling Enterprise Park
Stirling
FK7 7RP
Tel: 01786 449195
www.etl-ltd.com

Greenkeepers Training Committee
Aldwark Manor
Aldwark
Alne
Yorkshire
YO61 1UF
Tel: 01347 838640
www.the-gtc.co.uk

Institute of Groundsmanship
28 Stratford Office Village
Walker Avenue
Wolverton Mill
Milton Keynes
Buckinghamshire
MK12 5TW
Tel: 01908 312511
www.iog.org

Institute of Leisure and Amenity
Management
ILAM House
Lower Basildon
Reading
Berkshire
RG8 9NE
Tel: 01491 874800
www.ilam.co.uk

National Playing Fields Association
Head Office
Stanley House
St Chad's Place
London
WC1X 9HH
Tel: 020 7833 5360
www.npfa.co.uk

Sports Turf Research Institute
(STRI)
St Ives Estate
Bingley
West Yorkshire
BD16 1AU
Tel: 01274 565131
www.stri.co.uk

Turfgrass Growers Association
Corner House
The Square
Dennington
Woodbridge
Suffolk
IP13 8AA
Tel: 01728 638726
www.turfgrass.co.uk

Index